Secrets Of A Practice Consultant

Volume One:
1,000 & One Ways To Attract New Patients...

by Dr. Peter G. Fernandez

First Edition
International Standard Book No. 0-934616-21-3
Library of Congress Catalog Card No. 80-53738

NOTE FROM AUTHOR:
The words "he," "him," etc., are used throughout this book, regardless of sex of patient or doctor, etc. It is not meant as a slight to the female section of our society, as this author knows that female doctors are indeed good doctors and he values his female patients just as much as his male patients. It is used merely as the simplest way to get the points across.

Published by

Valkyrie
Publishing
House, Inc.

2135 First Avenue South
St. Petersburg, Florida 33712
U.S.A.

Secrets Of A Practice Consultant

Volume One:
1,000 & One Ways To Attract New Patients...

by Dr. Peter G. Fernandez

First Edition
International Standard Book No. 0-934616-21-3
Library of Congress Catalog Card No. 80-53738

NOTE FROM AUTHOR:

The words "he," "him," etc., are used throughout this book, regardless of sex of patient or doctor, etc. It is not meant as a slight to the female section of our society, as this author knows that female doctors are indeed good doctors and he values his female patients just as much as his male patients. It is used merely as the simplest way to get the points across.

Published by

Valkyrie
Publishing
House, Inc.

2135 First Avenue South
St. Petersburg, Florida 33712
U.S.A.

THIS BOOK IS DEDICATED TO

My wife, Cathy,
who lost her husband while this author spent many hundreds
of hours poring over reference material and dictating portions
of this book. I thank you, Cathy, for your patience and
understanding.

Dr. John T. Boutwell.
Dr. John raised me as a youngster in our profession. He was
my boss — and a good one. As his associate, he taught me:

★ How to take care of sick people.

★ The total scope of chiropractic, not just strains and sprains.

★ The principles of success contained in this book.

★ The use of the subconscious mind in attracting new and
   regular patients.

★ To follow the dictates of my innate mind to a more fulfil-
   ling life.

To you, John, and to my wife, Cathy,
I dedicate this book.

GIVING CREDIT WHERE CREDIT IS DUE

Special credits must be given the following people whose encouragement and ideas have helped my career and in the publishing of this book.

Dr. James W. Parker, Parker School for Professional Success, Fort Worth, Texas. Dr. Jim has been a constant source of inspiration and motivation to me during my practice career. He has picked me up when I was down and has kept me pointed toward success.

Drs. Gordon D. Heuser and Rolla J. Pennell of Clinic Masters, who changed my concepts and taught me to think "bigger."

Mr. Michael A. Jarvis, Chiropractic Management and Services, Phoenix, Arizona. Mike generously allowed me to consult his material. He has successfully guided me for the last eight years. It is from some of our shared experiences that a good portion of this book is derived.

Dr. John T. Boutwell of Augusta, Georgia, to whom this book is dedicated. Dr. John trained me as an associate when I was a youngster in this profession. Through observing him in his sideline business of managing chiropractic practices, I learned how to build and manage my own, and others.

Dr. Thomas A. Owen of Orlando, Florida. Dr. Tom voluntarily sent me his printed information on attracting new patients as soon as he heard that I was writing this book. Dr. Tom has personally set up, bought or sold over fifty chiropractic practices. His generosity in providing me with his notes and his encouragement will always be appreciated.

Dr. R. Wayne Pitts of Tampa, Florida. Dr. Wayne, my good friend, constantly offered me words of encouragement during the course of writing this book. His inspiration and friendship will always be remembered.

Mrs. Brenda Fernandez of Fort Myers, Florida. Brenda volunteered her time to edit this book. Her many suggestions on making it more readable will always be appreciated.

To these people — My Thanks!

INTRODUCTION

A wise man once said that there isn't anything new under the sun. The same is true of this book, which is a composite of ideas that I have been collecting and experiencing for twenty years. I do not endorse or recommend any of the ideas put forth in this book, as I am, in reality, a reporter who takes pleasure in reporting to you ideas and procedures that have worked in building a practice. I do know, however, that the ideas contained in this book *do* work.

The title of this book — *Secrets of a Practice Consultant: 1001 Ways to Attract New Patients* — doesn't actually denote that there are only 1001 ways to attract new patients. If the reader will take each and every practice-building idea presented and multiply those ideas by the many approaches possible, he will find that there isn't just 1001 ways to attract new patients, but THOUSANDS! Then, if he, the reader, multiplies the thousands of ways to attract new patients by the number of referrals from the new patients who will seek out his services because of the activities he will undertake after reading this book, he will find himself with a many-thousand-percent increase in his practice. The reader will soon see that there isn't any shortage of new patients — all he has to do is use his imagination and then apply action!

Some of the ideas presented herein may appear ethical, while other ideas may appear unethical. If an idea is disagreeable to you, forget it! Don't negate the rest of the book because of one seemingly unethical idea. Don't let one idea prejudice you against a future idea which may be tailormade for you. If an idea doesn't please you, just let it fly by. It is important to realize that none of these ideas will get you a new patient. *You* have to get the patient yourself! I can give you the ideas, but *you* have to put them into action. Any of these ideas will build a practice, but *you have to put them into use!*

TABLE OF CONTENTS

TABLE OF CONTENTS (continued)

A WORD FROM THE AUTHOR

It is an exhilarating feeling to know you have aided a fellow doctor in improving the profitability of his or her practice. Our practice consultancy: "Clinic Management Associates, Inc." (CMA) has given me many such experiences on a one-to-one level. Lecture tours have allowed me to reach and help an even larger audience.

Now, through this book and its sequels, I hope to put the message of improved profitability in front of every doctor wanting to improve his or her bottom line.

It is no secret that new patients equal increased profitability. The book you are holding will outline over a thousand and one tested and proven methods of gaining new patients. If you feel that the principles explained in this book have helped you improve *your* bottom line, you might want to investigate our CMA program. If you decide you would like more information, please write me personally: 4800-4th Street North, St. Petersburg, Florida 33703, or telephone: (813) 522-8066. I would welcome your inquiry.

Testimonials from several recent CMA graduates appear at the back of the book. Perhaps you'll recognize a few of their names.

Sincerely,

Dr. Peter G. Fernandez

Clinic Management Associates, Inc.
Dr. Peter Fernandez, Director

YES, There Is A SUPERMAN!

Yes, readers, there is a "Superman." Not the kind who flies through the air or leaps tall buildings at a single bound — but a man who accomplishes more than three, four, or five times the normal person, without working harder.

A Superman in our profession would be a chiropractor who has a practice of over $500,000 a year. And there are plenty of them around — approximately five percent of our profession.

As a lecturer, consultant, and author on Practice Management, I have made a thorough study of these Supermen and have found some striking similarities. How a Superman thinks, how he acts, his procedures, programs, etc., are the bases upon which this book is written.

Surprisingly enough, a Superman acts and thinks only slightly different from practitioners doing one-tenth of his volume. But, oh, what a difference his thoughts and actions make! The actions and thoughts of a $500,000-a-year man generates $500,000-*plus* in business for him, while at the same time, the actions and thoughts of his counterparts may only attract $50,000 a year to them.

The following pages will describe a Superman's actions, thoughts, priorities, convictions, and philosophies. If you, the reader, will match your thought patterns to his, you, too, will become a Superman.

Newton's *Third Law of Physical Science*, states: "For every action there is an equal and opposite reaction." This same principle applies to patient-referral activities. The secret lies in leading the patient to the desired reaction: referring a new patient. However, the action must be naturally right and complement the doctor's personality in order to achieve the desired results. Conversely, if the action used is foreign to his personality, exactly the opposite reaction will be achieved — that is, no referral.

One mistake doctors often make occurs after attending seminars with dynamic motivating speakers. Sometimes, doctors return to their offices and attempt to use the speaker's exact ideas, and they fail miserably. Why? The actions they tried to use did not match their own personalities. The majority of seminar speakers are domineering, out-going types with strong urges of self-expression. While there is nothing wrong with this type personality, ninety percent of people attending a seminar will have personalities different to that of the speaker's. An introverted personality who tries to use an extrovert's ideas or plans will not result in success, but only in dismal failure. The point I am trying to make is that a Superman will only use referral-stimulating ideas that are naturally right for him.

Doctors generally have one of three types of personalities: (1) Domineering; (2) Every Mother's Son; and (3) The Golden Rule doctor. These three basic types — and variations of them — will describe ninety percent of all doctors.

The Three Personalities

The first type of personality is the DOMINEERING personality. We have all, at one time or another, met someone who only has to say, "Stand up!" and we can feel our tails coming off the chairs. If such a personality says, "Sit down!" we feel our weight dropping to the chairs. This type person uses a straight, eyeball-to-eyeball contact, and with a deep voice, says, "Mrs. Jones, it is time that you referred some of your friends to this office." Sure, this takes courage, but if a doctor has a domineering-type personality, he can lead the patient and make him follow! People want to be led. Ninety percent of people are followers. They will do as they are told and refer patients to your office, and will like to do so. The reader can see, however, that another type personality could not be as blunt as the domineering personality. He would have disastrous results if he tried to mimic the domineering personality's referral stimuli.

The second personality type is EVERY MOTHER'S SON. This is the type of man whom every mother wishes their son had turned out to be. This type personality is typified by the shy, introverted, studious, quiet, non-forceful, self-conscious, worrisome, dedicated, good boy. This type personality will have the greatest success by making the patient want to "adopt" him.

Many people are disappointed in their own children. Possibly, their daughter married someone they didn't approve of; their son dropped out of college to run away with the circus, or any of a number of things. Now they meet a nice young man who made it through school, has become a doctor, is very considerate of people, is respectful, etc., etc., and they want to help him in any way they can, because they would like their sons and daughters to be just like him.

If a Superman has an Every Mother's Son personality, he makes the most of it and builds a large practice. Statements like, "If you were my mother/father, I would recommend . . . . ." or

"This is exactly what I would do for my own mother/father," etc., are the referral entrees that this type personality should use to be successful. A Superman doesn't try to be something he isn't. He does what is naturally right for him.

The third type personality is called the GOLDEN RULE doctor. This type personality is between the Domineering and the Every Mother's Son personalities. The Golden Rule type personality is more forceful than the Every Mother's Son type personality, but not as anxious to take command of any situation as the Domineering personality. The Golden Rule type personality uses a moral, Christian, sincere approach to practice-building. He makes his patients feel that it is their duty to humanity to refer other patients to him. He does so by saying something along the lines of: "You know, Mr. Jones, chiropractic has been good to you. It is your duty to let other people know how good you are feeling since you began chiropractic care. When something is good, you have to share it. Send your friends in here so they, too, can get well." The key to this personality's referral activities is the doctor's sincere belief that he can help his patients' friends to better health. If he is not sincere, his patients will pick up his attitude, with the resultant lack of referrals.

A Superman knows that while it is true that a Domineering personality can incorporate some of the referral stimuli which work for Every Mother's Son and the Golden Rule doctors, it is extremely doubtful that an Every Mother's Son doctor would have any success in adopting a Domineering doctor's referral activities. The various extremes are miles apart.

An achiever (Superman) knows that patients are usually of two basic types. They are either a retroflector (tough extrovert) or introjector (introvert).

The first patient type is the RETROFLECTOR. The retroflector is a boisterous know-it-all who does more talking than listening. He is usually the type person who walks into a bar and says, "Set 'em up! This round's on me!" Or he is the one who is always laughing and who always seems to have a big joke to tell. Anyone can see his actions, talk with him, but never really know him. His actions are an attempt to hide his true feelings. This type person has his ego surrounded by a thick shell. Usually he has been psychologically hurt in the past and has so set up a tremendous defensive shell around his ego to prevent anyone else from hurting him. To hide this, he puts on a false front, hence his boisterous, know-it-all, stubborn attitude.

This patient will not accept anyone telling him what to do. He will only do what he wants to do. In order to get him to cooperate,

13

a doctor has to "trick" him into doing what he needs him to do. In order to accomplish this, the doctor must try to make his idea appear to be the patient's idea. In other words, when presenting a package of care to this type of individual, a doctor gives him an option as to what he should do with his health, and lets him make the choice. Once this patient makes the choice, he will follow through and get the results he wants. If a doctor tries to force such a patient into doing something, that patient won't do it because his ego won't let him.

This retroflector-type of person is usually very difficult to handle. However, he is the type of person who isn't afraid to tell anybody anything. They are the ten percent of a doctor's patients who will send him ninety percent of his business. While these people are the hardest to handle, they are also the most rewarding.

The second basic personality type is the INTROJECTOR. The introjector is the patient who strictly follows the rules of society. He goes to church every Sunday, like he is supposed to. He follows all regulations and traffic rules. He obeys every law and fits very comfortably within society's mold. When this type of patient comes into a doctor's office, he expects — and wants — the doctor to tell him exactly what to do. He will follow instructions to the letter. These patients are the best patients in a chiropractic office because they follow recommendations exactly as outlined. However, being introvertish, they won't venture out to refer other people to their doctor, other than perhaps their immediate families.

This second basic type personality is the easiest type patient to care for, but they also refer less. See the section of this book on "Touch and Tell," which describes how to train the introvert to refer.

The Supermen recognize these two divergent personalities, and make special efforts to motivate each type to refer. They use different approaches and techniques that are naturally right for each personality. They keep in mind that what works with the extrovert may fail with the introvert, and vice versa.

The Superman Chiropractor has Philosophical Priorities

There is a certain "philosophical bedrock" upon which all successful practices are based. These philosophies, attitudes, principles, etc., govern all other actions of the doctor's professional life. When times of stress occur in his practice, as it always does, these philosophies set the priorities of the practice and keep the practice growing. These philosophical priorities are divided into BUSINESS Priorities and PROFESSIONAL PRACTICE Priorities.

A Superman looks at his practice as two separate entities. He makes this a rule: "Never think of the professional and the business portion of the practice at the same time, because they don't mix." The professional portion of his practice is the care of his patients, and the business portion is dollars and cents. When the two are mixed, they cloud the issues to be evaluated. The successful doctor never thinks of the different types of chiropractic care that he is going to use on a patient to get him well and, at the same time, thinks of how much money he can make on that patient. When the thought of money enters his mind, it messes up his treatment judgment. When the thought of the professional portion of his practice enters his mind, he thinks of the care of his patients. He demands the very highest standards of professional competence on his part. The best for his patient is the least he expects from himself.

The Superman chiropractor thinks of the business portion of his practice as if he were a private investor who buys practices and then manages them. Yes, he is concerned about the care of the patients, but he is also concerned about the net profit of his business enterprises. The Superman doctor dispassionately analyzes the plusses and the minuses of his practice and then systematically changes the minuses into plusses. And he does this routinely.

Business Priorities

Work simply. A Superman doesn't utilize complicated procedures, programs, etc. He takes any idea and quickly breaks it down to its most simple elements, because he doesn't have time to deal with anything complicated. Before an idea is added to his practice, it must be very simple and it must be proven to work well. It must produce a high return for the amount of mental energy expended.

He doesn't worry about making mistakes. He reasons that if he makes a mistake, so what! He already has a successful practice, and if an idea doesn't pan out, he'll simply drop it and add something else. He knows that the only way to be completely safe is to avoid trying anything new, for that would lead to a stagnant practice.

He never stops trying. The successful doctor fails more than a failure doctor. The difference is that the successful doctor tries one more time . . . and makes it! I know a Superman doctor who was bankrupt at the age of forty-three, but was a retired multi-

15

millionaire at age forty-seven! *He never stopped trying* . . . he did it one more time!

The Superman doctor is not emotionally involved with his goals. His goals are simply a destination he is taking himself. He makes plans on how to get to a goal and then simply moves forward until he reaches it. If an obstacle arises, he sidesteps it. He may take a short detour, but he still reaches his goal. Then he simply figures out where he would like to go next . . . and goes there!

He keeps his mind on production. All areas of his office must be productive. He "keeps his mind on the store" in other words. He eliminates waste. He is efficient. He doesn't see himself as a Superman, but rather thinks of himself as just an ordinary person who watches his practice. He watches what is going on throughout his practice, and he constantly strives to make it more productive, efficient, and profitable.

He doesn't waste mental energy. A really successful doctor doesn't waste his time thinking about that with which other men concern themselves. The average man makes plans and then worries about the many reasons why those plans might not work. A Superman doesn't waste time on why an idea may not work. He knows it will work, finds out how to do it, and then does it! He has a guide, a counselor, etc. (a friend or consultant who has already achieved high goals), in whom he has extreme confidence, one who can advise him. He usually "hitches his star" to this guide, for he knows that this guide can tell him how to succeed. He makes his decision, acts on it, and moves on.

He is excited . . . quietly excited. He thinks about all the avenues of his practice yet to be explored, of the different techniques he would curiously like to learn, the different specialty practices he would like to develop, or perhaps a new practice management procedure he would like to add to his practice. The Superman enjoys exploring these avenues, and mastering them. He enjoys making something new work. By adding these procedures, techniques, etc., he constantly has fun in his practice.

No gimmicks, come-ons, or bait-and-switches. The successful doctor doesn't waste his time on non-productive, self-defeating, reputation-tarnishing ploys, such as the above. The "big boys" don't use gimmicks.

He is a very good, technically competent chiropractor. He is more than up-to-date. He attends most of the seminars available. He is at the vanguard of chiropractic knowledge. A Superman is a seminar-attender. (See Practice Expansion Wheel in the next chapter for how a Superman increases his technical competence.)

He is as well-dressed as his best-dressed patient. He knows that if a patient is a fastidious dresser, of a middle- to upper-income bracket, and he is better dressed than his doctor, that patient will be embarrassed to send his friends to him. A patient will not refer his friends to a doctor who appears to be of a lower socioeconomic level than he is himself. Therefore, a Superman is always as well-dressed as his best-dressed patient, in order to appeal to the middle- and higher-income brackets, as well as to the lower-income bracket.

He isn't a flamboyant dresser. Cowboy boots, blue jeans, gold chains around the neck, purses, etc., etc., may appeal to some people but they *repel* the masses. A Superman reasons that if he is going to be a doctor, he should dress like one. He knows people have preconceived ideas of what a doctor should look like, and he matches this public image with his attire.

He drives a relatively new, status-symbol type of automobile. Patients expect a doctor to drive a nice, clean, and expensive car. In the patient' mind, if a doctor is successful, he should have all the trappings of a successful man. If he has all the trappings of being successful (clothes, cars, etc.), he, therefore, must be a good doctor, and that patient will go to him for care. The converse is true in a patient's mind: If his doctor is not well-dressed, has an unkempt appearance, and drives an old run-down car, that patient will feel that his doctor is not successful. The patient further reasons that his doctor isn't successful because he isn't a good doctor, and he won't continue going to him for care. The achievers put on the appearance of being successful; that includes car, appearance, and so on.

He concepts new patients into his office. This is a metaphysical principle that really works. What you think about all day long is what you will get. If a doctor thinks about new patients and taking care of new patients, he will have an influx of new patients flocking to his practice. If he thinks of golf or fishing, for instance, then that is what he will have, but he will NOT have new patients to keep his practice growing. What goes on in his mind, therefore, is what will manifest itself around him. It is his choice. The Superman uses this principle extensively. I refer you to the next chapter for an indepth explanation of this principle.

Results, longevity, and referrals. Any idea that a Superman thinks he would like to add to his practice must meet all three of the above criteria, or he won't use it. If an idea increases the results and longevity of the patient but not the referrals, he won't add it to his practice. He won't add an idea that will increase the longevity of a patient but which will NOT increase referrals.

17

The same is true of an idea that increases referrals but does not increase the longevity of a patient. To an achiever, any idea must comply with all of the above criteria before it is worth being added to his practice.

He adds new ideas to his practice rather than exchanging them for old. He knows that any idea added to his practice has to be an ADDITION to something he is already doing and NOT a substitution. He sees too often other doctors bringing new ideas into their practices and, at the same time, discarding true and proven ideas. A Superman doctor never adds ten cents to his practice and eliminates a dime. He always adds. He doesn't exchange!

He doesn't add dead-end procedures to his practice. Many times a doctor will add a procedure that results in a tremendous increase in his practice, yet becomes a bottleneck or stumbling block later on which will stop him from growing further. Thus, what first appears to be a practice-building idea may very well become a practice-building barrier.

An example of a dead-end procedure would be a blatant, tasteless, free x-ray program. Yes, it would attract many new patients and would increase a practice quickly. However, the overall reaction of the community would be "poor taste," "low class," "hucksterism," etc., and the people of moderate means, or the well-to-do people, would be turned off. They won't go to a doctor who utilizes "tacky" promotional schemes. This procedure, while seeming to be effective superficially, is counter-productive overall.

Other examples of procedural barriers would be: demanding large up-front cash payments, too much physiotherapy, too much nutrition, lack of professionalism, procedures that increase overhead excessively, fees too high, "tacky" advertising, high pressure reports of findings, cash-only policy, etc.

The larger a practice grows, the more problems these dead-end procedures will produce, until at some point, the doctor will place a "lid" on his practice because he has had enough problems and doesn't want to add more. A Superman doesn't add dead-end procedures!

A Superman only adds open-ended procedures. Open-ended procedures are procedures which increase a practice without resulting in hassles or stress. All practices have certain degrees of hassle and stress. It is inevitable. If a hundred-patients-a-day practice produces five times the hassles that a twenty-patients-a-day practice produces, no one would have a hundred-patients-a-day practice! However, the hundred-patients-a-day practice doesn't produce any more problems than does the twenty-patients-a-day practice. Why? The doctor who commands the hundred-patients-a-

18

day practice has systematically eliminated most of the barrier-producing procedures which bothered him at the twenty-patients-a-day level. Any Superman will tell you that he has fewer hassles now than when he had a smaller practice.

He knows that if he takes care of his present patients, the new patients will take care of themselves. He knows that if he takes good care of his present patients, they will refer new patients, and his practice will grow. He also knows that he cannot increase his practice by having a great influx of new patients and at the same time have a great exodus of former patients. It would be like trying to fill up a bucket which has a large hole in the bottom! It doesn't work! Therefore, the successful chiropractor will concentrate on his present patients, knowing that the new patients will take care of themselves.

He doesn't high pressure an individual patient to refer. He knows that if he pushes too hard for a patient to refer, that patient will resent the pressure. When a patient feels pressured, he won't refer because he'll feel that something is wrong with a doctor who has to pressure him for new patients. A Superman gives a professional impression that he is dedicated. He is there to take care of more sick people. His patients react to this "professional impression" by referring new patients to him.

Move the freight! Most patients of a Superman's practice don't know they are going to a volume practitioner. Their doctor is always on schedule and they never have to wait for their appointments. Supermen are very concerned about getting their patients in and out of their offices quickly. They don't keep people waiting.

A doctor can take an enthusiastic booster patient and completely turn him off by keepin him waiting too long. A patient's time is very valuable. When a woman schedules her day of shopping, picking up the children, taking them to one place or another, going to school, P.T.A. meetings, and so on, her time is extremely valuable. She only has so many minutes or hours in the day that she can devote to herself. Most busy people can only schedule a half-hour a day, three times a week, to go to their chiropractor. They cannot schedule a half a day, three days a week, to go to their chiropractor.

The Superman knows that if he makes it difficult for his patients to come to him by keeping them waiting, they won't come to him. He sets a schedule — and sticks to it!

To prove this point of "moving the freight," look at the fast-food restaurants: the successful ones have added "drive-thru" windows in order to serve their customers more quickly. It is effective. An eighteen percent increase in business is the result of the "move-the-freight" drive-thru windows. This same principle applies to chiropractic practices. If a chiropractor makes it convenient for patients to come to him, they will.

He cleans the slate. He gets everything in his office caught up. An achiever knows it is absolutely impossible for a doctor to attract new insurance and personal injury patients into his office if he has thirty insurance forms and five narrative reports yet to be done. In essence, this doctor is telling his subconscious mind that he doesn't want new patients because he can't handle what he already has. He knows if a doctor is behind in any aspect of his office, then he is not going to attract any new patients.

A Superman "cleans the slate." He has his insurance forms, narrative reports, and patient billings up to date. He has his office ready for new patients. He is ready to care for them. Besides, he prefers not to work in clutter, and patients surely don't like to see clutter in a doctor's office. All aspects of a Superman's office are up to date.

He gives $1.10 worth of service for every $1.00 received. The doctors of larger practices know that the more services and care they give a patient, for that patient's dollars spent, the larger their practices will be. Patients are like anyone else: they want more for their money. The Supermen give it to them!

He "touches all bases." In a baseball game, if the hitter hits a home run but doesn't touch all the bases, he will be called out. The same is true in a doctor's office. No matter how many home runs a doctor hits, if he doesn't touch all the bases, he will be called out. The "bases" in our offices are, of course, the many steps on a new patient checklist (covered in a later chapter).

Usually in a doctor's office, he will "touch all bases" when building his practice. However, once he has built his practice and he is busy, he quits touching all the bases, and soon finds himself not as busy as he would like to be. Then he again has to touch all bases in order to rebuild his practice. A Superman doesn't drop the steps that got him there. He touches all bases!

His office staff works together as a team. If a doctor desires to build a large practice, his entire staff has to help. Large practices are team efforts, not individual efforts. Any doctor of a large practice will tell you that he is only as good as his backup staff. Can you imagine a surgeon without an assistant?

He gives himself a Christmas present. Too often a doctor waits until Christmas before giving himself a present that he has wanted all year. Supermen give themselves early Christmas presents whenever they hit their goals. I know a Superman doctor who gave himself a Porsche automobile and his wife a room addition to their house when he hit forty thousand dollars a month. He found Christmas time in August!

Why not reward yourself for doing a good job? You deserve it! If it's good enough for a Superman, it's good enough for you!

A Superman has office goals to reach. He gets his staff involved. Once his goal is reached, he goes for another one.

He invests in his own clinic — before investing in something else. A Superman reasons that he lives in his office eight hours a day and, therefore, why shouldn't he live in nice surroundings. He knows that the nicer his facility is, the more patients he will attract to it.

He knows the ten most successful chiropractors in the country. A Superman visits with and learns from the most successful doctors in the country. He knows that a man who has done something outstanding in his profession can teach a colleague to do the same thing. It is a well-established fact that everyone shares at the top. Therefore, the achiever searches out and learns from the other Supermen doctors.

He gets to his office one hour earlier each day. The Superman doctor goes to his office at least one hour earlier each day. This time is spent organizing and planning his practice day. He never lets his patients or office staff run him; HE runs his office! This organizational time is spent catching up on insurance reporting, answering correspondence, looking over the day's patient schedule in case a patient needs extra service, and planning practice-building projects. He never lets his patients, his C.A.'s, or telephone calls interrupt his planning time.

Work. The average doctor of chiropractic only works twenty-four hours per week. A Superman, on the other hand, knows that if he wants to double his practice, he has to double his office hours. The more he is in his office, the more patients he can accommodate.

He "weeds out" his practice. Ninety-nine percent of practice problems are caused by one percent of the patients. A Superman eliminates these patients from his practice and so has a stress-free practice. Once these patients have been "weeded out," the Law of Vacuum comes into effect (as Nature always endeavors to fill a vacuum), and his practice increases.

He doesn't turn patients into "knockers." He goes out of his way not to create enemies. One "knocker" can destroy what ten "boosters" can contribute. The Superman chiropractor adopts the attitude that the patient is always right, even though he may be totally wrong!

He always settles accounts to the patient's satisfaction. If a disagreement comes up on how much a patient owes, the Superman always settles the account to that patient's satisfaction. He has seen other doctors actually lose patients because they, or their C.A.'s, forced a patient to pay fifteen dollars that the patient felt he didn't owe. Whether the patient actually owes the money is not important. The Supermen doctors feel that it is wiser in some cases to be kind rather than right. They always settle accounts to their patients' satisfaction.

If he is not getting results on a patient, he dismisses that patient. If a patient's symptoms or objective findings are not greatly reduced within thirty days of a patient's initiating care, a Superman chiropractor considers dismissing that patient. He knows patients don't like to be strung along. He simply sits the patient down and explains to him that he is not progressing as expected. He gives him the option of either going to another physician or staying under his care and expecting slower progress than originally anticipated. He offers to make the appointment with another physician for the patient and offers his cooperation with that other doctor by sending him x-rays, lab reports, etc. The patient usually will elect to stay with his Superman doctor, and that doctor will have stopped his patient from becoming a potential "knocker"; he is now a "booster" because of the doctor's honesty.

He doesn't treat more than one condition at the same time. Research studies have shown that eighty percent of patients accepted for care are relieved of their symptoms; ten percent are only slightly relieved; ten percent don't respond at all. A Superman knows that if he only treats one condition, he will have an eighty percent chance of success and a ten percent chance of failure. He also knows that if he elects to treat four conditions at the same time, his potential failure rate will be forty percent (four times the ten percent failure rate). Therefore, rather than increase his chances of failure, he treats only one condition at a time.

He replaces a bad habit with a good habit. The difference between the Superman doctor and the mediocre doctor is the achiever's excellent success habits. An achiever doesn't add a successful habit to an unsuccessful habit. He replaces an unsuccessful habit with a successful one. He finds out how the practice leaders in our profession are practicing, and does exactly like them. It will be uncomfortable at first, but he knows that if he perseveres, it will become comfortable for him, too.

He doesn't have a "help me but don't change me" attitude. This is the cry of a doctor who will not increase his practice. In order to grow, he must change — and most doctors want to grow without getting out of their comfortable ruts. A Superman knows that he has to change in order to grow, and he is willing to do so. That is why he is Super-successful!

Today, Not Tomorrow (TNT)! Supermen doctors do whatever they have to do — today, not tomorrow! They "clean the slate" for a smoother-flowing tomorrow. The larger producers in our profession "TNT" on a regular basis. They know that the more they can accomplish today, the more they will have tomorrow.

He carefully selects who he associates with. He knows that if a doctor **aspires to have a practice of $500,000 a year,** he should have friends who make that same amount, or more, a year. He won't associate with a $40,000-a-year doctor, because that man's concepts are only $40,000 a year, and a man will sink to his weakest friend's concepts. He has a choice of his associates. It is up to him. A Superman associates with people of like or higher calibre.

The doctor should do the doctoring and the C.A. should do the collecting. The doctors of larger practices only talk to patients about their health problems. Their sole concern is diagnosis and treatment. They feel that the C.A. is more competent to handle the collections. Remember: doctoring and collecting are separate arts.

The Superman chiropractor goes to one practice management seminar/program at a time. He doesn't try to get the "best" from four or five programs/seminars, and then add them to his practice. He knows it won't work, because every system has interlocking pieces and all the pieces must fit together to fill out the puzzle. He knows that by bringing together the best of four or five programs will only result in "pieces" that don't fit together. The result is confusion!

He takes his staff to practice management seminars and meetings. Not only do these seminars motivate his staff, but they also teach modern office procedures as well as elevating their concepts of chiropractic. A productive doctor knows that a well-educated, competent staff is absolutely necessary for a Superman's practice.

Professional Practice Priorities

One more time. When a patient expresses a desire to quit prematurely, the Superman always convinces him to come one more time. This extra visit may make the difference between the patient getting well or remaining sick. It also may turn a potential "knocker" into a "booster."

His office staff is enthusiastic. He has his entire staff enthusiastic about chiropractic. When a patient states that he is getting good results, the achiever says, "That's great! That's fantastic! I want you to tell my receptionist how good you are feeling." When the patient retells his story to the C.A., she responds, "That's wonderful! I'm very pleased for you. Isn't chiropractic great?" The successful chiropractor embellishes the enthusiasm in his office, making it a place where people want to go. He knows that if he can make his patients enthusiastic, he will end up with chiropractic "boosters" for patients.

He knows it is the enthusiastic patient, and not the satisfied patient, who sends him business. He knows that the patient has a contract with him. He has a health problem that the doctor can take care of. He pays the doctor money to take care of that health problem. The doctor corrects the problem, and both are even. The patient feels he doesn't owe the doctor anything. Therefore, something additional must be added to stimulate a patient to refer. This something extra is: "Only an enthusiastic patient will refer." To make a patient enthusiastic, the doctor and his staff must be enthusiastic themselves. For, when they become enthusiastic, it becomes infectious. When that enthusiasm spills over to the patients, they will become that doctor's "boosters."

He is therefore enthusiastic. To build a large practice for tomorrow, the successful doctor is more enthusiastic today. He knows that people don't like to go to stagnant doctors. It is depressing to be around people who are totally devoid of enthusiasm. Most people have strong desires to get away from them as quickly as possible. The Superman knows that if his patients feel this way about him, he won't have a practice. He doesn't repel patients with lethargy; he attracts them with enthusiasm!

The Superman doctor is more positive than his most negative patient. When a patient is extremely negative, as some are, he will respond very well to an extremely strong, positive doctor. When the doctor is more positive than the patient is negative, the negativism in the patient's mind is changed to enthusiasm and hope, and then the healing process can begin. The opposite is also true: if a patient drags the doctor down to the depths of that patient's negativism, making both moods negative, they will repel each other like two negative poles of a magnet repel each other. Therefore, an achiever is always more positive than his patients are negative in order to help his patients get well.

The doctor of chiropractic should always have a successful air about him. The successful doctor walks erect, holds his head high, and he is as well-dressed as his best-dressed patient.

He has developed charisma. Charisma is what separates the exceptional from the mediocre in the professional fields. One method of developing charisma is by being dedicated. When a doctor is dedicated, it shows. It shows in many facets of his life.

We have all observed the Supermen in our field of chiropractic. They have that charisma of dedication. They know what they are doing — there isn't any doubt. They have a glowing confidence and belief in the services they provide. They developed this dedication by finding a technique in chiropractic that really "turned them on" — and then they mastered it! This dedication and the mastering of a technique produced charisma. Once these doctors developed their charisma, it acted as magnets to attract new patients to them.

He specializes in certain conditions. A Superman knows that if he tells his patients that chiropractic is great and that all chiropractors handle similar conditions, those patients will refer their friends to another chiropractor who practices closer to their homes. However, if they know that their chiropractor specializes in certain conditions, they will refer solely to him. They will tell their friends that they would rather go to a specialist in [whatever condition] across town than to a general practitioner D.C. closer to home.

He specializes in a certain technique. If a Superman chiropractor uses a method such as Applied Kinesiology, Gonstead, Grostic, Pettibon, etc., he will tell his patients what it is and what the difference is between his technique and that used by other professionals in his area. His patients will then become "Bird-Dogs" (referring patients to him). His patients will sing the praises of chiropractic in general, but of him in particular. When he explains to his patients what he does in his specialty, they will pick up the impression that he is dedicated. The more dedicated he is and the more specialized he is, the larger his practice will become.

His patients will tell their friends or relatives, "I want you to go to my doctor because he specializes in this particular technique." That doctor's patients will tell everyone they know that their doctor is a tremendous chiropractor and that he specializes in the Grostic method, or whatever. They will also inform their friends and relatives that they can't get that particular technique anywhere else other than at their doctor's office. Obviously it will also increase that doctor's referrals tremendously.

He may develop an unusual expertise. I know a Superman chiropractor who specializes in the treatment of hemorrhoids. He has a reputation of excellence in this specialty and has all the professionals in his area referring to him.

A truly productive chiropractor doesn't have an "ivory tower" attitude. As previously discussed, a doctor should have confidence in what he does, and should radiate this confidence. But, at the same time, he should be careful that he doesn't project an "ivory tower" attitude showing the public that he feels he is the only panacea for all ills. Patients don't like a conceited, pompous, "ivory tower" attitude, and will not go to a practitioner who is so afflicted. All the Supermen doctors I know are "real" people who have not been adversely affected by their success. It is the "real" people's attitudes that attract patients to them!

The successful doctor gives V.I.P. care to his Bird-Dog, referring patients. There is a saying in chiropractic circles which states that only ten percent of our patients will send us ninety percent of our business. It is a true statement! A Superman takes extra good care of his Bird-Dog patients and he knows they will take extra good care of him. He never forgets who helped him attain success, and he takes care of them like a gardener takes care of a prized rose garden.

He goes back to the "well." Whenever a Superman finds his new patient volume down, he doesn't try to figure out new ways to get new patients. He just thinks of his most recent new patients. He finds out who referred them, and then he goes back to the "well," back to his referring Bird-Dog patients, and stimulates them to refer more new patients. He sends them Thank-U-Grams, makes telephone calls to them, gives them gifts (flowers, plants, etc.) — in other words, he lets them know how much he appreciates them. His Bird-Dog patients, thus stimulated, will refer more new patients to him, and his practice will start growing again.

He loves his patients. He uses lots of tender loving care (TLC) when taking care of a patient. He is not gushy nor super-sweet, but has a good deal of empathy for his patients, sympathy for their problems and TLC in his heart when he takes care of them. He has found that a great percentage of them come solely to him for the TLC he gives them. He has found that this is a very important aspect of doctoring and that the more he cares about his patients (like he would for his mother, father, sister, brother, etc.), the larger his practice becomes.

He is sympathetic and listens to his patients. He shuts his mouth and looks at his patients. Even if a patient bores him, he still listens to him. To the patient, his problem is the most important thing in his life at that moment, and he wouldn't be explaining it to his doctor if it wasn't. If the patient is having an emotional problem, the doctor counsels him, for he knows that many people come to his office not solely to be adjusted, but because he is the only one they can talk to. So he lets them talk!

He listens to his patients in order to pick up referral hints. He has found that the majority of his new patients come from his present patients and not from any outside source. Therefore, he listens attentively to them. They might tell him about a brother, an uncle, children, etc., etc., who have problems that he can treat. His patients might tell him about friends who have been involved in automobile accidents. As he concentrates on what his patients are saying, he picks up on their referral hints and he is able to tell them to schedule their friends or relatives for appointments. He pays strict attention to his patients because he knows that is where his future referrals are coming from. All Supermen's practices are primarily referral practices, and they obtain these referrals by listening for them.

He practices present-time consciousness. One of the most difficult things for anyone to do is to control his own mind. Too often we try to think of ten things at the same time and end up with mental confusion. The same is true when we take care of a patient. All kinds of other thoughts enter our minds, i.e., bills to be paid, family problems, the next patient, the last patient, etc. In order to stop all these extra thoughts from entering his mind, a doctor has to practice "present-time consciousness," which is total concentration on the task at hand, and not letting any other thoughts enter his consciousness. It has been found that doctors who have mastered this P.T.C. technique are able to care for more patients in less time without their patients feeling that they have been short-changed. Supermen doctors practice present-time consciousness.

He mentally overpowers his patients and gives them reasons to get well. Many times, when a patient's mind is magnetized to the hopelessness of his health problem, the doctor has to jar or shock that patient's mind in order to get it back on the track of getting well. He has to be more positive than the patient is negative. He has to be very forceful and dynamic in order to change the patient's mind from how hopeless his health problem is into a real hope of getting well. He has to transfer the patient's thinking from sickness to a positive attitude pointed toward getting well. Changing his mind can be done by asking the patient what his hobbies are, where he is going for vacation the next summer, or by turning his mind to something he wants to do, such as playing with his children or grandchildren, painting the house, riding a horse, going back into business, etc. Once he starts thinking of the answers, he is well on his way to health. The Superman doctor finds out what motivates his patients and then motivates them! He mentally over-

27

powers his patients for their own good.

He knows that patients go where they are invited and refer where they are appreciated. If you were one of your patients, would you refer your friends to your office? A Superman's office is the type of facility he and his family would like to go to. He gives his patients something extra to show his appreciation: unexpected blood pressure or spirometer checks, exercises to strengthen weakened muscles, etc. He shows his interest with his eyes as well as with his ears. He knows that the more he gives, the more he will receive. The successful chiropractor takes care of his patients!

He makes the patient feel important, wanted and needed. Indifference is the main reason why businesses lose their clientele. Inside all of us is a strong need that cries out for self-importance, recognition, love, security, etc. The practitioner who satisfies this need will be the practitioner who will create a strong clientele. A Superman goes that extra mile for his patients! They are his livelihood, and he takes care of them!

He gives them compassion and interest at their times of need. He knows that when patients are in pain or have serious problems outside the office, they will need extra TLC and time. He gives his patients this extra care.

He uses the power of being a doctor. Many times it is more effective to tell a patient with authority that you want him to make an appointment for his family than it would be to ask him! This is especially true of a man referring his wife, or of a woman referring her children.

If a patient tells a Superman doctor that he has a relative or friend who has a problem, the doctor would reply: "Of course I can help him. I want you to tell the receptionist to make an appointment for your relative/friend at the same time of your next visit. You can then bring him in with you." The Superman uses the power of a doctor's authority to get a patient to bring someone else to him. Also, if a patient tells him about one of his friends who has a problem which is similar to the one he is being treated for, the doctor tells him, "I want you to tell your friend that chiropractic definitely can help that problem. The longer he waits, the longer it will take to treat, and the more expensive it will become. As a matter of fact, what I would like you to do is to make an appointment with the receptionist for your friend for the same day and time as your next appointment. You can bring your friend along with you then." By using a strong, positive approach like this, the Superman doctor increases his number of referrals over and above what he would ordinarily get.

An exceptional doctor knows that this technique is only used with the best interests of the prospective patient in mind. He won't do it just to get a new patient. This technique is only used when the doctor honestly feels that it is imperative that he sees the prospective patient as soon as possible, i.e., pending surgery, developing a scoliosis, etc.

He makes commitments to himself. Whenever he decides on a practice goal, he commits all his mental and physical energies to accomplishing that goal. His commitment is what he does, whether or not he is tired, rushed, hassled, depressed, etc. To an achiever, a commitment is a "binding agreement" he has with himself, and it must be honored. A true professional honors his commitments.

He has a system of minimums. All Supermen have basic office procedures which are performed on each and every patient, regardless of how busy or tired they may be. These basic procedures are their systems of "minimums." The difference between the successful doctor and the mediocre doctor is that the former's system of "minimums" is higher than that of a mediocre doctor's. Perhaps, when the latter is rushed, he will put off a patient's post-examination, x-ray, etc., but a Superman doctor doesn't!

He raises his level of competency. Most of us would like to immediately double our practices and enjoy the fruits of a larger practice. We would like the prestige and the monetary rewards of a practice which is double the size of the one we presently have. However, most of us, if we doubled our practices, wouldn't be able to handle them. Our practices would, within ninety days, revert back to their previous levels. The reason why we wouldn't maintain our practices at twice their normal size is that we would be outside our "comfort zones," which are our present practice levels. In other words, we cannot handle more patients than we think we can, and if given more patients, we wouldn't be able to take care of them, and we would soon lose them.

I am sure we all can recognize the symptoms of a "comfort zone" in our practices. The tendency to stretch out our present patient visits when a large influx of new patients arrive in our practices, or the tendency to turn down or refer new patients to other practitioners more than we normally would, are signs that we have reached our comfort zones, or our competency levels.

A Superman knows that in order to grow, he must first raise his level of competency. Once raised, the Law of the Vacuum will automatically fill up his practice. One of the easiest methods of increasing competency is to take over a larger practitioner's practice when he is on vacation, or by stacking a day in your own practice. The stack-a-day procedure is explained fully in another section of this book.

A Superman chiropractor is not a seeker. He builds upon expertise, adding new techniques to his already existing treatment knowledge. He is not constantly seeking new chiropractic techniques, as this is counter-productive and destructive to a practice.

He knows that the worst thing a doctor can do is to get too excited about a new technique and try to convert all his old patients to this technique. Such type of action will only result in patient loss. He establishes his base technique first. This is the technique that he knows so well that it enables him to successfully treat eighty percent of his patients. Then, as he expands his expertise, he adds new techniques to his already solid base technique. He always adds to his base technique; he doesn't swap or exchange techniques. He is not a seeker.

HOW A SUPERMAN IS MADE

Many doctors build their practices to a certain level, run into a multitude of barriers, get discouraged, and never progress beyond that point. This chapter will describe how a Superman builds his practice above the practice level where the average doctor quits. Any Superman will attest that from this point onward, it is clear sailing to any practice heights a doctor desires.

How a Superman Conquers the Main Barriers to Success

Have you ever wondered why some men climb to the top of the ladder of success while the great majority (ninety percent) accept a lesser position in life? What is it that the so-called "gifted few" (the Supermen) have that the average man doesn't have?

He doesn't believe the introjections that people place upon him. Introjections are rules placed upon him by another person, agency, etc. — that is: rules, regulations, ethics, do's and don'ts, can's and can'ts, should's and shouldn'ts, etc., etc. The rules of you CAN'T give good service to over twenty patients a day; DON'T call yourself a chiropractor, call yourself a chiropractic physician; DON'T charge more than ten dollars per visit, or DON'T advertise, may have been true years ago but are not relevant today.

Similarly, a SHOULDN'T of 1492 was that a sailor shouldn't sail West for fear he might fall of the end of the earth! Once Columbus showed that one could sail West and return safely, fears vanished. People no longer believed the introjection of you SHOULDN'T sail West.

The Superman doctor reasons that if most of the rules of yesterday are no longer true today, perhaps the rules of today will be proven to be false tomorrow. In this spirit, he challenges today's introjections and forges new ground. What, then, stops other doctors from advancing like the Superman?

He conquers the Fear of Loss. Most doctors are afraid to gamble with the practices they have in order to build them up. Their fear of losing something prevents them from growing. There is a contradiction in their minds: they want to grow bigger to enjoy more of the fruits of life but at the same time they don't want to risk losing what they already have. Therefore, they never grow! Why, then, don't they take steps forward to larger and more rewarding practices? Obviously, the answer is that the fear of loss is a stronger emotion than the desire for gain.

How, then, does the Superman doctor handle this fear of loss that everyone is plagued with? He reasons that he already has the ability to maintain his practice at its existing level, and if he adds a new procedure and it doesn't work, so what! He simply will go back to the solid practice that he already has. The worst thing that could happen is *no growth* from a new idea, and a loss in his practice would never occur.

As the Superman forges new ground, he encounters a new fear: the unknown. Who wants to sail into uncharted waters? Who has to?

He conquers the Fear of the Unknown. Conquering the unknown isn't really a problem. A Superman merely attaches himself to someone who has already attained what he would like to accomplish, i.e.: a consultant, etc., and proceeds according to their instructions. By using this method, the Superman doesn't encounter any fears because the unknowns are eliminated for him.

There are many Supermen with practice incomes of well over a million dollars a year. Some of these doctors have insurance practices and some don't; some advertise and some don't; some have Personal Injury and Workmen's Compensation practices, and some have family practices; some are straights, and some are mixers. There are few unknowns in our profession. Someone else has conquered these unkowns and having done so, can teach others how to get there.

The achievers have found that those who HAVE can teach those who DON'T HAVE. Anyone can succeed if taught how. Some doctors, once trained, break loose from the pack and find that it's free and easy sailing to success.

The Secret Weapon of the Supermen:
CONCEPTING

Much has been written regarding the concepting of new patients. Most of it is mystical, far-fetched and, to some extent, unbelievable. While concepting new patients may seem too metaphysical, it is a proven fact that this is how the Supermen build and control their practices.

I cannot say that the method I am going to outline actually attracts their thoughts to them; however, it is a fact that when their minds are attuned to a certain topic, goal, ambition, etc., they become more aware of opportunities to attain their predominant goals. Concepting does work and it is the reason why the rich get richer, while the poor get poorer. One group is always looking for ways to make money, while the other group doesn't care.

The same principle is applicable to chiropractic. The doctor who concepts new patients, attracts new patients to himself, whether it be by metaphysical actions or by the doctor being more aware of opportunities to ask for referrals — the result is the same. The man who concepts new patients all day long is the man who gets the new patients.

The Mechanics of Concepting. Our minds are split into two portions: our conscious mind does all the thinking, reasoning, etc., and our subconscious mind attracts to us our dominant feelings, desires, ambitions, etc. The key to conception is: If we can consciously control the "feelings" of the subconscious mind, or at least control the thoughts that get into the subconscious mind, we will control what we get out of life.

How do we control the feelings that occur in the subconscious mind or the thoughts that get to the subconscious mind? The first step is to control those thoughts that we want to reach the subconscious mind. We can do this by following the five rules that will be explained later in this chapter. Once our thoughts are controlled by these five rules, we can then add a catalyst that carries our thoughts from our conscious mind into our subconscious mind. Once these thoughts, with the aid of a catalyst, reach our subconscious mind, they become a feeling. The subconscious mind then intensifies this feeling until it becomes all-consuming desire, and this desire drives us to our destination, regardless of obstacles.

In order to clarify this point, imagine a man's mind split into two portions. The front part is the conscious mind and the back part is the subconscious mind. (Illustration # 1)

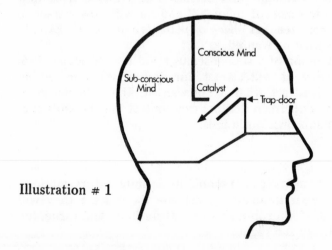

Illustration # 1

Connecting these two portions of a mind is a trap door that is activated by a catalyst. The catalyst is a powerful emotion, or an action which produces a powerful emotion. When someone wants something out of life, he thinks his dominant thoughts and adds a catalyst to open the trap door. The dominant thought then goes into his subconscious mind and becomes a feeling. The feelings in the subconscious mind intensify into a burning desire. The subconscious mind then attracts his feelings/desires to him. At this point, concepting seems quite simple. Add a catalyst to dominant thought, and this opens the trap door into the subconscious mind. The subconscious mind then attracts feelings. It seems easy — but it isn't!

The Five Rules of Thought Control. A word of caution: The subconscious mind is a non-thinking entity. It will attract to itself whatever our dominant thoughts are, whether good or bad. Unfortunately, it can also attract to us the negative aspects of life: sickness, poverty, misfortunes, etc.

To illustrate this point: If a doctor finds himself in a low income situation due to decreased patient volume, he will need more new patients in order to rebuild his practice. This doctor, in an effort to rebuild his practice, will set new goals and proceed to program his mind to attain his goals. He will tell himself, "The practice is down. I need more money, therefore I need five new patients per week to get my practice back where it should be." He will say it over and over mentally until he has the emotional state (catalyst) necessary to push his thoughts over into his subconscious mind. However, he has just programmed his mind incorrectly. The predominant thought and feeling was, "the lack of new patients" and "the lack of income," and he will now attract to himself his primary feelings —*lack of patients and money*. Exactly the opposite of what he wanted.

The programming of a subconscious mind is an exact art. Programmed correctly, it will attract our desires. Programmed incorrectly, it will attract what is not wanted. The following rules explain how the Supermen doctors can control the thoughts that reach into their subconscious minds.

RULE I: Your thoughts (goals) should be definite and crystal clear.
The clearer your thoughts (goals) are, the quicker they will come into being. If your thoughts (goals) are fuzzy and vague, the results will be fuzzy and vague.

RULE II: Only program positive thoughts.

All dominant thoughts should be formed with an expectancy of achieving them, i.e.: "This is where I am going," or "This is what will happen," etc. By commiting ourselves to our thoughts (goals), they will become a reality. Proper programming would be similar to: "I am going to take care of low back patients. I am ready to take care of two hundred patients a week. I will receive three thousand dollars a week," etc. And "I like taking care of co-operative patients. I have plenty of room for new patients. All my office activities are caught up and we are ready for new patients. I'm ready to serve five new patients a week," etc.

RULE III: Always instruct the subconscious mind to attain reasonable, prudent, and attainable goals.

Never ask for something that is unbelievabe or impossible to attain. That is the same as programming a *lack*, *need*, or negative emotion — it will attract the opposite of what is wanted. Example: If a doctor wants a hundred new patients tomorrow and yet won't do anything to attract them, who is kidding whom? Someone once said, "Whatever the mind of man can conceive and BELIEVE, it can achieve." If a doctor *believes* he can achieve something, he will be able to do so. If he doesn't believe he can accomplish something, then he won't be able to do so. Belief is what makes accomplishments possible.

RULE IV: Never program a need of anything.

Never program your mind in this manner: "I *need* new patients"; "My practice is doing poorly and I need new patients"; "I'm broke and need new patients"; "I have a lot of bills and need new patients." The predominant thought here is a LACK of new patients, and you will attract to yourself these thoughts . . . a LACK of new patients and money! Remember, negative emotions are more powerful than positive emotions, and the conceptors will attract their negative emotions rather than their positive desires.

When programming ourselves for practice growth, we have to be careful of our emotions on a slow day. We all have slow days. We should not tell ourselves that our practice is off and we need new business. Our primary emotions and thoughts revolve around lack of patients. This becomes a feeling, and we attract to ourselves our feelings — a lack of patients. When this slow day arrives, and it will, we simply say: "Great, I needed this free time to catch up on my insurance work and be prepared for all the new patients that will be coming in tomorrow," or next week, etc.

35

By using this technique, our primary desire is for new patients (not the lack of patients) and we will attract to ourselves these desires: new patients.

RULE V: Never ask for one desire when trying to avoid an even stronger desire.

The strongest desire is predominant and it will attract to itself what the conceptor already doesn't want.

If a doctor finds himself in a low-income situation, he will have two conflicting emotions: Fear of Failure (lack of income, etc.), and a Desire of Gain (more patients, income, etc.). In most cases, the Fear of Failure is the strongest of the two emotions, and the subconscious mind attracts to itself its primary thoughts: FAILURE (lack of patients, income, etc.).

The conceptor, instead of trying to avoid or escape from a failure situation, should ignore the poor state of his practice and only think of his desire for gain. If his desire for gain is his dominant thought, he will attract to himself only gain.

The All Important Catalyst

As previously stated, don't try to influence the subconscious mind with thought. Thoughts alone won't reach the subconscious mind. Every day we think millions of thoughts. Can you imagine the mess our lives would be if all our thoughts reached our subconscious minds and attracted to us all of our thoughts . . . daily? To quote an old joke: "If we became what we thought about all day, most men would become women."

We have to add a CATALYST. It is not thought, but a catalyst together with thought — that moves our PRIMARY thoughts from our conscious minds to our subconscious minds. Our thoughts then become a feeling. This feeling intensifies into a desire, and we attract to us our feelings/desires. The four most common catalysts are as follows:

CATALYST I: Emotion

Negative emotions, such as fear, hate, revenge, anger, etc., or the positive emotions, such as courage to achieve, consuming desire to be successful, commitment, drive, determination, single-mindedness of purpose, grit — are the emotions that penetrate the subconscious mind, carrying your thoughts with them.

CATALYST II: Action.

Many times an individual cannot conjure up an emotion strong enough to push his primary thoughts from his conscious mind to his subconscious mind. In this case, he should substitute "action" for the strong emotion. His thoughts plus his actions produce a feeling, and we attract to ourselves our feelings.

CATALYST III: Act as if.

Many times, an individual, in order to create a feeling, visualizes how it would feel to be successful, have money in the bank, etc. He then acts out his visions. This acting produces a feeling, and feelings are what attracts to us. Imagine the feeling you would have if you had money and success. Act it out, and it will become a reality.

CATALYST IV: Do a successful act.

The productive practitioner, instead of imagining the feeling of success, performs a successful act and he then *knows* the feeling of success. For example, he saves ten percent of his income until he has a sizeable amount saved up. This gives him the feeling of success. This feeling of success attracts to him more success. Try it! Ten percent saved never hurt anyone!

Summarized, concepting is crystalized, positive, definite thoughts (goals), with a catalyst added. The thought, aided by the catalyst, becomes a feeling which moves the subconscious mind into action and attracts our goals to us.

How It Works

The process by which our subconscious mind attracts to us has been likened to a radio transmitter that beams a message from our subconscious mind through the air into the subconscious minds of other people. If your subconcious mind is on "send" (ready to take care of new patients), and the other person's subconcious mind is set on "receive" (needs your care), you will attract this person to you. To illustrate this point: sometimes we can go to a party and feel attracted to someone else and, once having met this other person, find out that this attraction was mutual. Instant rapport! This is how subconscious attraction works.

By using this concepting principle, an exceptional doctor (a Superman) concentrates on his favorite type of patients (headaches, backaches, etc.), adds a catalyst, and his subconscious mind attracts to him his desires, that is, headache and backache patients. Better yet, his subconscious mind will only attract to him the type of patients he wants and not the type of patients he doesn't want. (Illustration #2) This is why two doctors can practice together and attract patients with exactly opposite type conditions and of opposite economic levels.

By attracting the type patients he wants, a Superman can have a stress-free practice. He can receive patients who are naturally suited to his ability, expertise, etc. The patients are happy because they are getting well, and the doctor is happy because he's helping his patients, his practice is larger, and his income is up — with less stress.

Illustration # 2

Does it work all the time?

If a doctor's subconscious mind is on "send" (ready for low-back patients) and there are five thousand people in town with low back pain, wouldn't all five thousand of these potential patients show up at his office at the same time? No. The number of patients who would come to his office would depend on a number of factors.

1. Strength of the doctor's mental signal. A very weak radio signal (low feelings on his part) will reach fewer people than with a strong signal.

2. A confused mental signal. Crystalized definite thoughts are necessary to attract like kind. A confused mind will produce confused results.

3. Whether or not the other person is receptive to the message. Using the principle of radio, it would depend upon whether or not the person receiving the message has his radio turned on. If his radio is not turned on, he can't receive the message.

4. Whether or not the other person has his receiver "tuned in" correctly. Again using the principle of a radio, if the prospective patient is slightly off-station or is listening to another station altogether, he will not receive the message. That is why radio advertisers keep advertising their messages — because people change stations.

These factors are why a "sender" can continue to beam out the same message and continue to receive the same benefit: a steady flow of new patients.

How a Superman Systematically Builds His Practice by Expanding His Concepts

The system I am going to outline for you here is the system a Superman uses to build his practice to the very heights of our profession. It is called the Practice Expansion Wheel.

The Practice Expansion Wheel

As the reader can see by Illustration # 3 on page 44, I have taken the practice of chiropractic and made it into a pie, with many slices to the pie. Each section of the pie (or between the spokes of a wheel) is labeled with the nine main conditions that a chiropractor treats and the five main variations to our chiropractic practices.

The nine main conditions that a doctor of chiropractic takes care of are: headaches — both migraine and tension, and greater occipital syndrome headaches; cervical problems, such as whiplash; thoracic problems, such as intercostal neuralgia; shoulder problems, such as tendonitis, bursitis, adhesive capsulitis, etc.; low back problems, such as strains, sprains, lumbago; disc problems; leg problems, such as sciatica; extremity problems; and internal problems.

There are also five main variations to chiropractic practices, i.e., insurance practices, Personal Injury practices, sports injury practices, pediatric practices, and nutritional practices.

The Superman carries out a frank appraisal of his abilities, and identifies those conditions to which he's become an expert. He then identifies areas in which he is weak but where he would like to be strong, and sets about a vigorous postgraduate educational program to make his weak points into his strong points.

Once a weak point becomes a strong point, it creates a new feeling of expertise and we attract to ourselves those needing our expertise.

Once this is accomplished, our doctor finds another weak point that he is interested in and sets about another vigorous postgraduate educational program until this weak point becomes his new strongest point.

This procedure is continued until all his weak points are his strong points. Each time he turns a weak point into a strong point, he increases his practice 25%. If he started with three strong points and increased his expertise the remaining 11 points of the Practice Expansion Wheel, he will have increased his practice 275%. The Practice Expansion Wheel is how the experts systematically expand their practices.

A Superman increases his practice by percentages. The illustration of the Practice Expansion Wheel shows that a doctor can increase his practice by 25% every time he develops a strong area from a weak area. If the reader will take this concept and enlarge upon it by adding office procedural differences, he will notice that the doctor can increase his practice by percentages that are astronomical.

As stated previously, a Superman doesn't get emotional about his goals, nor does he get emotional about the procedures he uses to build his practice. He *un*emotionally adds one office management procedure after another to his practice, and accepts the percentage of growth each procedure will produce.

He finds that it is best to increase his practice in a slow and consistent manner. He knows that if he only increases his practice one percent per day, this will result in a four hundred percent increase in one year. Therefore, he doesn't try to double his practice in one day when it can be comfortably done at the rate of one percent per day and still reach the same objective. Consistency is the key!

The following are the primary office procedures that these exceptional practitioners utilize to increase their practices, and the percentage of practice increases they expect from each procedure.

Management Procedures

30% **Examinations.** Orthopedic, Neurological and Chiropractic examinations added to a non-examining practice will add patient control, referrals, and income at a 30% ratio.

40% **Physiotherapy.** Once added to a practice, will increase that practice by 40%. Patients like the extra touch of gadgets and machines. A word of caution — don't increase overhead radically and don't overcharge!

165% **Increased Recommendations.**

25% If a doctor recommends **intensified care** to relieve his patients as quickly as possible, he will increase his practice by 25%.

100% If he recommends a series of care beyond relief, called **corrective care**, he will have a 100% increase in his practice.

40% If he recommends a series of care beyond relief and correction, called **rehabilitation**, he will add a 40% increase in his practice.

Note: People will come to an office for 80% of the recommended care.

20% **Pre-Report tape or audiovisuals.** This must be personally prepared by the doctor, explaining chiropractic, home care instructions, the do's and don'ts of how the patient is to conduct his personal life while under the doctor's active care, etc. This will produce a 20% increase in his practice. It is not necessary to have the tapes individualized to each patient. Pre-planned programs can be made up for cervical, lumbar, shoulder problems, etc.

40% **Written Reports.** The time spent making up written recommendations and instructions yield higher follow-through of recommendations — at least 40%.

30% **Multiple Appointment Systems.** Either cards or calendars. When patients have 10-20-30 office visits made at one time and see that it is posted in the appointment book, they have a tendency to follow through on their scheduling, at least 30% more.

40% **Recapture Programs.** A definite, consistent, and persistent program of preventing patients from resetting their appointments will increase your practice the stated percentage. This program of anti-self-destruction of patients is designed not only to prevent the patient from quitting care prematurely, but also to make up any missed visits.

30% Doctor Regimen Program. (See "The Toughest and the Best" page 119).

40% Patient Lectures. Patient lectures will increase any practice by 40%. The doctor should concentrate on teaching his patients how to care for their bodies and also the principle of chiropractic. He should talk about named conditions that chiropractic can help. He should NOT preach!

10% Patient Reminder Calls and Cards. This procedure is advisable when the patient has an appointment less frequently than every two weeks. This is done by having this patient fill out a postcard with his name, address and zip code when he makes his next appointment. The C.A. then places this card in a tickler file for four days prior to the patient's appointment date. When this card shows up on the date filed, the C.A. does one of two things: (1) calls the patient at home or work to remind him; and (2) mails the card. This will increase a practice by 10%.

10% Patient Letters. These are sent out on a pre-planned, regular basis, along with Thank You For Referral notes and Welcome to the Office letters. This procedure will increase a practice by 10%.

80% Liberalized Insurance Program. Allowing patients to charge their services as long as they have selective, assignable insurance, is advisable. An 80% increase can be expected.

5% C.A. Regimen. (See "The Toughest and the Best")

10% Courtesy Spinal Examination. Spinal examinations for patients and/or their relatives, at no charge or obligation, will increase a practice by 10%.

10% Recall of Former Patients. See section of book on "Telephone Recall of Former Patients."

10% Newsletters. If a doctor keeps in touch with former patients, they will return to him when similar conditions recur. If he doesn't keep in touch with them, they may forget who helped them get over their last episode of pain or illness.

10% Double Newspaper Routine. A method of spreading a doctor's name to the community by clipping newsworthy items out of a newspaper and mailing the clippings to people who are in the news. Usually a note is attached, re: "Thought you would like an extra copy," etc.

100% **Examining Doctor.** See "The Era of the Multiple Doctor Practice."

80% **Treating Doctor.** See "The Era of the Multiple Doctor Practice."

30% **Maintenance/Preventive Care.** Established doctors state that maintenance care patients make up 50-60% of their practices. Many patients cannot be cured, but they can be kept free of pain with regular chiropractic care. The more patients are convinced that maintenance care is necessary, the larger a doctor's practice will become.

* * *

When all of these management procedural percentages of growth are added together, they can increase a practice by 790%! (See Illustration # 4.) Multiply this figure by the number of times a doctor increases his expertise, and the result is a many-thousands-percentage increase in his practice. (See Illustration # 5 on foldout at back of book.)

Is this an easy way to build a practice? No — but it is the most sensible way in which to build a practice! By adding solid, long-lasting procedures to a practice, and laying out a plan for their implementation, *and following the plan*, a doctor can build an extremely large practice.

Productive chiropractors know that a practice based on occasional motivation, gimmicks, gadgets, and gizmos, is a practice which consistently has to be pumped up and pushed forward. A Superman doctor wants his practice built upon good, solid office procedures, correction programs, and rehabilitative programs. This type of practice is one that doesn't fail, has a consistent patient flow, and produces a steady income which the doctor can depend on. A Superman's practice is the most rewarding type of practice available.

Getting new patients into his office, stopping them from quitting prematurely, and getting them to refer, is how a Superman builds his practice from this point.

The following chapters describe many ideas that a Superman will utilize to build his practice. By doing the same, YOU, TOO, CAN BECOME A SUPERMAN!

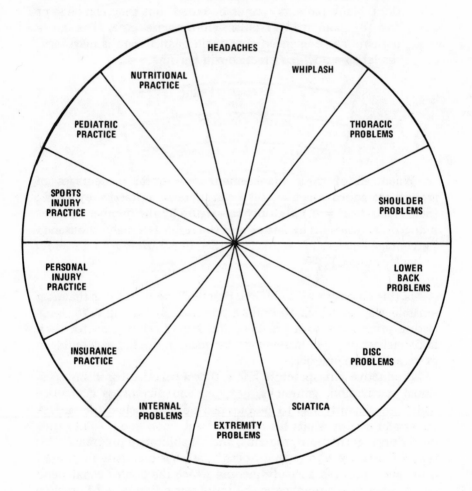

Illustration # 3 — PRACTICE EXPANSION WHEEL

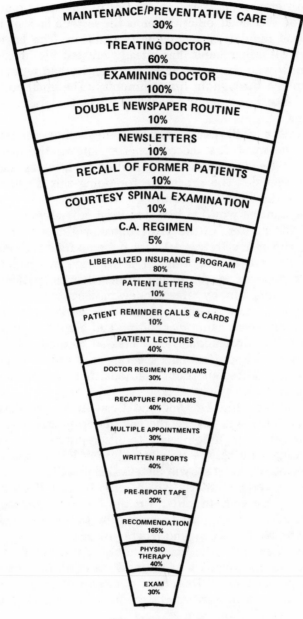

Illustration # 4

The difference between the success of the large practitioner and that of the small practitioner is the latter's lack of having a known good reputation and name recognition. The large practitioner, on the other hand, has already created his image: many people know who and what he is. His identity and reputation are already known throughout his community. The small practitioner generally has poor name recognition, little image, and less reputation.

Whenever a small practitioner competes against the larger professionals, he must first become better known throughout the community. He does this by attempting to meet as many new people as possible. The procedure for doing this is called "Bird-Dogging" or the "3-W" procedure.

In the hunting world, a bird dog is an animal which retrieves birds for the hunter. In the professional world, a "bird-dog" is someone who refers (retrieves) new patients for his doctor. This chapter is devoted to exploring the many ways in which a doctor can find supporters, or Bird-Dogs (other than his patients), who are willing to help him by referring new patients to him.

At the same time, a small practitioner needs to immediately establish an enlarged name recognition and a good reputation. In order to do this, professionals have created methods of becoming known quickly without actually meeting each and every person in their localities. These short-cut methods of acquiring an instant reputation are called "Busy Acts."

By using the "Bird-Dogging and Busy Acts" procedures, the small practitioner will invoke the law of action and reaction. He will make his community react to his reputation — building, image-creating actions. He will quickly develop a reputation of excellence and, in doing so, will increase his practice.

There are certain criteria which must be met if these procedures are to succeed. In order for the bird-dog contract to be successful, all 3 "W's" must be known by the person contacted: *W*ho you are, *W*hat you are, and *W*here you are.

At the same time, the doctor should give his contact a business card. The handing out of business cards we shall call "Whip Out Cards," or W.O.C. Therefore, a successful contact is made whenever the person contacted accepts your business card and learns the 3 "W's" about you.

Example:
"Hello, I'm Dr. Pete Fernandez. I'm a new chiropractor in

town. My office is at the corner of 48th Avenue and 4th Street North. [hand him one of your business cards before continuing] . . . I'm on a house call and can't seem to find the address. Could you help me?" If he agrees to help, thank him, and then continue: "Have you had any experience with chiropractors?" Many D.C.'s feel reluctant to ask a stranger about his experience with chiropractors because they fear a negative response. However, the response is rarely negative.

A well-known medical school in Boston, Massachusetts, conducted a survey in which its students walked up to total strangers and asked them, "What has been your experience with chiropractors?" They expected a negative response. The result, however, showed that fifty percent of the people approached, or their relatives, had used chiropractors, and that fully ninety-eight percent of these people were well satisfied with their chiropractic care. Doctors who have done similar surveys report that ninety-eight percent of all people met were favorable to chiropractic. The response is overwhelmingly favorable.

Usually the answers to your questions about chiropractic will fall into one of these four categories:

Too Good — This person is presently going to another chiropractor and thinks he's great. When he refers patients, he will refer them to his own doctor. Tell him you feel his chiropractor is great and end the conversation.

Good — This person went to a D.C. in the past, got good results, but is presently not going to anyone. This person is a source of new patients. Have him retell his experience with chiropractic and the seriousness of his problem. Teach him to testify. Rekindle in his mind how great his results were so that he will refer patients to you.

Bad — This person doesn't believe in chiropractic or has had a bad experience with a D.C. Don't waste time on this individual! Thank him for his help and time and end the conversation.

No Experience — To this person, simply state: "Chiropractors are doctors that specialize in back and neck problems, such as whiplash, and if you have any back or neck problems now, or in the future, or if you have any family or friends with these same problems, please contact me and I'll be happy to be of service. Do you have any problems now with your back or neck?" If this person does have a problem,· conduct a consultation on the spot! Make an appointment for him, write it on the back of two of your business cards, give one to him and keep the other until you get back to your office, where you will have your receptionist take the information off the back and transfer it to your appointment book. This two-card procedure seals the patient to you.

Bird-Dogging Contacts:

Utilize local tradesmen to remodel or repair your office. Don't make the mistake of doing your own painting, carpentry, rug cleaning, etc. If you do, you may save money but you'll lose an opportunity to go out and make friends and gain new patients.

Any work that needs to be done in your office should be looked upon as an opportunity for obtaining new patients. If you need electrical wiring for your new x-ray machine, call three conractors and ask them for bids on the job. When they arrive at your office, ask them, "Have you ever had any experience with chiropractors?" Do business with the man who has a favorable outlook on chiropractic. This principle extends to all people with whom you do business. Don't give your business to someone who has a negative attitude toward your profession.

Remember, people judge you by your appearance. When people see you in casual work clothes, they tend to question your image as a professsional man. If you don't look like a doctor, they may not come to you for chiropractic care. Therefore, you should not only hire contractors to do your remodeling, but you should also appear at your best when dealing with them.

After the work has been accomplished, you might offer that they can use your name as a reference to their work. This shows them that you are really proud of the fine work they have done for you.

Remember, send letters of appreciation to all repairmen, subcontractors, etc., for the same reason. Most people never think of sending a letter of thanks to their plumber, the electrician, or the carpenter. In this way you are getting your name known and liked throughout the business area of your community.

Whenever a service is performed for you, find something positive to say about it. We sell ourselves to other people by making them feel that they are favorably impressing us. We want to make them feel important, to give them a feeling of belonging and of being somebody. Everyone thrives on praise and encouragement.

Restaurant contacts. When you go into a restaurant, ask the waitress for advice when choosing from the menu. When she makes a suggestion, follow it. This will start a conversation and, before the meal is over, you will have found something nice to say about her . . . the cashier . . . anyone!

Have your lunches with business people every day. You have to eat lunch, so you might as well make your lunch break a productive time for building your practice. Many business associations or civic clubs meet at lunch time, and this is a good time to meet new people. Take attorneys to lunch — those who specialize in workmen's compensation and personal injury. When you meet these attorneys, and they like you, they will refer patients to you. In this manner, you will build up an industrial or negligence type of practice.

Do the same thing with claims agents, insurance adjusters, employers, and industry management personnel. Take one of these people out to lunch each day and ask him how you can help work with him to help build a better rapport between your profession and his industry. By doing this, you will build your practice through the patients referred to you by these insurance agents and adjusters.

Meeting with attorneys and insurance agents is a time-tested method for building practices. Don't be lazy! Put your lunch breaks to productive use by meeting as many potential supporters as you can!

Patronize your patients' businesses. If you have patients who own or manage restaurants, make sure that when you have a business lunch with an attorney, etc., that you go to your patient's place of business. Patronize their business and they will patronize yours. This mutual support promotes good rapport with other professionals and businessmen.

Have an abundant supply of business cards with you at all times. Whenever you go out to buy office equipment or supplies, ask for a cash receipt. Give the salesman your card, and say, "Can you make it out in my name? Here is my business card with all the information you'll need. I need a receipt for tax purposes." This will tell him who you are, where you are, and what you are — the 3 "W's"! Again, the more exposure you have in your community, the more productive will be your practice building.

Go to three bookstores and ask for specialty books, such as A Chiropractor Speaks Out, *by Dr. Chester Wilk.* Introduce yourself and give them your business card.

When you need new clothes, buy one item at three different stores. Never pass up an opportunity to discuss your favorite subject — chiropractic!

Visit churches. When you attend church, stay after service for any gathering or meeting, so that you can have direct contact with the people of the congregation. Make it a point also to arrive early at church and to be the last to leave. This will give you an extra opportunity to meet people. If you attend a church where they introduce visitors, be sure to take a visitor's tag, stand up (or do whatever is necessary for you to be recognized as a visitor), then make it a point to look around, try to catch people's eyes, greet them on the way out. Church is an excellent place to meet people! However, don't use the 3 "W's" procedure in church as it is too commercial. Only give out your business card if someone asks for it — and even then, don't elaborate.

Be active in civic clubs. You should get an invitation to every service club in town. When you meet other businessmen, inquire about their service club. Call the secretary of a designated club, and tell him that you plan to join and be active in a civic organization and that you have heard good reports of this club. Tell him that you would like to know when it could be arranged for you to visit his club. The secretary, who knows everyone in the club, will have the welcome mat laid out for you before you arrive. He will know that you are a prospective club member and will most likely introduce you around to other members.

Always write a letter of thanks to the secretary of the civic club after the initial visit. Tell him by letter how impressed you were with the hospitality and the spirit of the club. Tell him that you are visiting other clubs in the area, and will choose one soon.

It is possible for you to attend five or six service clubs in a week and be introduced before 250 to 300 businessmen. Again, the more people that know who, what, and where you are, the larger practice you will build.

Recommended civic clubs for leadership training are Toastmasters and the Jaycees. With these clubs you will gain a favorable reputation as an involved and civic-minded individual.

Go to the local Chamber of Commerce and ask for the names and addresses of all local civic clubs, union halls, churches, synagogues, condominiums, trailer parks; and ask for each program chairman's name, if any. Once you receive this list, write to each of the program chairmen, stating that you are a chiropractor located in their area, that you are a public speaker, and that you can speak on "How To Lift," "How To Take Care of Your Back," "Whiplash," "Neck Injuries," "Acupuncture," "Kinesiology," etc., and that you would be more than willing to speak to their club or organization. Have them simply call your office and make an appointment for you to speak. If you do this, you will have many invitations to speak. The more people that know you, the bigger practice you will have!

Become a committee chairman. Once you become a member of local civic organizations, volunteer your time for various committees. Run for a chair position, preferably program chairman, and use the opportunity to meet people — again, 3 "W's"

Go to every radio and TV station in your area. Tell them that if they would like a chiropractor to be on their talk shows, you would be happy to donate your time. Assure the TV or radio commentator that you will provide lively conversation that will help stimulate the listening or viewing audience. You'll be surprised at the number of invitations you'll receive as a result.

Do all your buying locally. Establish credit wherever you can so that they will have to investigate you . . . to find out who, what, and where you are!

Whenever possible, write checks for the smallest amount possible. Again, someone will have to know who, what, and where you are . . . and accept you.

Buying office supplies. Your office always needs supplies and you must shop for your own personal items, so use this factor to your advantage. Go to every hardware store, office supply store, discount store, etc., to price all the items you need. Learn the names of all salesmen you meet at these stores. Tell them who, what, and where you are located, and that you are pricing supplies to get the best deal. Once you have determined the costs of the miscellaneous supplies, make sure that you don't buy all your supplies from the same store. Buy two or three items from as many as twenty stores, if possible! Go back to the same salesman you met before, re-establish your contact with him, and give him another of your business cards.

Here is a list of some items which you may want to buy:

Paint — at 3 paint stores
Carpet — at 3 carpet stores
Electrical supplies — at 3 electrical supply stores
Hardware — at 3 hardware stores
Office supplies — at 3 office supply stores
Plastic signs — at 3 office supply stores
Books — at 3 bookstores
Clothes — at 3 clothing stores
Houses — see 3 realtors before choosing your house
Furniture — at 3 furniture stores

Your weekends can be of great assistance in promoting your practice growth. Stay in a local motel, talk to the desk clerk, tell him who, what, and where you are, and give him a business card. Motel or hotel clerks meet a lot of people in the course of their work! This way of using your 3 "W's" procedure is especially productive in tourist areas where there is a lot of transient business.

Call up every hotel and motel in your area and volunteer to be on call as a hotel and motel doctor. Send each a letter with your business card, telling them that if they have anyone in their establishment who needs chiropractic care, your business card with your home phone number is enclosed, and you'd be happy to be of service if they need you. They will put your card on file and on their bulletin board. When someone traveling through town needs a chiropractor, you are the one who most likely will be called.

Visit local auto dealerships to discuss future purchases. Salesmen will refer patients to you to insure your business. Go to all the local auto dealers and introduce yourself to the salesmen. Tell them you are interested in buying a new car, and that you are just checking out the different kinds of cars. Get their advice as to which ones break down the least, which ones the most, those with the best gas mileage, etc. When you get back to your office, write to the salesman and thank him for his help and advice. In every community, there are probably fifty automobile agencies you can visit. Hopefully, the salesmen will become patients of yours. These people will also refer patients to you in order to insure your future business.

Whenever you need an errand run, lawn mowed, etc., hire a local youngster, preferably the child of a patient.

Ask for items that you know a store does not carry. This will force an inquiry as to who you are and what you want. This permits you to introduce yourself. (Ask for a Gonstead parallel!)

Be seen at public events, such as town meetings, concerts, and other social events. Be recognized! How can you be known if you aren't there?

Be a leader. In every community there is a cry for those who are willing to lead. If a chiropractor responds, he can become one of the city's important personages.

Present awards. Personally award a local high school graduate a meritorious service award.

Meet every attorney in town. Volunteer referrals to them on workmen's compensation and auto accident cases.

Meet with union officials in your community. Ask to speak to union groups on "How to Lift." Give out posters. By speaking to such groups, you will increase your practice because union people

52

are very clannish and, if you take care of their people, they will take care of you.

Whenever you are away from the office, be sure to use this time for meeting people. Let them know who you are, what you are, and where you are! Talk about their health whenever possible. The idea is to make your community more familiar with you and to develop and enhance your name recognition.

Make this a rule: Never go anywhere without being paged. This affixes your name in people's minds — so be paged wherever you go. Make sure that when you answer the page, you attract some attention, but not at the risk of being obnoxious. Use the 3 "W's" procedure.

Whenever you're not busy, tell your receptionist that you are going to a certain supermarket and that you'll be there in ten minutes; tell her to have you paged at that store, as if for an emergency. Go to the supermarket, and when the page begins, let it be repeated two or three times before you answer it so that everyone in the store will have heard your name and will be waiting to see who you are. The store manager himself will probably tell you that there is an emergency call from your office. Thank him very much for taking the trouble of paging you, talk to your office on the phone, and then promptly leave the store. Go back to your office and don't forget to send the supermarket manager a thank-you note for being so thoughtful and courteous. The next time you enter that supermarket, you can be sure they'll know you! This paging procedure can be used fifteen to twenty times a day very successfully. If you've ever wondered why you've heard so many pages at football games for Dr. Jones or Dr. Brown, it is because they are medical doctors building their practices in the same way you are building yours. They know about the paging routines! You can use this procedure to your own advantage to become known throughout your community.

Every time you meet someone, write his/her name down in a little notebook. Send them Thank-U-Grams. Mail them chiropractic literature.

Build your practice in your recreational time. I know a doctor who developed sixty to eighty percent of his practice from the golf course during his first two years of practice. He played golf with a different person each time out on the course. Soon, everyone connected his name with chiropractic.

Chiropractic college catalogs. Place catalogs from the various colleges in the hands of student counselors. These college catalogs are very effective in high schools, junior colleges, and universities.

The counselor could be a good source of referrals.

Become a team doctor for a Little League and high school. Simply call the Little League coach or high school coach and offer to become their team doctor. Volunteer your services — offer to examine the kids prior to football season, basketball season, etc. On Friday nights, when the team plays, you won't be home watching television, because you'll be working with the football team. However, these children are covered by insurance and they often get hurt playing sports, and will become your patients. This results in a fantastic source of new patients because their parents will know who you are and what you are from their children. Also, spectators at the field will also learn who and what you are, as your name will be paged whenever you're needed. Many of the children you'll be working with will become your patients. When they grow up they will remain your patients and will refer their spouses and children to you. This is a dynamic way to build a practice!

Offer your services to local high schools. Tell them you will perform physical examinations at no charge for children who participate in sports. Every year, the coaches, during the months of July and August, have their entire football teams medically examined. Naturally, this applies to all other sports throughout the year. The teams have to be examined and the students have to be certified fit before they can play sports. If you volunteer to do these examinations free of charge — either at your office or at the school gymnasium — you'll soon find yourself examining one hundred to two hundred patients a year for the school system. Needless to say, the coaches will know who you are and what you are; the children you examine will know who and what you are; their parents will also know who and what you are. It is an excellent way to build a rapport with the community. When these children get hurt on the sports field, you will find some of them in your office as patients.

Be active in local political affairs; work for your political party. First of all, politics is fun, if you get out and meet the people! For years, the chiropractors in my county have walked door to door for political candidates. If you are a Republican, you will be furnished with a list of all registered Republicans in your district. Visit these people! Walk up to their doors, introduce yourself, and praise your candidate. This is a great method to become known. If you are a Democrat, the same applies. Get involved, and meet the people so they can meet you, and know who you are and what you are.

54

Cultivate centers of influence. Meet, know, and associate with important individuals in other walks of life. The more people you can meet and acquaint with chiropractic, the better known you'll become!

Join an adult bowling league, softball league, or any other sports league in your area. Many civic clubs have bowling or softball leagues. By joining one, it will allow you to share the camaraderie of many businessmen while, at the same time, letting them know who, what, and where you are!

Help with Scouting organizations in your area. These organizations always need volunteers. They appreciate and remember their leaders!

Stop in service stations and ask directions for an obscure address. Follow the 3 "W's" procedure. Let them know that you are making a house call and are looking for a certain address. Again, you are making an impression that you do make house calls and care for people. Thank them, and send them a note of thanks.

Buy your gasoline at different gas stations in your community. If you want to fill up your gas tank and you have, say, a twenty-four-gallon tank, stop at several gas stations and buy a few dollars' worth of gas at each one. Use the 3 "W's" procedure. When you do this, just tell them that you are a chiropractor in the area and are trying to find an address on a certain street. Make sure the address is on a street which almost no one knows exists — one that has to be looked up on a map. A sample conversation at a gas station would be: "My name is Dr. Jones. I'm a chiropractor in town. My practice is at the corner of 12th and Central." (You are establishing in the attendant's mind who, what, and where you are!) "Could you help me locate this address?" Then they will go to the map and look it up for you. When you get back to your office, write a letter thanking them for their thoughtfulness. Repeat this procedure at all gas stations. Next time you go to those gas stations, repeat to them how grateful you were for their help that day. This way, you are thanking them twice — once by letter, and once verbally. They will definitely remember you!

Go to the Post Office and get a bulk rate mail permit. 3 "W's" and W.O.C. (whip out card).

Go to farm stores and convenience stores. Buy milk, sugar, coffee, etc., for the office. Ask for a receipt with your name on it. (3 "W's" and W.O.C.)

Go to electronic stores and ask about tape recorders to record your examinations. (3 "W's" and W.O.C.)

Go to furniture stores and inquire about office furniture or home furniture. By pricing future purchases, you will meet many salesmen. These contacts will possibly become future patients. (3 "W's" and W.O.C.)

Go to different plastic fabricators and inquire about signs for your office. The more businessmen you can meet while purchasing signs, the larger your sphere of influence becomes. (3 "W's" and W.O.C.)

If you need to paint your office, visit three different paint stores in the area. Buy the different paints at three different stores, paint brushes at another, sandpaper at another, etc. (3 "W's" and W.O.C.)

Go to every carpet store in the area when purchasing carpets for your office. Ask the salesmen about their experience with chiropractors. (3 "W's" and W.O.C.)

Bowl (if you like the sport) with a different person each time. Use your recreation time to build your practice! (3 "W's" and W.O.C.)

Have two or three realtors take you around to look for houses or apartments. You'll be able to meet many community leaders this way and perhaps find the ideal house for you and your family. (3 "W's" and W.O.C.)

Meet every businessman in town with whom you'd normally do business. There are certain services and businesses that all D.C.'s utilize: banks, office suppliers, service stations, barber shops, restaurants, printers, stationery stores, etc. Use the 3 "W's" procedure. Ask them about their experiences with chiropractors. Only patronize businesses who have a favorable outlook on chiropractic. It is better to spend your money and do business with people who can be potential boosters for you, than it is to spend money where you will get possibly the lowest price, but never a referral! Only do business with potential boosters.

Coffee Caper. Have coffee in several different restaurants each morning before going to your office. Leave generous tips, and always slip your business card underneath the tip. You may write a short note on the back of the card, such as: "Susan, thank you for your smile!" Susan, the waitress, will be sure to remember you for your generosity and thoughtfulness!

I know a doctor in Florida who built his practice strictly by the coffee caper! He went to about fifteen or twenty restaurants a day, introduced himself, had a cup of coffee, paid for it and left a generous tip. He was very friendly. The restaurant staffs knew who, what, and where he was! Very soon, all these restaurant employees were referring patients to him.

Eat lunch at a different restaurant each day. Sit at the waitress' station and ask, "What has been your experience with chiropractors?" Remember, waitresses not only make good patients, but are also excellent sources of referrals. Follow the 3 "W's" procedure. Leave a tip and your business card.

Contact well-known barber shops and beauty parlors. They, in turn, can send you many patients. Get your hair cut at many different barber shops. (3 "W's" and W.O.C.)

When it is necessary to tell someone your name, give them a business card so that they don't forget it! This can be done when leaving your car to be repaired, when buying a new suit, when you leave camera film to be developed, when buying office supplies, etc. Always ask for a cash receipt with your name on it! This makes the person know you. Rather than spelling your name for someone, give them your card.

When making your "bird-dog" contacts, determine the health status of the people you meet. This is relatively simple to do as people always like to talk about their health problems. If they feel good, praise them! If they have a complaint, let them talk about it by asking leading questions. Lead the conversation so that you may say: "That certainly sounds like a problem a chiropractor could help." This gives you the perfect opportunity to conduct a consultation on the spot and make an appointment for them.

Telephone or visit the P.T.A. of your local schools. Offer to speak on scoliosis, drug abuse, family counseling, etc., or volunteer for back-to-school posture checkups and spinal checkups.

Telephone or visit all the restaurant managers in town and offer to furnish them with posters on the Heimlich Maneuver, as well as making yourself available to lecture to their employees on this technique. It is very simple and will only take about forty-five minutes of your time to lecture to thirty or forty of the restaurant staff. Naturally, they will know who, what, and where you are, and the Heimlich Maneuver charts (with your name and address on them) will be posted all over town. Needless to say, this will increase business. (See sample poster at end of this chapter.)

Go to your local newspaper and tell them that you are sponsoring a posture contest. This may be done in conjunction with your local chiropractic society. If you volunteer to do all the work, your local society will go along with you. By sponsoring this on your local level, you'll create a lot of good will. The posture contest should receive the support of all chiropractors in the area, because of the immense amount of free publicity it commands for your profession.

Telephone or visit your local grade schools, elementary schools, middle schools, and high schools, and sponsor a good posture poster program. Get your local society to support your effort in a good posture poster contest at the area schools. Offer to do all the work if they will sponsor the program. If your local society doesn't want to sponsor such a program, do it yourself!

Give out "How to Lift" posters. Obtain "How to Lift" posters from the A.C.A., SHARE, or some other national organization and supply them to area businesses which utilize manual labor. Contact the managers of these businesses and explain who, what, and where you are, and that you are doing this as a public service. Explain that by supplying people with information on how to lift correctly, there might be fewer injuries, thereby decreasing that business' workmen's compensation claims. Also explain that such claims do cover chiropractic care. Needless to say, if someone gets injured at that particular business, chances are you'll be the one who will get the patient. (See sample chart at end of this chapter.)

Offer to lecture to employees at businesses in your area on industrial safety. When supplying local businesses with "How to Lift" posters, tell the managers that you are also available to teach their employees the proper methods of lifting, job safety, etc. Also let them know that this program you are offering will reduce their workmen's compensation injuries, and thus their insurance premiums. The employer/manager cannot lose with these presentations, and will surely remember the doctor who cared enough to help them with this program.

Opportunities for handing out business cards are almost unlimited. Cards should be given to businessmen that you'll do business with, such as: other businessmen, store owners, tradesmen coming to your office, people you meet on the street, at church, in civic clubs, service station attendants, restaurant employees, dry cleaning operators, etc., etc.

Visit a series of restaurants, preferably right after church on Sundays, when the crowds are large. Have your wife call the restaurant at a certain pre-arranged time. She will tell them that there is an emergency call for you, and she'll ask them to see if you are at that restaurant. When they page you the first time, don't answer, but do answer the second page. If the restaurant doesn't page a second time, your wife will say, "I am sure he is there. Would you please page him again, just to make sure?"

When you answer the phone, you'll state: "Yes, I'll be there right away. Have her wait right there. Don't move the patient at all until I get there." Hang up the phone, go back to the counter and say, "It seems I never get to finish a good cup of coffee! Got to go." The waitress will never forget you.

Your spouse and receptionist should always have your business cards with them at all times. Whenever your spouse or receptionist has to go to the drug store or the supermarket to pick up supplies for your office, she should give your business card to the person at the cash register, and should tell him that she needs a receipt in your name for the supplies she is purchasing. Naturally, you don't want to buy too many supplies at any one store, because you'd rather go to five different stores and use the same procedure at each. This way, your card will be handed out to five different people and they will each know who, what, and where you are!

Personal checks should have your profession and office address on them. Your wife should also have her personal checks with your name, address and phone number on them, as well as her own name, so that when she pays for services by check, the people she does business with will know that her husband is a chiropractor. Sometimes they might mention that they need a chiropractor and she can tell them that she'd be happy to make an appointment for them, or if this is inconvenient for them, she should give them your business card and ask them to give you a call.

Meet three new people a day. It is not enough just to meet someone. They have to know the 3 "W's": who you are, what you are, and where you are! Usually, when a doctor starts his practice, he will meet twenty-five to thirty people within a very short period of time, and then spend the next ten years renewing the same number of acquaintances! Therefore, his practice will grow only very slightly. If you want to double your practice within a comparatively short time, you have to double the number of people who know you, who know what you are, and where you are located. It is difficult to do, but try to commit yourself to meet three new people each day.

SPECIFIC PEOPLE TO MEET

The Mayor of your town is one of the persons a doctor should know. It is surprising how few people call upon him/her for advice when the Mayor is the logical person to know many things about the town and its people. The Mayor will be pleased that the doctor is interested in civic affairs and the local political scene. While talking to the Mayor, ask for a referral to a local bank and for the name of the bank's president. Then take the Mayor's advice and call on the bank president. Never ask for advice if you don't intend to follow it!

When you call on the bank president, realize that he is a man of great influence in your community, and that he also knows many people. Introduce yourself, and say, "Mr. Banker, I'm Dr. Pete Fernandez, a chiropractor in town. My office is located at the corner of 48th Avenue and 4th Street North." Tell him that the Mayor referred you to him. (The Mayor may have already phoned ahead to tell the bank president that you will be coming in to do business. This can only impress upon the banker that the Mayor is interested in chiropractic.) While you are talking to the president, ask for the name of the editor of the local newspaper.

When you call on the editor, tell him that you were referred to him by the banker as one who really knows the town and its people. This will impress upon the editor that you, as well as the bank president, really think that he has a feel for the town and its people. You can inquire of him the rates for health columns and any other forms of advertising you have in mind. This inquiry about potential business can only put the editor in a good frame of mind.

You could then inquire about local civic clubs, saying that you would like to join one in the area. Chances are the editor belongs to at least one, and may invite you to accompany him to a meeting. After your first introductory meeting at the civic club, join it! Many times the editor will go out of his way to introduce you to people who can be very valuable contacts.

All of these people will be your powerful and influential friends, and will greatly help you in the future. The fact that you contacted them shows them that you are a stable and helpful resident of the area. You can continue this chain of contacts indefinitely.

Make it a point to meet as many policemen as you can. Policemen investigate accidents, and accidents create chiropractic patients. Policemen are also influential. Make friends with them. Stop and ask them for directions. Let them know who, what, and where you are (3 "W's"). Invite them to stop by your office whenever they are in your area. Let them know that you have a great appreciation for policemen.

Visit the local pharmacist and try to get his good will. Compliment him on his stock of vitamins and orthopedic supports. Tell him you'll be happy to refer your patients to him for these products. Introduce yourself and give him your business card; he can become a good source of referrals.

Reinforce all "bird-dog" contacts by calling them a week to ten days after your initial contact. Call them by name. They will be impressed that you remembered them. You have their name in your notebook. People like the sound of their own names and will always remember someone who remembers them. Keep this in mind: only the people who know you, are the people who are going to refer to you. When making the second contact, simply say: "Hello, Mrs. Brown. Remember me? I'm Dr. Pete Fernandez, the chiropractor on Hillsborough Avenue at the Town and Country Shopping Plaza. I met you a few days ago. I certainly appreciated the help you gave me the other day, etc., etc."

Send Thank-U-Grams to all these people for the help they have given you. Have your name and address on the envelope, and enclose your business card. Sign the Thank-U-Gram clearly.

DEVELOPING MUTUAL SUPPORT
AMONG CHIROPRACTORS

This section is designed for the new practitioner. However, if an established doctor were to follow these guidelines, his practice would also grow.

To promote good relations among the established chiropractors in your area, you should call your fellow professionals and arrange convenient times to visit their offices and become acquainted. While you are in a D.C.'s office, *ask him for his referrals when he has a patient in your end of town who can't travel to his office. Volunteer your services to cover his practice when he is at seminars, away on vacations or weekends, for night calls, emergencies or house calls.*

Some D C.'s with well-established practices, are anxious to refer patients to another chiropractor when a situation warrants it.

Should another D.C. refer a patient to you, *show your appreciation with a phone call or by some other means.* Never try to steal patients from a fellow doctor! That is the surest way to promote bad relations. You should inform his patient that you are taking care of the emergency only.

The feedback received on this idea has been very positive. Many doctors have said that the seasoned practitioner was happy to have someone available for emergencies, night calls, on weekends, etc. The "emergency only" patients referred many new patients to the other doctor who wasn't quite as busy as their established doctor. These additional referrals got their practices growing quickly.

Ask the established D.C. if you can consult with him on difficult cases. The largest compliment one doctor can pay another is to be asked to serve as a consultant. This also shows concern for the well being of a patient.

Join your local chiropractic society. Established doctors who enjoy considerable success, praise association membership as a definite and positive aid in their professional growth. It is seldom that meetings of chiropractors fail to provide a number of valuable contacts or ideas which can be used in your own practice.

A practitioner should never criticize his colleagues. A D.C. should never tell his patients about his new, superior training and make all other doctors' training seem obsolete. Let your training speak for itself. Do not drop hints that other colleagues have failed to keep up with chiropractic progress, etc.

Never criticize the medical profession. They are just as dedicated as any chiropractor, and just as competent. You will never successfully build yourself up by tearing someone else down. In all your contacts with the public, be pro-chiropractic, but don't appear critical of others.

BUSY ACTS TO PROMOTE YOUR NAME

Get brightly colored "Keep Smiling" cards printed with your name and address on the front, and a blank space on back so that you can write notes on them. Sample: "Mary, this doctor cured my headaches. I had suffered with them for ten years! Joan." Leave these cards, with similar comments, all over town, in obvious places, such as in phone books, on people's desks, etc.

Imagine the good impression these cards will make when people pick them up and read the message. If a thousand of these cards are read, you will get some new patients within sixty days. The effect of an "instant reputation" is not only immediate, it is long-term! The benefit is now as well as in the future!

You should have a sufficient quantity of high quality, expensive and tasteful business cards. These should be left all around town — anywhere you find the opportunity to leave one. For instance, leave one with a tip at a restaurant, with a note of thanks for good service; with a service station attendant who helped you find an address, etc. In other words, create your own image and reputation in your community. Nothing happens unless someone makes it happen!

Always park your car in the same parking place at your office. If a patient drives by and sees that you are there by recognizing your car, he/she may stop in for an adjustment.

Keep the cars of your staff off of your parking lot. You don't want patients, who might be driving by, to be deceived by a "full" parking lot, when actually the parking lot was only filled with the cars of your office staff.

Write notes on the backs of your business cards. Take your business card and write on the back of it: "John, this doctor cured my back problem. He is terrific!" or "Mary, this doctor cured my son's asthma. He is a great doctor!" Just write messages such as these on the backs of a thousand to two thousand business cards, and then travel through your community, dropping them in obvious places — places where people are going to pick them up in their curiosity. You will obtain patients from the scattering of these cards because people are basically nosey. They will see the message, and they will read it, and look to see who the doctor is and where he is located. Hopefully, when they need to see a chiropractor, they will remember that note and will refer to you. These cards can be left just about anywhere.

Write notes on good chiropractic literature. Write on the literature with a red pencil: "John, this man cured my headaches. Go to him!" or "Bob, this is the best doctor in this whole town! He cured the back problem that I have had for the past 15 years!" Then take this literature and lay it all over town: in phone booths, on people's desks, etc. This can be done very easily, and will bring you many new patients. Be sure to stamp your name, address and phone number on the literature.

In many cases, you do not necessarily have to go to a place to become known. Example: Your wife or receptionist may call a hardware store and say, "I am trying to get hold of Dr. So-and-So. He is on a house call in your area of town and we need him very badly at the office. He said that when he finished with the house call, he was going to stop by your hardware store and pick up something. He's a tall fellow with gold framed glasses and has on a white shirt and red tie. Would you please see if he is there?" They will usually page for the doctor, then come back and say he is not there. "Well, would you watch out for him? We have someone here who needs him urgently. If he comes in, please tell him to call his office right away."

This procedure has made the people in the hardware store familiar with your name and your profession. You are on their minds for the rest of the afternoon, as they are watching out for you. They know what you look like, that you make house calls, that you are busy, and that you are needed.

Have some of your friends or relatives stop at various places in town and ask for directions to your office. They could say that they are from out of town and that they need your services and would like to know how to get to your office. Someone will have to look up the address, and in doing so will now know who you are, what you are, and where you are!

Put your card on any bulletin board you see. Many restaurants have bulletin boards for their customers' cards. Place your card on their bulletin board. Make sure your card is unusual — not flamboyant or extravagant, but something that will catch the eye in order to attract people's attention. Another business place that has a lot of people reading the bulletin board is a laundromat. While the people are waiting for their laundry, they have time to spend, and usually pass the time reading the cards on the bulletin board. Also, some supermarkets have bulletin boards for their customers' use. Check with the managers of these establishments before placing your card on their bulletin boards; there may be a small fee.

You can make many contacts without leaving your office. Your wife and/or receptionist can dial any phone number and say, "Is this Dr. So-and-So's, the chiropractor's office? I hear he is tremendous with treating headaches and I've got a terrible headache." Obviously, they will tell her that she has the wrong number. She should then say, "I'm sorry, is this —[she then gives your phone number] . . .? No, well I'm sorry."

I know a doctor who employed a woman to make these calls eight hours a day. It was her only function on his staff! He built a large-volume practice in a short time using this technique.

Letters to the Chamber of Commerce. A letter should be sent to the Chamber of Commerce from someone out of town, stating that they know you are an outstanding chiropractor, and that you are located in their town. Would the Chamber assist in locating you?

Circle your name and telephone number in the yellow pages of every phone book you come across. Use a red grease pencil. Go looking for them!

Don't remain in your office during slow periods. When you are not busy, don't sit behind your desk and wait for new patients to come into your office. Get out and meet your community! Have your receptionist cover the phone while you go out and make new contacts.

People don't like to go into an office that is empty. If you act busy, you will become busy! One method of giving an illusion of being busy is to have a friend call your office on cue. Example: your receptionist sees a patient entering the office. She dials your friend and says, "One is coming," and hangs up. A few minutes later, the friend calls the office and the receptionist talks into the phone, following this script: "Yes, Mrs. Jones, Dr. So-and-So has been very successful with headache cases. However, in your individual case, it will be necessary to arrange for a consultation to see if you are a chiropractic patient. Would you like to come in today or tomorrow? Very well, Mrs. Jones, we will put you down for 4:30 tomorrow afternoon. Thank you for calling."

Your receptionist then writes the appointment down in the appointment book *with a different color pen so she will know it is not an actual appointment.* Patients do not like to glance at an appointment book and find it blank.

People who appear busy, become busy! Have a coat hanging on the rack in the reception room. When the patient is in the reception room, the doctor can open and close doors in the back of the office, giving the impression of being busy. The patient doesn't know whether there is one person or ten people in your office. If you are not busy, at least create the impression of being so. People do not like to go to a doctor who is not busy.

Go to the bank daily. Let the bank personnel see you. The banking officers and personnel can be excellent sources of referrals.

Survey of business people. Arm yourself with a clipboard and get out to meet all the businessmen you can in your town. Ask them what they would consider a good site for your new office building, etc. This is an excellent method of making new contacts.

Survey of residents. This procedure is the same as the one above, except that the doctor is meeting all the residents who live within five miles of his office, asking them questions regarding public awareness of chiropractic. The more people a doctor knows, the larger his practice will be!

Any office equipment that you are thinking of buying should be demonstrated at your office. Always compare prices of three or four manufacturers. You'll be surprised how much money you'll save and the number of people you'll meet during these demonstrations.

IF A PERSON STARTS CHOKING ON A PIECE OF MEAT, THE DR. HENRY HEIMLICH TECHNIQUE MAY OFFER A WAY IN WHICH YOU CAN HELP

THE CLUE TO RECOGNIZING A CHOKING ATTACK IS THAT THE VICTIM CANNOT SPEAK.

STANDING BEHIND THE VICTIM, PLACE YOUR ARMS AROUND HIS WAIST, SLIGHTLY ABOVE THE BELT LINE. ALLOW HIS HEAD, ARMS AND UPPER TORSO TO HANG FORWARD.

GRASPING ONE WRIST WITH THE OTHER HAND, PRESS INTO THE VICTIM'S ABDOMEN RAPIDLY AND FORCEFULLY, REPEATING SEVERAL TIMES. THIS "REVERSE BEARHUG" PUSHES UP ON THE DIAPHRAGM, COMPRESSES THE AIR IN THE LUNGS AND EXPELS THE OBJECT BLOCKING THE BREATHING PASSAGE.

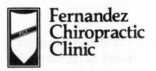

Fernandez Chiropractic Clinic

— Display In A Prominent Place! —

Learn how...
TO LIFT PROPERLY

WRONG

RIGHT

TO KEEP THOSE KINKS OUT OF YOUR BACK!

1. SQUAT DOWN
2. BEND KNEES
3. BACK STRAIGHT
4. ARMS CLOSE
5. KEEP LOAD CLOSE

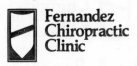

BECOMING KNOWN:
THROUGH PUBLIC RELATIONS OR
PAID ADVERTISING

Years ago, advertising was the norm for the chiropractic doctor. Then, with the advent of stringent state laws, it was eliminated in most states. Recently, the Supreme Court of the United States struck down the bans on advertising for professionals, and it is once again coming into vogue.

When advertising was outlawed, doctors had to resort to promoting public relations in the form of free media publicity. This free media publicity was something for nothing, because the doctors, using a little ingenuity, obtained the same media publicity they had originally paid for with little or no cost. Public relations, if properly utilized, is just as effective as advertising, and it's free! All it takes is a little work and imagination.

This section of this book will not attempt to judge the ethics of advertising versus public relations, since this is largely a subjective determination. I will simply enumerate the various methods of media publicity available to the professional. How you obtain your publicity is an individual choice.

For your ease in reading this section, I am taking the liberty of abbreviating the various methods of public relations into:

N — News releases (to media)
N — Newsletters (to patients)
E — Enclosures (cards, literature, etc., in mail to non-patients)
L — Letters (postcards, Christmas cards, Thanksgiving cards, letters to the editor, etc.)
S — Signs (plaques, signs, notices on bulletin boards, etc.)
A — Announcements
P.S.— Public Service (teaching, lecturing, speaking, writing, sports, etc.)

At the same time, in order to describe the various methods of advertising that may be applied to an idea, I will use the following initials as abbreviations:

R — Radio
T — Television
N — Newspapers
S — Shoppers (free neighborhood newspapers)
N — Newsletters (to non-patients)

O — Occupant mail (mail sent to non-patients)
B — Boards (bulletin boards, billboards, information boards)
T — Telephone book listings
M — Magazines
W — Welcome Wagon

Whenever a practice-building idea is discussed and public relations or advertising may be applied, the initials NN, EL, SA, PS and/or RT, NS, NO, BT, MW, will be placed at the end of that particular practice-building idea. All, or some, of these public relations and/or advertising methods may be applicable.

Public Relations
This section describes the many "freebees" that are available to you in the public media, and other areas. A number of doctors get consistently "good press" in the newspapers simply by utilizing many of the following ideas. Most of these options are available for no charge. All it takes is a little work and initiative. It is actually easy for a doctor to secure inches of free publicity in the newspaper.

Send birthday cards out to all your patients. Do it every year, year in and year out. You will be surprised at the number of patients who will receive no other birthday card except the one you send. These cards bring much joy into your patients' lives. The doctor should sign the cards himself. Doing so will reinforce in the doctor's mind a memory of that patient, a patient who may soon reappear in his office. This is a metaphysical principle that works. NN - EL - SA - PS. (See example on Page 236.)

Send out Thanksgiving, Easter and Christmas cards. The patients will remember the doctor who remembers them. Sending out Thanksgiving and Easter cards is more effective than sending Christmas cards, because your card will probably be the only one the patient receives. Christmas cards should be sent out November 30th, so that it will be noticed. Otherwise, your card will be lost in the mass of Christmas cards arriving at the patient's home. A rubber stamp, saying, "I'll bet this is your First Christmas card!" could be stamped on the envelope as an additional attention-getter. NN - EL - SA - PS - RT - NS - NO - BT - MW

Have a Neurothermograph card. These cards are the size of a business card and offer a free neurothermograph examination to determine if there is nerve pressure and if chiropractic care will be of benefit to the prospective patient. This card is handed out all over town, dropped everywhere, sent out to people through the mail, given to patients to give to their friends, etc. When the prospective patient comes into your office and you find nerve pressure, you can tell him, "Yes, I did find pressure on your nerves, and if you want me to see what is causing the pressure, I will have to x-ray and examine you further. Of course, there will be a charge for these services." This is a great way to attract new patients. NN - EL - SA - PS - RT - NS - NO - BT - MW

Utilize complimentary consultations, examinations, or x-ray cards. These cards can be a practice-builder. They can be handed out to patients, friends, or anyone the doctor meets. Please refer to section on Referral Procedures for further information on these cards. NN - EL - SA - PA - RT - NS - NO - BT - MW

If you have a hard-to-find office location, print a map on the back of your business cards. Your patients will appreciate your thoughtfulness. NN - EL - SA - PS

Enclose your business card whenever you mail anything from your office. Absolutely nothing should be sent from your office without a card or literature enclosed. It is going to cost you a certain amount to mail a letter; you might as well make it more productive by educating the party who is to receive the letter.

Send literature in the mail when paying bills. This rule applies to any mail leaving your office. As long as you are paying for the stamp, you might as well send some promotional literature.

Insert Workman's Compensation pamphlets to the employers and insurance carrier with the initial insurance forms. This can be a good practice-builder.

Become a local author. Write stories for local newspapers, magazines, or trade journals. The more people who know what you are, where you are, and who you are, the more people you will have as patients. NN - EL - SA - PS - RT - NS - NO - BT - MW

Some newspapers will place health columns free for a doctor. If you provide newspapers with ten or fifteen health columns that are well written, they will add your name, address, picture, and phone number, and it will be done as a courtesy of the newspaper. If you must pay for them, health columns are a great method of building a chiropractic practice. There are many professional sources for these health columns. NN - EL - SA - PS & RT - NS - NO - BT - MW

Write professional articles/papers and get them published in your professional journals. These articles/papers may be of a technical or procedural nature. When they are published, your colleagues around the country will know where you are practicing, and will be able to refer to you. Also, if your article/paper is of patient interest, you could have it printed and sent out to your patients. NN - EL - SA - TS & RT - NS - NO - BT - MW

70

Have a practice brochure. A simple, complete, and direct practice brochure should be made up, explaining who the doctor is, his training and background, and the type of service he renders. However, be certain that this brochure is written in layman's language. Do include the doctor's photograph, the office address, phone number, business hours, and any other information you feel is vital. NN - EL - SA - PS & RT - NS - NO - BT - MW

Mail monthly newsletters to patients and non-patients. Inform them as to the happenings in your office and your profession. This will let the patient know that his doctor is still practicing. It can contain such items as the seminars the doctor is attending, the introduction of a new associate or C.A., new equipment in the office, or testimonials of patients, etc.

Mail seasonal newsletters to your patients. Heart Month, Hypertension Month, Flu Month, Hay Fever Month, etc., would be good topics to include in a newsletter. NN - EL - SA - PS & RT - NS - NO - BT - MW

Have a monthly magazine (enlarged newsletter) published each month and available only through your office. Have patients contribute articles, poems, recipes, etc. This creates great interest and referrals. People appreciate the person who places their name in print. NN - EL - SA - PS & RT - NS - NO - BT - MW

Send testimonial-type magazines or newspapers to your patients. This tells them what chiropractic is, and what conditions chiropractic can help. NN - EL - SA - PS & RT - NS - NO - BT - MW

Make up your own testimonial newsletters. Once made up, they should be mailed out to your patients and your community, and placed in your office as a hand-out. This idea has proved to be very successful in stimulating new patient flow. NN - EL - SA - PS & RT - NS - NO - BT - MW

Have a Physical Fitness Day, Week, or Month. RT - NS - NO - BT - MW & NN - EL - SA - PS

Organize a Chiropractic Lay Group. This type of group can promote your name, and may result in many referrals. At the same time, you will be serving your profession. NN - EL - SA - PS & RT - NS - NO - BT - MW

Lecture on an unusual topic. One doctor built a large practice by being a lecturer on acupuncture; not ordinary acupuncture, but laser acupuncture. People were very interested in how he could treat people with a laser gun. If you are going to do something, do it in a unique way to attract attention. NN - EL - SA - PS & RT - NS - NO - BT - MW

Thank-You notes. Be certain to send thank-you notes to the newspaper editor, your local Chamber of Commerce members, or any other individuals for whatever assistance they may have rendered in establishing your practice.

Have well-organized "booths" at state fairs, shopping malls, shopping centers, etc. Check the public's blood pressure, posture, etc., at these booths and pass out your cards. It is a great way to build a practice while providing public service. NN - EL - SA - PS & RT - NS - NO - BT - MW

Give your patients growth charts for their children. These charts are used to measure the children's growth. A message, "Courtesy of the Fernandez Chiropractic Clinic," could be printed on the chart. Give the parents one chart for each child in the family and also extra charts for their friends. The more you can get your name out to the community, the larger your practice will become. The A.C.A. has "Bunny Growth Charts" available. NN - EL - SA - PS & RT - NS - NO - BT - MW

Send out letters to your patients explaining the chiropractic benefits of your state's insurance laws. Also, explain to them the different types of insurance that pay for chiropractic care, i.e.: Homeowners, Medical Payments, Major Medical, No Fault, Sickness and Accident, etc. The more the patient knows about his insurance coverage, the more new patients you will receive. You may also place ads in the newspaper, TV or radio explaining insurance benefits regarding chiropractic.

Have a "Welcome to the Office" letter sent to each new patient. People go where they are comfortable and refer where they are appreciated. The extra touch of a letter from their doctor welcoming them to his office, an office that cares and welcomes patients, produces big results.

Send a thank-you letter to each person who has referred a new patient. Everyone likes to be thanked, and usually become annoyed if they aren't thanked for a good deed. Make sure that you acknowledge the referrer whenever he/she sends a new patient to you. Referring patients are hard to develop — and easy to lose! Thanking others repeatedly is the way large practices are built.

Send announcements to your patients stating that you are available during the months of June, July, and August for back-to-school physical examinations. Soon you will find your office filled with patients needing these examinations, at your normal office visit fee. If you are examining twenty students a day for three months in the summer, you will find yourself with additional income for this simple type of examination. Remember — youthful patients become adult patients! NN - EL - SA - TS & RT - NS - NO - BT - MW

72

Have a series of letters mailed to each new patient. These letters may be on any topic you choose: welcome to the office; reaction; retracing; referrals; re-examinations, etc., etc. These letters should be sent out on a weekly basis to educate the new patients. Practices that utilize such a procedure report consistently increasing referrals.

Send automobile accident or Workmen's Compensation letters and pamphlets to patients involved in this type of accident. The doctors who have built automobile accident or Workmen's Compensation practices report that the majority of these patients were referred by their regular patients. If you hear of any of your patients who are involved in this type of accident, send them appropriate literature. It will pay big dividends. NN - EL - SA - TS & RT - NS - NO - BT - MW

Send letters to your friends when opening a practice. If you had to work at another job prior to opening your practice, use the following letter outline to design a letter to be sent to previous fellow employees. The ideas to be included in the letter are:

1. Thank them for all their assistance and encouragement which you received while you were working to earn the finances necessary to open your practice.

2. Thank them for the confidence they have shown, by not only coming to you with their health problems, but also by referring their friends.

3. Let them know that you are always happy to be of service.

4. Enclose a business card with your home phone number, letting them know you are always available in an emergency.

5. Enclose a general information pamphlet on chiropractic, stating that you hope they will find time to read it.

News article when opening an office. When you first set up a practice, if you are a member of the A.C.A. or I.C.A., write an opening announcement and send it along with your resumé, stating that you are opening your office at a certain address. Also include a 5x7-inch black and white glossy photograph of yourself. Ask them to retype the announcement on their stationery and mail it to the business editor of your local newspaper. The newspaper will usually print it word for word as they receive it. The more qualifications you can list in your resumé, the larger the write-up will be in the newspaper, and the more it will attract new people to you.

Contact the society editor of your local newspaper. Explain that you are a professional in the area and you have noticed in the past that the newspaper has written up professionals newly-arrived in town or who had opened new offices, etc. Ask the editor to interview you and do an article on you. This is extremely good public relations. (See Page 223 for example.)

Letters to the editors. Have a regular program of writing to the editor of your local newspaper. Your letters should be written on topics of local interest: police department, fire department, city employees, city services, etc. These letters should be positive, constructive, and interesting.

Call your local newspaper and ask them to print an article on your particular expertise in chiropractic. Some of the subjects you might wish to expand on are: nutrition, kineseology, behavior modification, etc. These articles will provide excellent publicity. NN - EL - SA - PS - RT - NS - NO - BT - MW

Write all the restaurant managers in town and offer to furnish them with posters on the Heimlich Maneuver. Also tell them you are available to lecture to their employees on this procedure. This is very simple and will only take about forty-five minutes of your time to give a lecture to thirty or forty restaurant employees. Naturally, they will know who you are, what you are, and where you are, and the Heimlich Maneuver posters, with your name and address on them, will be posted all over town. Needless to say, this will increase business. (See sample poster at end of previous chapter.) NN - EL - SA - PS - RT - NS - NO - BT - MW

Write all the business and manufacturing plants in your area and offer them "How To Lift" posters. Obtain these posters from A.C.A., SHARE, or some other national organization, and supply the posters to area businesses which require heavy manual labor of their employees. Contact the managers of these business firms, explaining who, what, and where you are, and that you are doing this as a public service. Explain that by supplying employees with the information on how to lift properly, you hope to prevent injuries, thereby decreasing their Workmen's Compensation claims. Also explain that such claims do cover chiropractic care. Needless to say, if someone is injured on the job, chances are you will be the one that will have this Workmen's Compensation patient. (See sample poster at end of previous chapter.) NN - EL - SA - TS & RT - NS - NO - BT - MW

Offer to lecture to employees on industrial safety. When supplying local businesses with "How To Lift" posters, tell the managers that you are available to teach their employees the proper methods of lifting, job safety, etc. Also point out that this program should reduce Workmen's Compensation injuries as well as their insurance premiums. The employer/manager can't lose with such presentations and will surely remember the doctor who cared enough to help him with this program.

Write to the schools, colleges, civic clubs and tell them you are sponsoring a Posture Contest. This may be done in conjunction with your local chiropractic society. If you volunteer to do all the work, your local society will go along with you. By sponsoring this on your local level, you will create a lot of goodwill. The Posture Contest should receive the support of all the chiropractors in the area because of the immense amount of free publicity it commands for our profession. NN - EL - SA - TS & RT - NS - NO - BT - MW

Write the schools, colleges, etc., and tell them you are sponsoring a Good Posture Poster Program. Have your local society sponsor this program at your local grade schools. Offer to do all the work at no cost to your local society if they will sponsor the program. If they don't want to sponsor such a program, do it yourself! NN - EL - SA - TS & RT - NS - NO - BT - MW

Write the P.T.A. of your local high schools and offer to speak on Scoliosis, Drug Abuse, Family Counseling, etc., or volunteer for Back-to-School Posture check-ups and Spinal check-ups. NN - EL - SA - TS & RT - NS - NO - BT - MW

Send letters to your local high schools, middle schools, grade schools, colleges, Little League, Pony League, etc., etc., and volunteer to do free athletic examinations. At the same time, volunteer to become their team physician. This procedure will result in many patients covered by the school athletic insurance. NN - EL - SA - TS & RT - NS - NO - BT - MW

Write all high schools and colleges and offer them chiropractic college catalogs. The counselors will appreciate your interest in placing their students. Once the counselors express interest, you can personally take the catalogs to the school, where you will meet the counselor, the principal, etc. W.W.W. and W.O.C.

Write to all high schools and colleges and offer to speak to the Health classes. Schools are always looking for free outside speakers. By utilizing this procedure, you will meet many people. W.W.W. & W.O.C., NN - EL - SA - TS & RT - NS - NO - BT - MW

Write to the local high schools, colleges, trailer parks, condominiums, etc., and offer to teach a free first-aid class. If your knowledge of first aid is "rusty," take a refresher course at your local Red Cross. The more people you meet, the larger practice you will have.

Write the Mayor, Governor, etc., and ask them to declare a "Spinal Health Week" or month. Usually they will be happy to do this, as it only entails a proclamation. They will be pleased to have their pictures taken with you while presenting you with the proclamation. Your local press will be happy to take these pictures and print a newspaper write-up for you.

Send letters to the various Little League teams. Volunteer to coach a Little League team. You could help coach football, baseball, basketball, soccer, etc., etc. The more people you meet, the larger practice you will have.

Write letters to all civic clubs, trailer parks, condominiums, churches, radio stations, TV stations, etc., and offer your services as a speaker. This can be written on your stationery. However, you will increase the response if your local chiropractic society will type these letters on their stationery on your behalf. Again, it may be better received because the society has recommended you. The list of local civic clubs, trailer parks, etc., and their program chairmen, can be obtained from the area Chamber of Commerce. Write a letter similar to the following:

Dear Mrs. Smith:

It is my pleasure to announce that Dr. John Doe, who practices at 4800-4th Street North in St. Petersburg, is available to speak to civic clubs.

Dr. Doe is from Kansas City, Missouri, where he not only maintained active practice, but continually advanced his knowledge by attending postgraduate seminars sponsored by the Missouri Chiropractic Association, in conjunction with the Cleveland College of Chiropractic, Postgraduate Division. These seminars dealt with the latest techniques and scientific advances in Chiropractic Orthopedics, Nutrition, Acupuncture, Examination, and Diagnosis.

We are most fortunate to have Dr. Doe, not only because of his tremendous ability as a Chiropractic Physician, but also because he has completed years of extensive training in the theory and practice of Chiropractic Orthopedics and Nutrition.

Dr. Doe has completed the prescribed one hundred hour course of training and has successfully written an examination prepared by the New York Institute of Chiropractic to receive his certification of proficiency in Acupuncture.

Because of Dr. Doe's knowledge of Acupuncture and Nutrition, and specifically because of his proficiency in the application of Acupuncture without needles, I feel he could present a very interesting program for your organization.

I would like to invite you and other members of your organization to meet Dr. Doe in person and hear some of his theories on Chiropractic treatment, Acupuncture, and Nutrition.

Then I think you will agree with me that he will present an outstanding program for your members.

Please call 525-1141 for more information.

Very truly yours,

Write a letter on your office stationery to all your local Realtors. Describe a piece of property you would like to purchase for a new chiropractic clinic, or home. Ask them if they would know of such a property. You'll be surprised how many people you will meet using this method. You will also learn about property values and — who knows? — perhaps you'll locate your next office or home site!

Whenever you want a new piece of equipment, write the various dealers in your town. Describe exactly the type of equipment you want and the functions you want it to perform. Ask the dealers to call your office to arrange a convenient time to demonstrate their product. This method will allow you to meet many salesmen. Remember, salesmen are extroverts and will refer to you. Send them a thank-you letter for demonstrating their equipment.

Send out referral appreciation letters to the wrong names! I know a doctor who sent out thousands of letters to the *wrong* people, thanking them for referring someone to his office. He received many new patients from this one idea alone!

Meet with local radio and TV station managers and ask them to run A.C.A. Public Service material — if they are not already doing so. This material is available by writing to the A.C.A.

Look around your town to find the most beautiful areas. When you see a business building that has beautiful landscaping, jot down the address. Write to the person who owns the building and tell him how much you like his landscaping. Also tell him it is always nice to have people in town who care about their surroundings. You can do the same thing in a residential neighborhood with homeowners who keep up their lawns, etc. Also, if you see someone who has built a new office, write him a letter and tell him how great his new office looks and how it is an asset to the neighborhood. If you see a building being remodeled, do the same thing. Look for any excuse possible to write a letter to someone to compliment any action they may have taken. If you follow this procedure, you won't be forgotten by the people in your area. NN - EL - SA - TS & RT - NS - NO - BT - MW

News Releases

A doctor can receive much personal publicity from well-written news articles. These news releases should be written on any professional event, topic, or anything pertaining to the doctor or his family. It is not difficult to write news articles, nor is it hard to get them published.

If a doctor is a regular paying customer for newspaper advertising space, then his chances of news releases being printed by that newspaper are increased. The doctor, his wife or secretary, should be the press agent.

Whenever a doctor's article appears in the newspaper, it is comparable to a monthly mailing: it brings his name to the attention of the community, his former patients, and to people who met him when he was bird-dogging or performing the "busy acts."

If you want your name to become well known, repetition and consistency in the local newspaper is the key. Try to get your name printed at least weekly by some genuine news article. Be forever conscious of ways to build your public relations image. Do not let an opportunity pass you by. Keep in mind:

1. Maintain current articles;
2. Utilize photographs;
3. Be active in newsworthy events.

When you attend meetings, seminars, etc., prepare your news releases along these guidelines: Explain where the meeting was held, who the speaker was, what subjects were taught, how many D.C.'s attended, etc., and mail these articles to the business editor of your local newspaper.

If outstanding speakers attended the meeting, include their names, titles, and possibly a quote from them. This is always newsworthy and creates positive public relations. If possible, have your picture taken with this famous person and include it with your news release.

Another option would be to have your local chiropractic society write up an article to send to the business editor of your local newspaper, explaining that you are going out of town for four days to attend a seminar. They should inform them where the seminar is being held, what the seminar is about, what you are going to learn at that seminar, and who the instructors are. The business editor will be happy to put it in the newspaper. If you type the news release on your stationery, the chances are that it would get into the newspaper, but if it comes from a third party, such as your local or state association, your chances of it appearing are greater.

When you're going to address a group meeting or a service club,

78

or when you have received an honor from an organization, be sure that you or the group's public relations secretary sends an article to the newspaper describing the topic of your speech, or your honor. Once your speech or reception of an honor is over, prepare a news release, describing the occasion. These letters should be typed on the club's stationery.

There are many ideas, topics, events that would prompt a news release. The following subjects are only a small fraction of the possibilities. Just use your imagination: Any honors you may receive; story about a new clinic; placement in Hall of Fame; joining your state and national associations; passing national and state boards; charity projects; C.A. training; anything regarding a doctor's family; receiving certificates; doctor's opinions on a subject; talks to chiropractic groups; new programs added to your office; articles about women chiropractors; anniversaries, birthdays, etc.; treating athletes, celebrities, etc.; describing chiropractic techniques; marriages; teaching courses or classes; husband and wife teams; brother and sister teams; attending college homecomings and conventions; certification in specific subject; out-of-town doctors visiting you; purchase of site or building for office; forming of partnerships or corporations; becoming a sports trainer; taking and returning home from a trip, vacation, etc.; treating children; scoliosis examinations; spinal care classes; free spinal examinations; listing in *Who's Who*; awards received; conducting a correct posture clinic; elected to any office; appointed to a board of examiners; elected Chiropractor of the Year; chairman of committees; length of time in practice; cardiopulmonary resuscitation training; graduate from college or course; entering practice; relocating practice; opening practice; new doctor joining practice; new C.A. or therapist; talks to civic clubs; treating the handicapped; famous patients lauding you; engagements; running for a chiropractic-related office; helping with local politics; delivering babies; explaining chiropractic; chiropractic progress; chiropractic education; use of new equipment; addition of new equipment; free x-rays; free contour analysis; starting a health column; debate with M.D.; participating in sports; dean's list, *cum laude*; lecturing to grade-school class; tying in with Holistic trend; career days; health fairs; nutrition; spinal care week; sleeping habits; free blood pressure checkups; chiropractic legislation; Medicare and Medicaid; positive report on chiropractic; patients' rights; testimony in court; expanding clinic; advice on spinal problems; Medicare has pay increases for D.C.'s; resuming practice; remodeling; going to seminar; joining research group; football training clinics; attending a conference; returning from a conference; legal/chiropractic meetings; speaking engagements; serving special interest groups; hobbies; groundbreaking for new office or home; receiving post-graduate degree; chiropractic booth at state fair; poster contest; free testing at schools; posture; sponsoring of anything; how to properly shovel snow; health systems agencies inclusion; beneficial legal rulings; participating in state government; endorsements of chiropractic; petitioning of something; new health care methods; D.C. & M.D. ties; new and different chiropractic laws; running for public office; D.C. qualifications; having open house; assuming a practice; becoming member of foundation; visiting a college; famous person speaking to group of chiropractors; any condition chiropractic can help . . . as I have said, the possibilities are endless!

Get a double subscription to your morning and evening newspaper. The reason for *two* subscriptions is that you are going to cut out all newsworthy items, and there may possibly be some that are printed on opposite sides of the same page. Clip out any newsworthy articles in your town, and write a letter to the person who is the subject of each article, congratulating him/her on whatever was written.

Look for reasons to write letters. There are thousands of reasons and thousands of letters that you can write! Do it! It will pay great dividends. And, do it on a daily basis.

The following are examples of this procedure:

If a serviceman was just promoted to lieutenant and was written up in the newspaper, you would send a little note to his parents, who reside in your town. Example: "Dear Mrs. Jones, I read in this morning's newspaper that your son [name] has just received [the honor received]. You must be very proud of him. All Americans are so deeply indebted to our boys in the service. I share your pride in his accomplishments."

Acknowledge school board members and congratulate them on their public-spirited interest. "Permit me to express my sincere admiration to a person, such as yourself, who has chosen to serve the community."

Send the following to your Senator: "Dear Senator [name], I note in the newspaper that you have recently been elected to the Senate of the United States. I congratulate you on your spirit of public interest. Please permit me to express my sincere admiration to a person who has chosen to serve our community in this demanding way."

How about your legislator? Just tell him you congratulate him for contributing to our system of government. I guarantee that if you send a letter to a legislator, he'll send one back.

Letters to club presidents. "I note in the newspaper that you were elected and installed to the position of President of [name of club]. May I join the many well-wishers in offering you my heartiest congratulations. Sincerely. . ."

Personal congratulations. "I note in the paper that you were [honor or accomplishment]. Let me add my congratulations and assure you that I am personally delighted with your . . . . Wishing you success in all your endeavors, I remain . . ."

Wedding anniversaries. "I noted in the paper that you recently celebrated your golden wedding anniversary. I'm sure your years together have been a wonderful reward in themselves, and let me offer my sincere congratulations."

Welcome to new residents. "It has recently been brought to my attention that you are a new resident here. Let me welcome you to [name of area]. Also, let me extend the services of my office if, at any time, we can be of assistance."

Birthdays. "It has been brought to my attention that you recently celebrated your 80th birthday. I am taking this opportunity to extend my best personal wishes."

This type letter could be sent for the "sermon of the week", *etc.* "I noticed your letter to the editor in the *Daily Sun*. I appreciate your comments, and share your views."

There are many reasons for sending out letters of this nature. For example: If someone has done something noteworthy in a charity; a high school athlete, a college athlete who has excelled; a civic club officer who has excelled; someone elected to political office; students who excel in spelling bees or who are on the Honor Roll or who become Eagle Scouts; people who retire; new business opening; charitable contributions made; industrial development; employee development; achievements of a personal nature, and so on.

Paid Advertising

Hire a local public relations firm. These professionals can easily obtain maximum publicity for the minimum dollar outlay. The public relations firm can arrange for twice the local publicity that you can possibly get as a private individual. Their connections produce greater dividends for you.

Newspaper Advertising

All newspaper ads should be placed on the top half of the page. The ad should be placed on page two or three of the first or second section of the newspaper if possible. It naturally follows that the doctor should only advertise those ailments or conditions with which he has been successful. It is essential that the doctor can perform what the advertisement proclaims.

Advertise conditions that get remarkable and immediate responses to chiropractic care. For example: headaches, back problems, whiplash, bursitis, leg pains, asthma, nervousness; rather than a very rare condition such as locomotor ataxia. NN - EL - SA - TS & RT - NS - NO - BT - MW

Open-minded and progressive chiropractors place ads in local newspapers, alternating the topics, and thereby improve their practices. Are YOU one of these? If not, you are cutting down on your practice volume. Here are a few ways that you can correct this:

On-the-job injuries. Place an occasional ad in the newspaper, informing the public that chiropractic care is readily available for on-the-job injuries. NN - EL - SA - TS & RT - NS - NO - BT - MW

Back-to-school examinations. You can advertise in the newspaper that your office is available for back-to-school examinations. These examinations are required in some states in order for the students to be re-admitted to school. NN - EL - SA - TS & RT - NS - BT - MW

Changing office hours. Place ads in the newspaper whenever you change your office hours. This could be for extending your office hours, winter or summer office hours, evening hours, weekend hours, etc. NN - EL - SA - TS & RT - NS - NO - BT - MW

Place display ads and imprinted tabloids in the newspaper. These ads and tabloids are available from the A.C.A. or the I.C.A. They educate the public regarding the benefits of chiropractic. The more educated the public becomes, the more new patients you will acquire. Obviously, if your name is imprinted on the ads and tabloids, the immediate response will be yours. The tabloids can also be used as handouts at your office, distributed to your community by mail, or hand-delivered. NN - EL - SA - TS & RT - NS - NO - BT - MW

Place an ad in the newspaper asking for volunteers for a Good Posture contest. Ideally, these contests should be sponsored by local or state societies. However, if your society doesn't wish to be involved, sponsor the contest yourself. See chapter on "Bird-Dogging" for more information on this idea. NN - EL - SA - TS & RT - NS - NO - BT - MW

Organize a "Chiropractic Information Bureau." Doctors around the country are joining together to form information bureaus. These bureaus perform various functions: referral service, answering service, clearinghouse for a speaker's bureau, etc. Place an ad in the newspaper offering these services.

Place an ad offering free spinal check-ups. These check-ups can be done in your office, or through the schools, examining for scoliosis or for other spinal problems. If you find a problem, you can notify the parents and tell them that they should go to their doctors for spinal corrections for their children. Naturally, when you write to them on your letterhead, quite a few of them will choose you. NN - EL - SA - TS & RT - NS - NO - BT - MW

Free x-ray ads. An old standby in the chiropractic profession is the free x-ray program, which is available to any member of a patient's family or to any member of the community. This lowers the cost barrier for chiropractic care by offering x-rays free of charge. I have known doctors who have used this program and their results were very successful. When you think of it, if a set of x-rays cost from seventy dollars to ninety dollars, this charge may keep people away who would normally utilize chiropractic care, but who just can't afford the entrance fee.

This x-ray program can be carried out in many ways. It can be advertised in newspapers, on television or radio, etc. It can also be done solely in your office by offering your patients, their relatives and friends an x-ray examination for a certain period of time at no charge. Or you could associate with a national chiropractic research firm and carry out the x-ray program under their name. It is highly effective and it really does work. *Caution:* Only implement this program if you can comfortably assimilate eighty to a hundred new patients a month into your practice *and retain them.* Otherwise, you will lose most of the new patients gained. NN - EL - SA - TS & RT - NS - NO - BT - MW

Advertise free laboratory procedures. During Heart Month, advertise free EKG's, blood pressure, urinalysis, etc. These type advertisements are effective in producing new patients. However, the patients who respond to "freebees" are usually of the lower socioeconomic levels and want something for nothing, as you may find out in the following visits. Although this method is highly effective, the hassles associated with this type of patient make the results questionable. NN - EL - SA - TS & RT - NS - NO - BT - MW

Free contour scanning as a method of attracting new patients. This idea uses a method of light projection that results in lines superimposed upon the bare body of a patient. The patient is then photographed. This photograph will reveal high or low muscle tissue, torsion of the body, etc. Chiropractors have utilized this idea as part of an actual nationwide screening program. This method of spinal or physical screening provides danger-free data to the doctor without harm to the patient. If the doctor finds physical problems with the scanning device, he recommends chiropractic care and, if he doesn't, he states so. This method of new patient procurement has proven very effective. NN - EL - SA - TS & RT - NS - NO - BT - MW

Random Access Information machines. These machines will play numerous taped messages, produced by the doctor, to people who are interested in hearing them. The doctor usually places an ad in the newspaper, etc., and lists the tapes and their topics. Prospective patients responding to the ad, call the D.C.'s office and request the tape by topic or by topic number. NN - EL - SA - TS & RT - NS - NO - BT - MW

Closing ads. Place an ad in the newspaper stating that your office will be closed while you are attending a postgraduate seminar in [city] on [subject.] This is excellent public realtions as people will see that you are keeping up-to-date on your science of chiropractic. NN - EL - SA - TS & RT - NS - NO - BT - MW

Re-Opening ads. Place an ad in the newspaper announcing that your office has re-opened after attendance of a chiropractic postgraduate seminar. NN - EL - SA - TS & RT - NS - NO - BT - MW

Announcements. When opening a new office, moving your office, adding a satellite office, etc., place an announcement in your local newspaper stating that you are opening your office at such-and-such an address. This will supplement the news write-ups that the local editor can place for you. Keep this printed announcement moderate in size and very professional-looking. NN - EL - SA - TS & RT - NS - NO - BT - MW

Place opening announcements in the local "shopper." Each area of town usually has a local, giveaway newspaper or "shopper" that is delivered free to each household. By placing an opening announcement ad in these "shoppers," you will supplement, again, the news write-up that the local editor has placed for you. NN - EL - SA - TS & RT - NS - NO - BT - MW

Mail opening announcements. When you have moved your office location or have just set up your practice, an opening letter, accompanied by some chiropractic literature, should be sent to as many households as possible. This letter should be brief, to the point, but personal and dignified. Write this letter as if you were writing to a friend. A sample letter follows:

Daniel W. Piney, D.C.
1701 Park Boulevard
Bradenton, FL 32701
(813) 505-1101

Dear Resident:

We feel very fortunate to be a part of Bradenton, and to have been given the warm welcome that everyone gave us when we arrived. This warm welcome reinforced the decision we made to make our home here. My wife, our two sons, and I congratulate you on having such a productive and pleasant community and promise that we will do our best to make a positive contribution to it.

We have been able to find the right location and facilities for the practice of Chiropractic Health Care. With the assistance and cooperation of Bradenton's professional, technical, and business people, all the x-ray and related scientific equipment are properly installed and functioning. Office hours are daily from 9 to 6 and on Saturday from 9 to 1 by appointment.

Since you have resided in Bradenton much longer than we, we're sure you are aware that the area is unequalled as a happy place to work, live, and raise children. We certainly agree with this, which is why we chose it as our home after carefully considering virtually every part of the state. We hope to serve as good fellow citizens, but we also look forward to making friends with everyone.

Sincerely,
Daniel W. Piney, D.C.

Child Health and Fitness Week or Month. Place an ad in the newspaper stating that free fitness examinations will be given to children, commencing the month prior to school, in the fall. This could be carried out in combination with scoliosis check-ups, free spinal examinations, back-to-school check-ups, etc. NN - EL - SA - TS & RT - NS - NO - BT - MW

Advertise in the newspaper that you are conducting free (or at nominal fees) the following classes: Physical fitness class, spinal care (and spinal hygiene), women's fitness class, exercise class and weight reduction class. These classes are normally taught once a week for six weeks. While performing a valuable service to the community, you are increasing your "sphere of influence" by teaching these classes. Once your students become familiar with you, your staff and your facility, and they accept your expertise in the classes taught, then they usually become regular patients. NN - EL - SA - TS & RT - NS - NO - BT - MW

Place an ad in the classified section of your local newspaper for a receptionist, and interview many people. Ask the applicants their experience with chiropractors. Find out their qualifications. Tell them you need someone who can type eighty words a minute, take shorthand, has chiropractic assistant training, hospital training, etc. Keep all applications that look promising for future employment. Send Thank-U-Grams to all who apply.

Mail advertising. Various localities differ in results produced from direct mail. Persevere! Repetition is the key to a good public relations program.

Postcards to patients. Send your patients postcards when you are away at a seminar. If you have a large mailing list, mail the postcards to your "bird-dog" patients and your active patients. Say, "I'm learning new methods of treating conditions such as yours."

Postcards to prospective patients. If you have met people who have physical problems while using the W.W.W. procedures, send them postcards from your convention hotel similar to the cards you sent to your regular patients.

Establish a monthly program of mailing literature to the people you have already met. Remember — "out of sight, out of mind." People will forget you unless you remind them who you are, what you are, and where you are.

Send out testimonial newspapers. These testimonial newspapers inform people what chiropractic is and the conditions chiropractic can help. Place them in your office. People love to read the stories of celebrities who use chiropractic and how it helped them. I personally like to see Robert Goulet getting his adjustment. I like to hear James Arness saying something nice about chiropractic. I like to see articles about the care of our Olympic athletes. Testimonials from these celebrities will definitely please your patients. These testimonial newspapers can be sent to your mailing list or to the general public. NN - EL - SA - TS & RT - NS - NO - BT - MW

Opening announcements. If you have moved your office, set up an office, or have built a new office, send opening announcements or open house announcements to the community leaders. Be sure to include business firms, dentists, optometrists, and other professionals, such as attorneys, podiatrists, hair stylists, bank managers, accountants, civic leaders, newspaper editors, etc. NN - EL - SA - TS & RT - NS - NO - BT - MW

Mail "opening literature" to everyone else. Don't waste your money sending opening announcements to the general public. Opening announcements say little and aren't worth the expense. Whenever you mail something, make it work for you to the fullest. Send out a pamphlet of chiropractic literature, not an announcement of your opening. Save the professional opening announcements for only the community leaders. Always make sure your name and address are clearly stamped on each piece of literature — *twice!* NN - EL - SA - TS & RT - NS - NO - BT - MW

Healthways. Send the monthly publication, *Healthways,* as well as other chiropractic literature, to your area beauty salons and barber shops, as well as to your regular patients. NN - EL - SA - TS & RT - NS - NO - BT - MW

Check newspaper daily for reports of automobile accidents. Send the victims appropriate literature.

Advertise in magazines. Many national magazines have local advertising space available. Usually this can be found through a public relations firm, as professionals and merchants band together to buy space in these national publications.

Mail Survey. Do a survey of your area through the mail. Determine the section of town you want to mail to by using a cross-reference index. Then mail to the homeowners in the predetermined sector a letter similar to the following:

Dear Mr. Smith:

Your name has been selected at random to participate in a Health Survey on Physical Fitness and Posture. We have set aside a certain time each day to discuss any health problem you may have. You will receive a complete examination, plus a physical fitness and posture check and a detailed, written report. This public service is only available within the months of . . . . . . and . . . . . and there is no charge or obligation. If you have any questions, don't hesitate to call and, if you wish, arrange a convenient time for an appointment.

Sincerely yours,
John Doe, D.C.

Send out a practice-survey letter. Usually this comes from a third party asking questions regarding your practice. For example: Did the patient feel the examination was good, poor, thorough, etc.? Was the patient treated warmly and courteously in your office — yes or no? Does the patient have any suggestions to make for improvement in your office? The patients (approximately twenty percent) will reply either positively or negatively to each of the questions. Using this method, you can evaluate what is going right or wrong in your practice.

Yellow Pages, Telephone Book advertising. The phone company will be happy to assist you in designing and placing an effective display ad in their Yellow Pages. This also pertains to information bureaus, answering services, etc. Reference should be made in the doctor's individual telephone listing that he is available for emergency calls. Also, the doctor's home phone number should be included in case he cannot be reached at the office number. These procedures will produce additional new patients for his practice.

Advertising on the information boards at new shopping malls. These boards are usually at the entrances to the malls and usually have displays for the restaurants in the malls, the plays or movies appearing at local theatres, etc. Doctors have placed displays pertaining to their offices on these information boards, sometimes attaching literature racks for appropriate literature. They report increased new patients from this type advertising.

Television spots. If chiropractors would form groups to place spot announcements on TV, and keep at it, a tremendous increase in the number of new patients would occur. This is very expensive but very effective media advertising.

Radio spots. This media is effective, as you can tailor your ads to exactly the market you desire. Manual laborers, blue-collar workers, white-collar workers, religious people, etc., listen to different radio stations. For instance, the manual laborers would generally listen to country and western or rock stations, while white-collar workers may listen to FM stations playing primarily classical music, etc. The A.C.A. has programmettes available for radio advertising. These short radio spots are professionally made to aid the doctor of chiropractic.

You can use the Welcome Wagon service for your business cards or for a complimentary consultation. Whenever a new person moves into the neighborhood, the Welcome Wagon meets them. They welcome the newcomers to the neighborhood and give them all kinds of free services from the many businesses in the area. You can welcome them also with a letter (which will be included in the Welcome Wagon packet). Give, in the letter, a courtesy consultation as a welcoming gesture to the newcomer. This same kind of approach could be utilized in cities where city halls give couples getting married a packet (similar to that given by the Welcome Wagon) introducing them to various businesses and services in the area. Check your city hall to see if they give these packets to newlyweds, and if they do, ask if you can include a congratulatory letter and courtesy consultations to these couples.

Billboard advertising. This method is usually used to establish a theme, i.e.: Try Walking, Availability of Insurance Coverage, etc. Many doctors of chiropractic have reported excellent results when using this media.

There are certain rules and ideas that, if followed, will guarantee the constant growth of a practice. These are the procedures, programs, etc., that are contained herein. They are not dependent upon your mood at a given time. Rather, these rules are "Do It" rules. By following them on a daily basis, regardless of circumstances, you will build a larger practice.

Commit yourself to inform your patients: (A) that you want their assistance in building your practice by referring patients to you; (B) by discussing their need of chiropractic; (C) of the value of chiropractic for their friends and relatives; (D) of their obligation to bring their friends and relatives under your care.

If you are serious about building your practice larger, discuss all of the above points with your patients. Everything you ever wanted in your practice is attainable if you commit yourself to covering each of these points with your patients.

Commit yourself to building your practice. A *rule of thumb* measurement used by all management consultants is:

0-10 New Patients a Month = Failure Practice

10-20 New Patients a Month = Below Average Practice

20-30 New Patients a Month = Average Practice

30-40 New Patients a Month = Good Practice

40+ New Patients, along with a decent visit average per patient (30 or over) = a successful "Superman" type Practice.

What level of practice are you at? Why not move up a practice level?

Be positive about your recommendations. Tell your patients how long you want them to stay under your care, what you expect them to do to help themselves, and what you are going to do to help them. Give them a good, positive prognosis of the results they can expect. However, don't promise them a "pie in the sky." Tell them that in your experience the majority of people with problems similar to theirs are going to improve eighty or ninety percent, or whatever your recommendations may be. Be very firm, definite and positive in what you tell your patients, because this starts the healing process.

Impress your patients with the seriousness of their conditions. I do not suggest that you alarm your patients. However, most people come to a doctor hoping that they only have a little problem which will need only a very little amount of care. If you find a problem that is going to be long-lasting and which is going to take quite a while to straighten out, tell that patient so. Tell him what is wrong, what needs to be done, and what will happen if it is not done. Tell him about the normal progression of pathology if a condition is not arrested. Don't exaggerate — just tell the facts as they are, and explain to the patient the seriousness of his condition.

The doctor should take the patient's condition seriously himself. When a doctor is in practice for a number of years, he knows, generally, how a patient's problem is going to respond. This often creates in the doctor a very relaxed, almost careless attitude. "Oh, your condition isn't anything. I've taken care of that before." Remember, to a patient his condition is the most important condition in the world. What may appear to be minor to a doctor is major to the patient. Take the patient's problem seriously. That's how he wants you to take it, and if you don't, he will go to someone else who will.

Give the patient relief as soon as possible. Don't stretch out the relief phase of a patient's care. Relieve his pain in the first two days of care if possible. If it is necessary to treat the patient twice a day for the first two days in order to relieve him, do it, and charge for it. Patients come to you because they are in pain. They want you to get them out of pain, and as quickly as possible. The immediate relief of pain should be your objective. It is absolutely disheartening for a patient suffering from a hot low back with sciatica, to have his doctor place him on a three-times-per-week schedule, taking two weeks to relieve his pain. What the doctor should do is treat the patient twice a day for two or three days, thus breaking the pain cycle in the first week of care. The obligation of the doctor is to get the patient out of pain as quickly as possible. Patients don't have any objection to paying for two office visits on the same day if it provides pain relief.

Be thorough. Patients would rather their doctor be overly thorough and cautious than for him to be careless and miss something that possibly could affect them for the remainder of their lives. I know of a medical doctor in Florida who, on every patient, performed an examination that cost $350. He examined everything and anything that could possibly be wrong with the patient. All his patients said the same thing: "My golly, this man is expensive — but boy, is he good!" Whether the doctor was good or not is irrelevant. The fact is, because he was thorough, his patients thought he was good. When a patient thinks his doctor is good, he will refer his friends and relatives to that doctor. Commit yourself to always giving thorough consultations, covering all that could possibly be wrong with the patient; give thorough examinations and thorough reports of findings. The patient will appreciate your thoroughness, will stick with you, get well, and refer.

Take all the time necessary when examining a patient. This impresses the patient that his doctor cares and is thorough. This is a seed that will generate referrals.

Do a talking examination. Remember, the patient is paying for your examination. He wants to know what is going on. When you are doing a straight-leg raising test, tell him you are going to check to see if a nerve is swollen. When you raise the patient's leg and it hurts, he will automatically know that the nerve is swollen. Tell him the next test will indicate whether or not he has a disc problem. When you perform that test and it hurts, the patient will know that he has a disc problem, and so on.

The patient will add up in his mind the results of all your tests and will know what his problem is. Then, when you give him a report of findings, he will already know what to expect from it. All you will have to do is to clarify what the patient already knows. This eliminates the mystery of a doctor's office.

Patients get angry when they go to a neurosurgeon and are examined with a pinwheel or feather and are charged a hundred dollars for the examination. They feel that they were cheated because the examination looked simple and the doctor didn't inform them what he was doing or how he was interpreting the tests. All the doctor had to do was say a few words explaining his tests, and the patient would have been satisfied. Explain what you are doing and keep your patients satisfied.

Do not treat a patient without having taken x-rays first. You are not functioning like a doctor unless you know what is wrong with your patient. The only way you can really know what is wrong with a patient's spine is to look at it. Therefore, x-ray all new patients. The only possible exception might be someone passing through town on vacation, etc., who is presently under the care of another D.C. in a different locale. If this patient hasn't had any falls or accidents since he saw his previous doctor, you should telephone his doctor and ask him how to treat his patient.

Explain lab findings during the report of findings. When you give a report of findings, go over each lab test and explain to your patient whether the findings are normal or abnormal, what they indicate, and what you are going to do to bring the abnormal findings back to normal. After a period of care, retake the lab work and show the patient how he has progressed between the two lab reports. This shows the patient that you are thorough. The more thorough you are, the more patients will be referred to you.

The simple step of adding lab work to your practice will increase your practice services and income. If you feel that you do not understand laboratory procedures well enough to do a credible job, purchase a reference text on the subject, or attend one of the many postgraduate seminars available through your state or national associations.

Pre-plan the number of office visits for your patients. If you are not currently doing this, you will be able to increase your practice by properly controlling and motivating your patients. When patients are placed on a schedule, they get better more quickly, stay well longer, and refer.

Offer more care than just relief. Don't have an "acute only" practice. These emergency type practices are very stressful. It is the doctor's responsibility to emphasize corrective care in his office. Explain to your patient that you will get him relief as soon as possible. However, the underlying cause of his condition will still be there and has to be corrected. Further explain that relief of pain may take a week, while fixing the real problem may take ninety to a hundred and twenty days. Also tell him that you want to fix his problem in order to give him as much of a normal life as possible. Emphasize that if you only relieve his pain, his condition will degenerate and he will be coming back again, but in worse shape. This lets the patient know that you are concerned about him and he will appreciate it.

Patients appreciate a doctor's efforts to "correct a problem," rather than simply relieving pain. Even if a patient does not follow through with the recommended corrective care, he will know that his doctor was interested in his welfare.

To determine the type of practice you presently have, read the following chart devised by the top chiropractic management consultants in the country:

Office Visit Average — (Divide your monthly new patients into your monthly patient visits.)

0-10 Office Visit Average = Emergency Care Only Practice.

10-20 Office Visit Average = Below Average Practice, barely above an Emergency Care basis.

20-30 Office Visit Average = Average Practice, mostly Emergency Care, but with some corrective measures. This type practitioner treats patients until they complain, then he dismisses them.

30-40 Office Visit Average = Good Practice. Good balance of Emergency Care and Corrective Care.

40+ Office Visit Average = Successful Practice. Ideal combination of

Emergency, Corrective, Rehabilitative, and
Maintenance Care. This visit average, plus a
40+ New Patients a Month average, equals a
"Superman" Practice.

Patient control via reports of findings. If you don't presently
give thorough structural reports of findings to your patients, you
will increase your practice if you do so.

*Give the patient a report of findings only after you have re-
ceived the "green light."* If you notice the patient is reluctant to
start care, don't treat that patient. In such a case, examine . . .
examine . . . examine! Impress him with your thoroughness! When
that patient exhibits faith, confidence, and belief in you, *then*
start treatment.

Never treat a patient before a report of findings is given. This
statement doesn't indicate that you should leave the patient in
agony for three days while you make up a report. You can
examine, x-ray, and report to a patient on the same day if necessary. However, always examine, x-ray, and report to a patient
before treating him.

*When giving a patient a report of findings, explain to him
other conditions that respond to chiropractic.* This will expand the
patient's knowledge of the various conditions that a chiropractor
can successfully treat. This is especially true if you know the
health problems of other members of his family (see "Family
Health History). In this case, your report of findings should
explain the chiropractic benefits for the health problems of
the patient in front of you, as well as the health problems of his
family.

Give pamphlets during the report of findings. When giving a
report of findings, at the same time give the patient a pamphlet regarding his relatives' health problems and write their names on the
pamphlet. Ask him to give it to his relatives and to relay a message
to them that you feel you could help them too.

Don't expect perfect results from your care. Accept less than
a hundred percent results on a patient. The chiropractic profession
is the only profession that has the audacity to expect that it is
going to get a hundred percent result on each and every patient,
which in reality is actually an impossibility. Therefore, after you
have examined a patient and have determined the percentage of
results you can expect, tell it to your patient. He will understand.
Patients appreciate frankness and honesty from their doctors. If
you tell a patient you expect seventy-five percent correction in his
condition, you will be a big "hero" when you accomplish a *ninety*
percent correction. However, if you promise, insinuate, etc., a

94

hundred percent result and can only deliver seventy percent, you will become a "failure" in that patient's mind. Hero or failure — it's your choice!

Give your home phone number to your patients. It is this author's standard procedure to write my home phone number on the backs of my business cards and give them to my patients. I tell them that if they ever have an emergency or one of their friends has an emergency, they should feel free to give me a call at my home. I tell them that I'm not hiding from them. I'm there to take care of them if they need me. I can state emphatically that my patients have never abused this privilege. They appreciate being able to reach me at home if they need me, but they almost always stick to their regularly-scheduled office visits.

If a patient is uncomfortable at home and calls me at my home, I give him a home remedy to relieve his pain. For example: "Lay down on the floor"; "Take a tub bath"; "Apply ice," etc. I also tell him, "If it doesn't work in an hour, call me right back and I will be happy to come to the office to see you." This helps the patient get over his symptoms until the following day. Most people do not abuse this privilege.

Use the "patient in pain" phone procedure. Whenever a patient in pain is treated in my office, he will be called at the end of our workday to determine how he is feeling. Before we go home at the end of the day, the receptionist or I will call that patient and ask, "How are you? How are you feeling after your adjustment today?" If he states that he is feeling better, we tell him that we are pleased he is doing better and we'll see him at his appointment the next day. If the patient says he is still in pain, I prescribe home remedies such as ice, heat, etc., until his appointment the following day.

Use this "patient in pain" telephone procedure on each and every patient who is in pain. They will appreciate your thoroughness. Also, call all new patients after their first adjustments. Ask them how they are feeling. Did they have any stiffness in the areas you treated? Is it looser, etc.? Tell them that you are just checking on them to make sure they are all right.

These patients will tell all their relatives and friends how thoughtful their doctor was to call them. Patients have never had doctors who cared enough about them to call them. They appreciate thoughtfulness in a doctor. This is the stuff that referrals are made of!

Use "twins" in the beginning of care. When initiating care on a patient who is in pain, don't push for referrals at that particular point. Patients in pain don't want to hear anything about sending additional patients to your office. Remember, when a patient is in pain, the most important thing in his entire world is his pain. The patient in pain wants to hear about himself and how he is going to get free of that pain. In such cases, use the "twins" approach. When a patient starting care is discouraged, tell him of a similar patient (twin) of similar age, sex, and health problem, who you cared for, and tell him how that patient responded. Keep using one "twin" after another to keep your patients encouraged until their pain has been broken. Once the patient's pain cycle is broken, then you can proceed with referral stimulation.

Constantly talk about the progression of degeneration of patients' problems. A good example of this is whenever a patient is involved in a whiplash automobile accident, explain to him that the joints of his neck are sprained, the discs are stretched and, if he doesn't receive the proper care, his neck will become kyphotic. Further explain to him that arthritis will develop at the posterior elements of his spine and the intervertebral discs will degenerate, causing nerve root compression. Eventually, the nerve root compression in the cervical spine will cause headaches, brachial neuralgia, etc.

All doctors of chiropractic know that the above facts are true, but we are reluctant to tell our patients of the onward progression of degeneration that happens when somebody is not cared for properly. It is your professional obligation to explain to each and every patient how degeneration progresses and what their spines will be like in two years, five years, ten years, etc., without proper chiropractic care.

The explaining of the progression of degeneration can also be done when a patient tells you that he has a friend who was involved in an accident. Tell him about the progression of degeneration and how important it is for his friend to come under your care to prevent this from occurring.

Don't go to extremes with this issue. Don't elaborate more than necessary. Don't try to scare the patient. Just be a doctor and remember, a doctor is a teacher. Teach your patients what happens when care is not initiated soon enough, or when not enough care is given to a patient. Don't scare your patients needlessly — just report the facts as they occur.

Use multiple treatments for multiple problems. When a patient has more than one problem, design a treatment program for each. This may involve using a different therapy on each area where applicable. When you explain to a patient the problems he has and the treatment/therapies that you are going to use on each problem, you will impress upon that patient the seriousness of his condition, and he will appreciate your multi-faceted treatment plan designed to correct his problems.

No improvement. If you have a patient who is not responding to care, change the frequency and/or the roughness of your adjustments. Sometimes fewer adjustments or more intensified adjustments get results. Also, sometimes rougher or gentler adjustments are needed to have a patient respond. If your patient is not responding, do something different.

Treat the patient's mind as well as his body. We've all heard of psychosomatic conditions where a patient is mentally ill and this mental illness is making his body ill also. The doctor can treat the body forever, but if he doesn't work with the mind first, the body will not respond. It has been said that "you have to go through a patient's mind to get to his spine." The reverse is also true. Sometimes a patient will start with a physical condition and the pain lasts for such a long time that he gets very discouraged, and it affects him mentally. This is a physical condition causing a mental aberration. Therefore, a doctor has to treat both mental and physical conditions. Treat your patients' minds by utilizing procedures that will increase the patients' confidence in your ability to get them well, and then the mental process of healing can begin.

Many doctors feel that it is their sole function to treat the patient's organic problem. However, with every organic problem there is a concomitant mental problem that accompanies it. It is just as much a part of being a doctor to treat subluxations above the atlas as it is to treat the subluxations that exist below. If you can overpower a patient's negativism or his sickness concept and get him to think about health, you have started the healing process. Once your patients start thinking they are going to get well, they will, in fact, help themselves get well.

Talk about chiropractic in your office. If you relieve a patient who has been suffering with migraine headaches for twenty or thirty years, tell *all* your patients of the great results you achieved with that particular patient. Don't mention the patient's name, but you can say, "Hey, I'm excited! I want to tell you something." Then tell them the story of your patient. Once you have told all your patients this story, they will go out and tell their friends how you cure migraine headache sufferers. Do this every day of your practice career.

Talk a little, but only about chiropractic. Whenever you have an opportunity to explain how chiropractic can help problems, do so with enthusiasm. Show the patients your indepth knowledge regarding health problems. Many referrals will result. Don't talk about anything other than chiropractic in your office. Remember, you are an expert in one field: chiropractic. You are not an expert in politics, religion, etc. If you talk about topics that you don't have expertise, you will only show the patient that you don't know what you are talking about. Talk a little, but only about chiropractic.

Talk about a case of the day, week, month. Your entire staff should have a topic of the day/week/month to talk about to your patients to systematically educate them. The more educated a patient becomes, the more patients with various disorders he can refer to you. Follow up this procedure with appropriate literature.

Shake hands with all your patients at each visit. Make your handshake a warm, friendly, firm handshake. Don't use a fish-like, wilted or limp handshake. At the same time, don't squeeze the patient's hand forcibly as if to crush his knuckles. Make your handshake firm and friendly, letting the patient know that you welcome him to your office and that you are happy to see him.

Compliment your patients whenever you can. Don't compliment the person, compliment the act he has performed or a thing (hairdo, clothes, etc.). Don't be too direct; it will make the patient feel uneasy, i.e.: "Kathy, you are the most beautiful woman I have ever met in my life"! Obviously, such a statement would make that patient feel uneasy and she would question your motives. However, if you say, "I like your dress. It is really beautiful," you are, in essence, complimenting that patient by complimenting her choice of clothes, and she will appreciate it. Or, you can say, "I like your hairdo. It really looks good today," or "I like your perfume. It really smells good." You are complimenting her choice of hairdo or her choice of perfume, and she will appreciate your compliments. Or, you can say, "John, I read in the paper the other day about the project you did for the Junior Chamber of Commerce and I want you to know I appreciate what you are doing and I think you did a great job." In this case, you are complimenting an action on the part of a patient and not the patient directly.

Patients appreciate these indirect compliments. We all like to be appreciated for our acts. By using these techniques, you will be able to compliment the patients without making them feel uneasy. When you say nice things about your patients, they in turn will reciprocate and say nice things about you to others. It is these little things that help a practice grow.

Ask patients to refer to you. Have enough audacity to simply ask for more business. You can tell your patients that you are there to take care of sick people and that is what you want to do.

If they have anyone — friend or relative — who is in need of chiropractic care, you would appreciate them putting in a good word for the services that you render. You don't have to project a begging attitude, only simply state that you are there to take care of sick people and that if they have friends or relatives who need care, you would be happy to take care of them. If you make your request in a begging manner, the patients will think something is wrong with their doctor who has to ask for more business, and it will backfire on you. If you make your request sincere, as a dedicated professional wanting to help sick people, that's how the patients will interpret your comments and they will therefore refer to you.

Use statistics in your practice. Explain to your new patients that a national survey shows that such-and-such percentage of patients who were accepted for chiropractic care with problems similar to theirs got well or were much improved. Also, point out that these statistics were also on patients who were worse, older, weaker, etc., etc., than they, thus increasing your patients' odds of recovery. This gives them new hopes of recovery and thus starts their healing process.

Utilize the seasons or the weather to stimulate referrals. If a patient complains about the weather, you should use the patient's complaint as a springboard to stimulate referrals. For instance, if it is raining, tell the patient that rain washes the pollen from the air and is a big aid to your hay fever and asthma patients. Rain also results in slippery streets and automobile accidents, etc., etc. If a patient complains about the weather, you should use the patient's complaint as a springboard to stimulate referrals. For instance, if it helps your arthritis patients, etc., etc. Always use the weather as a springboard to give a positive referral plug.

Tie in local events to chiropractic. Whenever a popular football game is being played and it is the topic of the day, use this to your advantage. Explain how football injuries are similar to whiplash injuries, which is your specialty. If boating is a popular topic among your patients, explain how the jarring of boats on the water aggravates the necks and lower backs of your patients, etc. Always turn your patients' comments to a chiropractic referral stimuli.

Explain chiropractic research. Explain our profession's various research projects to your patients and dovetail the research projects into the various conditions that chiropractic can help. This broadens the scope of chiropractic in the patients' minds, resulting in referrals.

Educate your Bird-Dogs. As previously explained, a Bird-Dog is a person who is an enthusiastic booster of your services. Bird-Dogs don't just happen — they are trained and educated by you. The more Bird-Dogs you have, the larger your practice will be.

Train the Bird-Dog to see the bird. Bird-dogs in the hunting world are dogs that retrieve birds for the hunters. In the professional world, a Bird-Dog is a person who retrieves new patients for his doctor. An actual bird-dog doesn't learn its talents easily and neither do professional Bird-Dogs. Actual bird-dogs have to be trained to see and retrieve the birds. Our Bird-Dogs have to be trained too. A hunter trains his bird-dog in the woods; a professional trains his Bird-Dog on an adjusting table. Every time you talk with a patient, teach him something new about chiropractic. When you adjust a patient, teach him why you are doing so, what you are doing, and when he can expect results. In other words, in order for us to have Bird-Dogs retrieving patients for us, we must first train the Bird-Dog to see the bird!

Teach patients to testify. When a patient starts telling you how much better he is feeling, tell him, "That's fine, Mr. Jones. I'm really pleased that you are feeling better." Act enthusiastically to let the patient know how appreciative you are that he is responding. Then say, "Mr. Jones, I would like you to tell my receptionist exactly how good you are doing." The patient will then tell the story for a second time to the receptionist. This time, testifying becomes easier for him. He will tell the receptionist his story with a little more enthusiasm and gusto, and also with a little more elaboration. The receptionist then responds enthusiastically about how great the patient is doing and says, "Listen, Mr. Jones, we have another patient who is a little discouraged. Would you please tell him how good you are doing, as a favor to me?" The patient has already testified twice, and by the time he testifies for the third time — this time to the discouraged patient — he will be even more enthusiastic in telling his chiropractic story.

By using this method, you can teach your patients how to testify and then they can go out into the community and testify for you, because they have successfully done it three times inside your office, thus removing some of their inhibitions. This is the best way to get introverted patients to testify to people other than their immediate families. Teach them to testify.

Inform as you perform. Tell your patients what you are doing when you are doing it, and what they can expect for results. When you take a patient's blood pressure, tell him what it is. When you take x-rays, show them to the patient. In this way, people will clearly understand what is happening to them. Do everything you can to establish trust. Use sentences such as, "I want you to do this because . . ."; "This is necessary because. . ."; "The answer to your problem is . . ."; "Your x-rays show . . .," etc., etc. Inform as you perform! Patients like to know what you are doing and why you are doing it.

Show and tell chiropractic techniques. If you use the Gonstead technique as your primary adjusting method, you should add a little kinesiology on one visit, some Nimmo on another, Rolfing on yet another, and some DeJarnette on another visit. Explain to your patient that you are using different chiropractic techniques and explain what each technique does to help him. The patient will then go out and tell his friends, "Boy, my doctor knows everything!" If you can impress the patient with your expertise, you will increase the size of your practice.

Have supportive evidence of patient progress. Normally, when a patient comes to a chiropractic office, he is examined, x-rayed, and then placed on a treatment plan that continues indefinitely. The patient usually has to keep asking the doctor, "How am I doing, doctor?" or "Am I improving?" The doctor usually replies, "Why, sure you are." This doesn't satisfy the patient.

You should regularly re-examine and re-x-ray all patients. After re-examination and/or re-x-ray has been performed, you should give the patient a progress report, saying, "Mr. Jones, when you originally came to this office, you had [problems] and, after your examination today, these have been eliminated. We've done a good job up to this point. Now let's continue to treat you to relieve the problems that remain."

If the patient doesn't respond as well as expected, you should say, "Mr. Jones, these [problems] have cleared up. However, these [problems] have NOT responded. Therefore, we are going to change the type of treatment that we are giving you in order to correct the problems that haven't responded yet." Patients appreciate progress reports and will usually continue treatment until the next examination.

After the next examination has been performed, explain to the patient what has improved and the problems that need further attention. Further tell him, "There are a few problems that are clearing up, but slowly. The treatment program that we have outlined for you is correct. Let's continue and we will examine you in a month to see how you are doing at that point."

Re-examine, re-examine, re-examine — throughout the patients' care, so that you can properly inform them of their progress. Examinations and progress reports keep your patients under your care and keep them happy. These re-examinations also let you know what has improved, what hasn't improved, and whether you will have to change the type of adjustment/therapy, etc., in order to complete the patient's healing process.

Ask your patients to telephone the person who referred them . . . to thank them. When a new patient starts to get results and is enthusiastic about chiropractic, tell him, "Mr. Jones, I would like you to call Mr. Black who referred you to me, and thank him for referring you to my care. If it wasn't for him, you wouldn't be in the good condition that you are now. Why don't you give him a call? I know he would appreciate it and that he would love to know how you are doing." Needless to say, when Mr. Jones calls Mr. Black and thanks him for being referred to you, Mr. Black will be more enthusiastic about referring more new patients to you, because he is now receiving a positive feedback. He will now refer even more patients to you because of this telephone call from Mr. Jones. This is a great way to increase referrals.

Make notations of prospective patients on your patients' file folders. Whenever a patient tells you of someone else's health problems, tell him that chiropractic can help his friend, and then make a note on your patient's file as to who the prospective patient is and what is wrong with him. A week or two later, if the prospective patient has not been referred into your office, you can casually mention to your patient, "How is your friend, the one with the low back problem?" The patient will be impressed that you remembered a casual conversation made with him a few weeks prior, and this will motivate him to re-contact his friend and refer him to you.

Give chiropractic literature to your patients for their friends. Whenever a patient states that he has a friend/acquaintance/relative with a health problem, give him appropriate literature to take to his friends. Write on the top of the literature the prospective patient's name. Also write the prospective patient's name and condition on your patient's file folder. Then, if within two weeks the prospective patient hasn't initiated care, you can ask your patient how his friend is doing, etc.

Scold patients if they miss appointments. Emphatically tell your patients that regularity in their treatment schedules is necessary for proper progress and that when they miss one appointment, their progress is lost and will necessitate two office visits to make up their lost progress. Control your practice and your patients. Don't let them control you.

I'm sorry. When a patient wants a quick cure, tell him that you are sorry but you didn't expect his condition to be so involved, etc. Also tell him that you are on his side, but express regret that it will take longer to treat his problem than you expected.

Put the monkey on the patient's back. Don't allow a patient to place the responsibility of getting well on your shoulders. It is the patient's responsibility to get well, not yours. Many people wish that someone else would be responsible for their actions, health, etc. These people are obese, drink too much, smoke too much, are over-medicated, don't exercise, don't follow their doctors' orders, etc., etc., etc. These same people have the audacity to expect someone else to get their mistreated bodies back in shape! They want someone else, the "white knight" in a doctor's uniform, to do for them what they refuse to do for themselves . . . take care of their bodies! This is impossible! A doctor's duty, and only responsibility, is to render the very best service he can to his patients. The patient's responsibility is to follow his doctor's orders to the letter. If you find a patient is trying to dump his responsibilities onto your shoulders, don't accept it; put the "monkey" on the patient's back — where it belongs!

Counteract patient dissatisfaction. If you sense patient dissatisfaction, immediately re-x-ray, re-examine, and re-evaluate his case. Do it at no charge if necessary. This will save fifty percent of your patients from quitting your care. Perhaps a potential "knocker" will be changed into a "booster."

Don't accept the blame. Whenever a patient states that since his last visit to your office he developed pain in a certain area, or if he states that he is in a worse condition, etc., ask, "What did you do to aggravate the problem?" If he states that he didn't do anything, further ask, "Think hard . . . something you did aggravated your condition." Usually he will then tell you, with a sheepish grin on his face, that he was involved in some action or accident which aggravated his condition.

Don't accept the blame for a patient's condition worsening. He usually did something, disobeyed your orders, etc., to aggravate his symptoms. If you let a patient put you on the defensive, he will immediately lose confidence in you and, even though he did something to make himself worse, he will quit your care because he has lost confidence in you.

Use text book selling. Find reference texts with paragraphs and page numbers, whose authors have similar opinions to yours. Memorize the paragraphs, the authors' names and the page numbers of these important paragraphs. When giving a patient a report of findings, you could quote a paragraph and state, "On page . . ., the author states . . . . ." Then reach behind you and grab the text and say, "Let me show you," then open the book to the page you have already stated and show the patient the important paragraph to back up your words. The patient will be highly impressed, and you now have a "booster." Actually, all you have done is memorized a few paragraphs, the page numbers on which these paragraphs are printed, the name of the text, and the author's name. It's simple and it works!

Check and re-check your patients. Examine your patients before adjustment and re-examine him afterwards to determine if the adjustment accomplished what you wanted it to. When you treat high blood pressure patients, take their blood pressure before and after the adjustment to see how much it has been reduced. If your patient has a restricted range of motion, check it before and after adjustment to see how much it has improved. The same would be true of grip tests, bilateral scales, and many other tests performed in your office. Check and re-check on each and every visit. Your patients will appreciate your thoroughness.

Do post-x-rays, exams, and chemistries. Re-examine at least every thirty days of active care, and re-x-ray in ninety days. Tell your patient in the report of findings that you will be doing these procedures to monitor any change in his progress. Practices which have monitoring examination systems are usually the larger practices.

REFERRAL PROCEDURES

The following are the procedures used by successful practitioners to build their practices. These doctors view building a practice as a business. They design procedures such as the following, methodically implement them, and double, triple, even quadruple, their practices.

The basics. There are certain basic procedures used in all doctors' offices, i.e.: examinations, consultations, reports of findings, etc. However, there are extra variations that may be added to the basics which make a practitioner more prone to stimulate referrals and attract new patients. The following are some of the extras that may be of benefit to you.

Consultation. Whenever you take a history on a patient, you should include a FAMILY HEALTH HISTORY and list all the members of that patient's family, and the conditions that these people are suffering from. Ask if the relatives live in your town. The reason you should ask if they live in your locality is that similar weather conditions may affect their problems. Explain this fact to the patient. Do not let him think that you are looking for referrals. When he says that his relative *does* live in your area, this lets you know that you have a potential new patient. If the relative does not live in your area, this is a chance for you to refer that relative to a friend of yours in that locale. You should also tell the patient: "Sometimes conditions are inherited, and I want to find out if we are dealing with an inherited condition in your case. This will have an affect on the response we can expect in your case."

Ask the patient during consultation who referred him to you. Once a patient tells you who sent him, you should say something nice about the referring patient, and ask the new patient to thank him for you. This instills the referring concept in the new patient and reinforces the "right decision" of your Bird-Dog patient to refer to you.

Written reports. Many management programs recommend the use of written reports. This is an excellent procedure. Write down what is wrong with a patient, the treatment you are going to give, the results that patient can expect, and how much it will cost. Give this to the patient. He will appreciate your thoughtfulness and will be impressed with how thorough you are. When you give written reports, it shows the patient that you are serious about what you are doing. This definitely helps build a practice.

The $200,000-a-year doctors see approximately 12 patients an hour. Have an appointment book that will allow you to see 12 patients per hour. As you are practicing, check the appointment book hourly to see how many patients per hour you are treating. If you are treating 12, you are practicing at the $200,000 level for that hour. Once you impress yourself and your staff that you are capable of a $200,000 level, you will be well on your way to attaining it.

Have an appointment-only office. Don't let patients walk in the door and be treated without an appointment, or take a walk-in patient ahead of a patient who has a scheduled appointment. Determine what your maximum work-load is. Perhaps you can treat six, eight, or ten patients an hour and still remain on schedule. Once you have determined your maximum work-load, schedule your patients in groups according to it. If a patient walks in without an appointment, tell him you will be happy to see him at your next available appointment time, perhaps three-quarters of an hour from then . . . or whenever it may be. Then take care of your regularly-scheduled patients, waiting until there is a gap in your schedule to take care of the walk-in patient. The patients who have scheduled appointments are the ones who really care about you and your time. The patients who just walk in the door without appointments should not be treated at times which cause inconvenience to your scheduled patients. Give first consideration to your regular patients. Have an appointment-only practice.

Group your appointments together. If you only see four patients per day, schedule them all at the same time so that they will see other people being treated. A patient doesn't like to think that he is the only patient a doctor has. Also, it is extremely tiring to treat a patient, sit down to do paperwork, treat another patient, then sit down to do paperwork again, and so on. This up-and-down routine wears a doctor out both physically and mentally. It is a lot easier to schedule patients in groups, treat them one after the other, and then do paperwork procedures when you are through with the patients.

Group your patients together. It is easier on the receptionist, it is easier on you, and psychologically better for the patient.

Review your daily appointment sheets to determine whether there is any extra service that can be rendered to the patients scheduled that day. Concentrate on the extra service. At the beginning of each day, review the schedule of patients who you are going to see that day. While reviewing this patient list, think about the extra service you could provide each patient. What procedure, x-ray, examination, adjustment, etc. was not given to a patient on a previous visit because it slipped your mind? When you review your list daily and then provide the extra services for your patients, they will think that you've gone the extra mile for them. When a doctor goes the extra mile for his patients, they will return the favor.

Patient lectures will increase your practice forty percent. When a doctor develops a busy practice, he doesn't have the time to explain the scope of chiropractic to his patients. When this occurs, he will have his headache patients referring other headache patients to him while, at the same time, they'll send their relatives and friends with another chiropractic problem to an M.D. The only reason they didn't send these friends to you is that they didn't know the scope of chiropractic. If you initiate a program of regularly-scheduled patient lectures, you will be able to effectively explain the total scope of chiropractic to your patients. When they know the various conditions you can effectively treat, you will increase your practice by forty percent.

Ask your patients to bring their spouses, their friends, and their neighbors to the lay lectures. This will result in many others becoming patients and also potential Bird-Dog referrals.

Note: Don't turn your patient lectures into church services. Don't preach. You are a professional. Conduct yourself as a professional. Teach the patient what chiropractic is, the conditions chiropractic can treat, how to care for their own spines at home, etc. Also, show good quality pre- and post-x-rays to the audience as proof of chiropractic results.

Free x-rays. Whether or not this type of program is utilized is up to the individual doctor's sense of ethics. I have known doctors to use this program very successfully. If a set of x-rays costs seventy dollars, this charge may keep many people away from chiropractic care. Many people just cannot afford the entrance fee.

This x-ray program can be carried out in many ways. It can be done through advertising in the media. It can also be done exclusively in your office. You could inform your patients, and the relatives and friends of your patients, that you will not charge for x-rays during a certain period of time because of a research project being conducted during that time. Perhaps you could even become part of a national chiropractic research firm and do the x-ray program under their name.

This program is highly effective and really does work. However, a word of caution is needed: If you have a maximum ability to examine and x-ray twenty-nine new patients a month and then add a free x-ray program, you may increase your new patients by fifty. If so, you may not be capable of handling that many and, consequently, may lose the majority of them. If you decide to do a program of this type, space the new patients out so that you can properly take care of them.

Another cautionary note: A free x-ray program appeals to people of a lower economical status. People in a higher income bracket may see a free x-ray program as a gimmick and may choose to take their business elsewhere as a result. Therefore, you should carefully consider all aspects of such a program prior to initiating it.

Accept insurance assignments. This is a tremendous stimulant for referrals. If a patient makes $175 a week and has a wife and three children to provide for, he cannot afford a tremendous amount of chiropractic care. Health doesn't fit into his budget! The middle-income and lower-income people don't have large savings accounts to pay for your care. However, eighty percent of these people are covered by some type of major medical insurance — either through a group where they work or through a private plan. Simply tell these people that you will accept insurance assignments on their claims.

Your first step would be to call the insurance company of that patient and verify his chiropractic coverage. Once verified, tell the patient that he has one of three options. The first option is to pay cash for his care. The second option is to sign the assignment form and to pay the hundred dollars deductible and the twenty percent of his care that his insurance company won't cover, and to bill the insurance company for the remainder. The third option is to sign the assignment form and then charge his services. Whenever the insurance company doesn't pay, the remainder will be billed directly to that patient.

If the patient chooses either of the last two options, you will increase your referrals. As long as a patient can charge his services, he will continue coming and will refer others. Not only will he refer people from his place of employment, but he will also refer his family, because they, too, will be able to charge. By using this assignment method, the financial barriers to chiropractic care are lowered and, therefore, more people will avail themselves of your services. A good example of how this principle works is seen in Workmen's Compensation and automobile insurance patients who don't have to pay for their services because their insurance pays everything. These patients are hard to dismiss because they are getting free care. If you can place your major medical insurance patients into a similar category, you will have a more streamlined practice and will increase your referrals.

Allow selective charging. If your practice is cash only, you can liberalize your practice by allowing selective charging. If a patient shows a willingness to pay, let him charge his services and pay you on a monthly basis. This procedure will increase your practice volume. The more easily patients are able to charge their services, the more likely they will be to utilize your services.

To determine if your charging policies are too liberal or too restrictive, check your accounts receivable. These should be three times your monthly gross plus ten percent. If they are less than this figure, you are too strict in your collection procedures. By liberalizing your procedures, you will increase your practice. If your accounts receivable are more than this figure, you are too liberal and your collection procedures need to be more stringent.

Offer a family plan. Most family plans have the first member of the family paying a standard office fee, with all other members paying a reduced fee. Imagine the financial burden placed upon a family if they have five members being treated on the same day at fifteen dollars per patient. Compound this figure as though it were necessary to see all of these patients three times a week. Obviously, this family will not be able to afford to continue under your care as a group and will only send the sickest member to you for treatment.

Many doctors feel that it is better to have a family plan where the entire family can have chiropractic care, with some family members being treated at a reduced rate. It is important to remember that the children you care for now are going to be your adult patients in five or ten years' time. (Please refer to chapter on "Building The Pediatric Practice.")

Have a family health history questionnaire. If you utilize a family health questionnaire, you will find many relatives of your patients with problems that chiropractic can help. Make a note on the patient's chart as to the health problems of his relatives. During the course of that patient's care, you can subtly drop suggestions, such as, "Remember that uncle of yours with a bad shoulder? Why don't you bring him here? I feel I could fix that shoulder for him." Hints like these will definitely increase your referrals.

Give prospective patients a trip through your office. Most people who shy away from doctors do so because of a fear of the unknown. Whenever a patient has a friend or relative accompany him to your office, the C.A. should immediately take this opportunity to escort the friend of this patient through the office. She should show him the equipment, explaining the function of it and, perhaps, if the doctor is free, introduce the prospective patient to him. Once the fear of the unknown is eliminated, the prospective patient may feel free to come to your office for care.

Have regular staff meetings. At least once a week, go over office goals, problems, programs, etc., that are pertinent to practice growth. This should be a motivational and instructional meeting, not a "gripe" session.

Bonus systems. There are many varieties: percentage of gross, percentage of net, new patients, regular patients, recaptured patients, recall patients, cash collected, number of insurance forms completed, amount of slow collectibles collected, etc., etc. Whatever bonus system fits your office, implement it. It is unreasonable to ask your staff to work harder for the same pay. Salaries should be twelve percent of income. Give your staff a percentage of your growth in the form of a bonus system, but keep this percentage within the twelve-percent guidelines.

Examine family members free. Give an initial examination to any member of a patient's family at no charge and at no obligation. If the examination proves negative, ask the patient to return in a year for another courtesy checkup. However, if the examination reveals a problem, ask him to make an appointment for x-rays to determine the extent of that problem. This is a very effective way to obtain new patients.

Back-to-school examinations. Most states have procedures in which school children have to be medically examined prior to entering school. Usually the examinations are prior to the first grade, the third grade, the seventh grade, etc. Write to all your patients and tell them that you are setting aside certain time periods during the summer months for pre-school examinations. Also tell them that you will be examining their children for scoliosis at the same time in order to determine if they are starting to develop this problem. This examination should be at a minimal cost, comparable to the cost of a normal office visit.

Conduct scoliosis-screening examinations. Scoliosis is progressive, crippling, and degenerative. It affects five hundred thousand children between the ages of ten and nineteen. If left untreated, it can result in deformity, back pain, disability, heart problems, degenerative arthritis, disc disease, and sciatica. It affects girls far more often than it affects boys (at a ratio of 8:1).

It can be prevented by early detection.

1. Offer free spinal examinations and scoliosis screening examinations for this age group by way of newspaper, radio, TV, and direct mail advertising. Or, at far less expense, ask area school principals to include your offer in flyers sent home to parents.

2. Offer free spinal examinations to your patients, either by discussing with them, when they are in the office, or by mailing to former patients.

3. Call former patients with children of this age bracket and

4. Give patients pamphlets on scoliosis. Explain the program.

5. Hang plaques around the office, stating: "Look at your posture; others do!"

6. Post notices of your scoliosis checkup program on your bulletin board.

7. Have the C.A.'s explain the program to your patients.

8. Offer a complimentary examination, not only to all your patients' children, but also to their friends' children.

9. Have tickets made up for the scoliosis-screening examinations. Hand fifteen to twenty of these tickets to each mother, and have her pass the tickets out to her friends.

10. Keep names and addresses of all children who have had the examination in your tickler file. These examinations should be done yearly for children of ages ten through nineteen.

These examinations can be performed by x-ray, plumbline, physical examinations, contour photography, etc.

Broaden your base. Don't offer only one type of service or adjustment. If your practice has a specialization, add different techniques, such as nutrition, weight reduction, spinal exercise classes, etc. Please refer to the Practice Expansion Wheel

Show other people's x-rays in your office. Place x-rays with a bad curvature, compression fracture, etc., on lighted viewboxes in your adjusting rooms. These viewboxes should be kept illuminated during the day. When a patient is in an adjusting room, waiting for his adjustment, he will see these x-rays. When the doctor walks into the room, the patient will usually ask, "What is wrong with the person on that x-ray?" The doctor will then explain what was wrong with that patient, how he treated the patient's problem, and how he responded to care. By using this method, a doctor can be constantly telling a new chiropractic story to each patient on each visit. The better educated your patients are, the better able they are to refer to you. This same procedure can be followed by having *before-and-after x-rays* in illuminated viewboxes in your adjusting rooms.

Complimentary consultation cards. These cards are the same size as business cards, showing your name, address, phone number, etc., but they also have space for "Complimentary Consultation for" and a line for the prospective patient's name. Another space should be made with "Valid Through" and a line under it for a date:

Whenever a patient asks if you can help a friend's or a relative's condition, simply give him a pertinent pamphlet and a free consultation card. The doctor should put a date on the card for two to three weeks hence.

He should explain that there will be no charge for the patient's friend to come to your office and find out if chiropractic can help him. Let the patient know that you are doing this especially for him. Also, tell him that if you find that you cannot help his friend, you will tell him so.

Cards of this type can be used in many ways, for example, as an extra plus in a recall program, as a "thank you" for referring patients to your office, to give to prospective patients you might meet while Bird-Dogging, to use when giving patient lectures, etc. These cards may also be labeled for a free examination, free adjustment, free x-ray, or free laboratory.

Use comparative questionnaires to evaluate patients' progress. When you have a patient with a lower back problem, fill out a comparative questionnaire and, if it reveals that other problems have cleared up while the patient has been under your care, take credit for the resolving of it. At the same time, explain to your patient how chiropractic helped this problem. This is an excellent opportunity to educate your patients. If you follow this procedure, your referrals will increase.

Give questionnaires to prospective patients. If a patient mentions a friend or relative who has a health problem but who is reluctant to come to your office, give him a questionnaire for that prospective patient to fill out. Tell him that once it is filled out, you will be able to determine whether or not you can help him.

Your patient will be impressed, the prospective patient will be impressed, and you will obtain a new patient.

Patient convenience is always a top priority, but is particularly important when you're seeking referrals. If you are treating a lady patient for a cervical problem, don't require that patient to get into a gown, because it takes time for the ladies to get out of their clothes, it messes up their hair, etc. Also, many women find it embarrassing to wear the gowns. If you can possibly treat the patient without her being required to disrobe, do so. Every trip to the doctor should be free of embarrassment and any inconvenience if possible. The same principle applies to male patients. If you are treating only the man's low back, don't have him strip completely. If you can treat him effectively by simply having him pull up his shirt, do so.

Have phone teams. Ask your Bird-Dog patients for their permission to give their telephone numbers to discouraged patients. Tell them that you would like them to relate their chiropractic stories to these patients. Find a male and female Bird-Dog patient with each of the five or six main conditions that you take care of in your practice, i.e.: headaches, migraine headaches, bursitis, sciatica, etc. Ask your patients something similar to the following: "Mrs. Jones, you have been an excellent patient of mine. You've sent me many people with migraine headaches. I would like you to do me a favor. If I have a patient with migraine headaches and he is not sure that chiropractic can help, could I have your permission to give him your phone number so he can call you? I would like you to tell him your story. You might be able to help me to help him get well." The patient obviously will be flattered at your request and will give you her permission to give her telephone number to discouraged patients.

Whenever you have a patient who is discouraged, consult your list of Bird-Dog patients and find one with a similar problem. Ask your current patient to call your Bird-Dog patient for information on what he did to help his similar problem. Obviously, your Bird-Dog patient will tell him how great chiropractic is, how great you are, and he will encourage the discouraged patient to continue under your care. Usually the discouraged patient will respect the opinions of another patient and will continue under your care until results are obtained. The list of Bird-Dog patients is called your Phone Team.

Key to patients' problems and key treatment. Tell the patient when examining him that the purpose of the examination is to find out what is wrong with him. Also, that once you find the source of his problem, you will be able to get him well by selecting

113

the correct key for treatment.

When a patient has been coming to you for quite a while, tell him that you have found the key to his problem and, if it ever comes back, you know the answer in his particular case. Tell him, "We have found the key to your problem and we will be able to take care of you from now on."

When treating a patient, say: "I just gave you the 'key' treatment. This certain treatment is what works for you. It may not work on someone else, but it does work for you. I'm writing this treatment on your file folder so that if it comes back I'll know that this is the treatment that works best for you." This technique builds a unique binding loyalty between doctor and patient.

The C.A. should make a social profile on each patient. Notations should be made by the C.A. on each patient's file of important social facts that pertain to that patient, i.e.: birthdays, anniversaries, children, grandchildren, pets, hobbies, trips, vacations, etc., etc. Once these notations are posted on the files, the C.A. will always be able to strike up a good heart-to-heart conversation with any patient. Remembering small facts about a patient will help increase that patient's referrals.

Review your previous patients' files. Go through your previous patients' files and refamiliarize yourself with their health problems. Once you have done this, you may notice many of your former patients have returned for care. Do this on a daily basis. (Refer to chapter on "How a Superman is Made," Concepting, for an explanation of this principle.)

A doctor should always buy his products, supplies, furniture, etc., from his patients' businesses, even if he has to pay more than he would if he went to a discount store. I would rather spend twenty dollars more for a television set, buying from a patient's business who refers his friends to me, than I would buying from a discount house to save twenty dollars. Can you imagine what would happen if this patient found out that I bought a TV set from a discount house? I would lose his business as well as his referrals. It is always better to do business with patients because it keeps reminding them of you and they will continue referring patients to you.

Refer patients to your other patients' businesses. If someone says, "Doc, I need a new television set," write on the back of your business card the name and address of a patient who sells television sets. Tell your patient, "Go see Mr. Jones at his appliance store. He is a real good man. He is a patient of mine and will take good care of you." When this patient goes to the appliance store with your card and says that you told him to go there to buy his

114

TV set, Mr. Jones, the patient who owns the appliance store, will be appreciative that you sent him a customer. When you send business to your patients who own businesses, they will send business to you. This is a seed from which many referrals grow. This is an excellent way to increase your practice. Support the patients who are supporting you!

The basic six points of an office visit. A good rule to follow when adjusting patients is the basic six points of an office visit. It is not sufficient just to administer quality chiropractic to patients; the doctor should also treat the patients psychologically. These six points will describe the six bases that should be touched upon during all office visits. These points will not require an hour per visit. They can be done very easily and, in doing so, you will have a more successful practice and increase your referring patients.

Every Visit a Six-Point Procedure:

1. Body — Physical — a good adjustment. Try to keep your explanation simple as to how the body heals.

2. Mind — Mental — the best way to free the mind is with happiness and laughter (not off-colored jokes). People who laugh, don't go insane. Happiness spreads as well as gloom. People like a laughing man or one who can make them laugh. Make sure the patient at least smiles once during an office visit.

3. Soul — Spirit — give patients hope. Your chiropractic philosophy and results are great sources of hope and faith. I'm sure it has affected your life and health understanding — so share it with your patients! They could catch the big idea too!

   To make a lifetime patient, just teach him the chiropractic principle. Take some time and explain to your patients what chiropractic really is. Give your patients hope — understanding, assurance, and faith.

4. Make sure the patient is fully aware of a need. Pain is the main motivator of people who come to your office. Make sure a tender area is located each visit and that the patient is made aware of this tender area. Pain lets the patient know without words the need for care. It justifies the reason for each visit.

5. Awareness — be certain that your patients know something happened on each visit — and let them know this through their own senses.
   (a) "Did you hear that?"
   (b) "Did you feel it move?"
   It isn't necessary to wrack the entire spine, just one simple feel or sound. Just make the patient aware that something did hap-

pen and that he is conscious of it. The simpler you can keep your procedure and treatment, the better. A large variance of care can confuse the patient as to what helped him get well. Keep it simple! Your objective is to have the patient say, "He found my trouble. It was a pinched nerve, right here in my back. He adjusted it and I felt it when it moved, and I felt the difference. I'M BETTER!"

6. Be sure the patient is aware that there was a change — by his own admission. This is accomplished by the doctor stating:
    (a) "We sure got it, didn't we?"
    (b) "How's that?"
    (c) "Do you feel that warm, more relaxed feeling?"
    (d) "Does that feel easier?"
    (e) "Do you feel any different?"
    (f) "Does that feel easier?"
    (g) "Stand up and try that out. Does that feel any better?"

These six points justify the money spent in your office for each visit. There isn't anything else more important to be said during the course of an office visit than talking about chiropractic.

You can use whatever time necessary (two to twenty minutes) to touch all six points. Don't be excessive, because it will water down the effectiveness of the office visit with the patient. There are some chiropractors who like to hear themselves talk (self-expression urge), or who simply want to pass time until the next patient arrives. If this is done, a vacuum will not be created. It is necessary to have a vacuum in order to fill that time with another patient. Some D.C.'s think they are giving more service by dragging out an office visit. This is not true. The more you talk, the more the patient will be detained. The only real way to render service to more people is by creating a vacuum — and filling it!

Practice-building at vacation time. How much does a vacation cost a doctor? Most doctors, when asked this question, will reply with a figure of the total dollars spent on vacation, usually fifteen hundred dollars for two weeks. This figure is only one of four factors necessary to compute how much a vacation really costs a doctor. The first factor is how much income loss will result from the doctor being out of the office (divide yearly income by 52 weeks). The second factor is how much the doctor's weekly overhead is (subtract net taxable income from yearly gross, then divide by 52 weeks). The third factor is the loss of new patients and the income derived from these patients (average weekly new patients multiplied by income per patient). The last factor to be considered is the out-of-pocket expenses spent on vacation. Therefore, a two-week vacation would cost a $100,000-a-year doctor the following approximate amounts:

Factor #1
Income loss ($2,000 a week)...................... $4,000.00
Factor #2
Continuing overhead ($1,000 a week)............... 2,000.00
Factor #3
New patient loss (3 new patients per week @ $500.00
    per new patient x 2 weeks)..................... 3,000.00
Factor #4
Expenses while on vacation........................ 1,500.00

    TOTAL COST OF VACATION............... $10,500.00

Obviously, when a doctor considers all of the above factors, he should give much thought to planning a vacation so that it doesn't become too costly. The following paragraphs will aid him in this.

If a doctor has an associate practice, he won't encounter any difficulty at vacation time. He simply reschedules only those patients who are emphatic about being treated solely by him. All other patients are told that he wants them to be seen by his associate on exactly the schedule of care they presently are on — emphasizing that it is the schedule of care and NOT the doctor providing the care that will get them well. The associate doctor will therefore have a full schedule of regular patients and whatever new patients and emergency patients who call the office while the senior doctor is on vacation.

If a doctor practices solo, he has four options at vacation time. The first option is to have a colleague come to his office and treat his patients while he is away. The second option is to refer his new patients and emergency patients to another D.C.'s office. The third option is to have his C.A. use therapy on his patients. The fourth option is to close his office and leave it unattended.

Obviously, only the first two options warrant consideration. The first is the best method of handling a solo practitioner's vacation time. By using this method, similar to the associate practice procedure, the vacationing doctor will have peace of mind in knowing that his patients are cared for, that his practice income is continuing, and that he will have new patients ready for him when he returns. The second option will give the doctor peace of mind because his emergency patients are cared for, but his vacation remains extremely costly. The third and fourth options are unacceptable and are not worth discussing.

If a solo practitioner chooses to refer his emergency, new, and acute patients to a colleague, the following steps should be followed. Give the files of the acute patients — or anyone who needs to be seen — to the fill-in doctor. A financial arrangement can be worked out between the two doctors. Perhaps the doctor going on vacation will be reciprocating with the fill-in doctor when *he* takes his vacation. It is to the advantage of the substitute doctor to give good patient care and to make sure that all the vacationing doctor's patients return to him as soon as he comes back, because the vacationing doctor will serve as his fill-in doctor in the future when he wants to be out of town. This procedure helps assure the vacationing doctor that he will have a full patient-load upon his return.

Pre-vacation activities. Send postcards to all your patients thirty days prior to your vacation. Example:

"It's vacation time again! I will be out of the office from_____ to _____ ."

Send out another postcard two to three weeks prior to your vacation. Example:

"If you have been putting off your adjustments or have had another accident since your last visit, call _____ so we may treat you prior to our vacation, from _____ until _____."

Another example:

"Dr. Fernandez will be going on vacation from _____ until _____. Please call 525-1141 if you want to be treated prior to vacation time."

These postcards will stimulate former patients who have been putting off their appointments and will motivate new patients to schedule their appointments before you leave for vacation.

Also, address postcards to all your Bird-Dog patients. Write a message similar to: "Having a great time. Wish you could join me. See you in one week." Don't forget to sign your name.

Telephone procedure. Leave instructions with your C.A. or answering service that Dr. [fill-in doctor] will be seeing Dr. [vacationing doctor's] emergency patients. Also tell your C.A. that if a patient does not want to see Dr. [fill-in], please take his name and phone number and that Dr. [vacationing doctor] will call upon his return.

On-vacation activity. Mail the postcards.

After-vacation activity. Send Thank You notes to all who helped make your vacation a happy and successful one.

The following procedures are the very best of the referral-stimulating, new patient-obtaining programs that can be initiated in a doctor's office. They are the best because they provide immediate return, yet, at the same time, they are the toughest because they demand self-discipline for their implementation.

An iron-willed determination and persistence will propel these procedures into the top priority bracket for use in building your practice. These procedures will provide more new patients to your office than you can possibly assimilate. Self-discipline is the key.

Doctor's Regimen Program

Everyone is looking for an easy way to increase their business, increase referrals, increase income, etc. Unfortunately, these "easy methods" are also short-lived and often work poorly. The best methods are usually the hardest methods. Hardest, because it takes discipline and work on the doctor's part to accomplish these objectives.

The word "regimen," short for regimentation, denotes exactly the intent of this program. The doctor regiments (disciplines) himself to cover a certain topic with a patient each and every visit. He will educate his patients bit by bit until they understand the scope of chiropractic and, therefore, refer more patients. This program also results in a fifty percent increase in the patient-visit average.

The regimen program is simply a list of things to be said to the patient on each visit. This program will not only prevent early self-destruction of the patient during course of care, but constantly re-programs him with the scope of chiropractic and the referral concept. In my office, the key "phrases" are printed on gummed labels which are pasted onto the patient's file. These phrases are checked off after each visit and the file is ready for the next visit.

Following are a listing of the abbreviations of my phrases and a description of the meaning of each.

1. PPC — Patient Phone Call
2. PNC — Private Number on Card
3. OPP — Other Patients' Progress
4. LTB — Leaping Tall Building
5. PAM — Pamphlets
6. TYF — Thank Your Friend
7. FM — Family Member
8. MXR — Mini-Exam and Report
9. MSP — My Specialty

10. REX — Re-examination Today
11. INR — Interim Report
12. STS — Schedule To See
13. SOD — Story of the Day (ulcers)
14. RNC — Results of No Care
15. AWM — Angry With Me
16. OPP —Other Patients' Progress
17. TTT — Teach to Testify
18. GTY — Good to You
19. SOTD — Story of the Day (Allergies)
20. WHYT — Who Have You Told?

Visit No. 1 — PATIENT PHONE CALL

Telephone the patient on the evening of his first adjustment. Simply ask him how he is feeling. Most patients will be surprised as they have never had a doctor who was concerned enough to call them at home. Please refer to "Patient in Pain" telephone calls in another section of this book.

Visit No. 2 — PRIVATE NUMBER CARD

Write your home phone number on the back of one of your business cards and give it to the patient. Tell him that if ever he should need you outside of regular office hours, to please call. Patients don't want to take advantage of their doctor and therefore won't call you. However, it gives them a feeling of security to know that they can reach you if they need to.

Visit No. 3 — OTHER PATIENTS' PROGRESS

Tell your patient of the progress other patients have made who have had conditions similar to his. This encourages the patient during the beginning phase of care.

Visit No. 4 — LEAPING TALL BUILDINGS

Predict some unusual or absurd activity for the patient due to his returning health. Say: "John, you are doing so much better that we will have you leaping tall buildings before you know it."

Visit No. 5 — PAMPHLETS

Ask the patient: "Have you noticed all the pamphlets we have in our treatment rooms? Please feel free to take any that interest you. Perhaps some of your friends have health problems that may be helped by chiropractic care. Why don't you take a pamphlet to them?"

Visit No. 6 — THANK YOUR FRIEND

Tell the patient: "Mrs. Jones, you are doing so much better since you started chiropractic care. Have you thanked Mrs. Brown who sent you to us? I am sure she would like to know how well you are doing and that you appreciate her caring."

Visit No. 7 — FAMILY MEMBER

Ask to see other members of a patient's family to see if they have any health problems which can be corrected by chiropractic care. This is especially effective with mothers of small children when you point out that many spinal problems are hereditary.

Visit No. 8 — MINI EXAM AND REPORT

Perform a few brief tests on the patient's main area of complaint. Advise him how much better he is doing.

Visit No. 9 — MY SPECIALTY

Tell your patient that if you were to specialize in any one particular area of practice, it would be in the area of his chief complaint since you have had great success with this type problem.

Visit No. 10 — RE-EXAMINATION TODAY

Perform a comprehensive re-examination on the patient. Tell him that this will enable you to monitor his progress in order to see how well he is doing.

Visit No. 11 — INTERIM REPORT

Go over the findings of the re-examination and tell the patient what has improved. If you are going to be changing your treatment routine, explain the changes you plan to make.

Visit No. 12 — SCHEDULE TO SEE

This point is primarily used in a multiple-doctor office. After the re-examination and interim report have been performed, the patient will be scheduled for one of the other doctors. The other doctor will perform a mini-exam, acting as a consultant, and will make recommendations to the treating doctor as to a change in care he recommends, etc.

Visit No. 13 — STORY OF THE DAY (Ulcers)

Tell your patients the "story of the day" about an ulcer patient who discontinues care before he should leave. Explain how degeneration progresses and that the problem will return and worsen.

Visit No. 14 — RESULTS OF NO CARE
Explain to your patients the poor outlook for a patient who discontinues care before he should have. Explain how degeneration progresses and that the problem will return and worsen.

Visit No. 15 — ANGRY WITH ME
Say: "Mrs. Jones, are you angry with me? Usually by this point in a patient's treatment program he or she has referred at least one patient to me. I just wondered if something was wrong."

Visit No. 16 — OTHER PATIENTS' PROGRESS
Tell your patient of the progress of another patient with conditions different than his. This is particularly effective when teaching your patients the scope of chiropractic.

Visit No. 17 — TEACH TO TESTIFY
Ask your patient: "Mrs. Jones, have you noticed how much better you are walking? Why don't you tell someone what chiropractic has done for you?"

Visit No. 18 — GOOD TO YOU
Tell your patient: "Mrs. Jones, chiropractic has been good to you. You now have a wonderful opportunity to express your appreciation by telling others about the benefits of chiropractic."

Visit No. 19 — STORY OF THE DAY (Allergies)
Tell your patients the story of the day. In this case, talk about a patient with allergies and how he responded to chiropractic care. Ask them if they know anyone who suffers with allergies. Tell them that you would appreciate their friends/relatives being referred to you.

Visit No. 20 — WHO HAVE YOU TOLD?
You should reply when a patient tells you how good he is doing: "I'm proud of you, Mr. Brown. Who else have you told about how good you are feeling?"

One alternative to the twenty-visit regimen was developed by Dr. Tom Owen of Orlando, Florida. This is basically the same format as used in our office, but is only for ten visits.

FIRST TEN VISITS (ADJUSTMENTS)

Visit No. 1 — WHAT TO EXPECT

(While adjusting): "Mrs. Jones, you will have some good days and some bad. The good days will come more often and last longer. You might experience some sore spots you didn't have before. Don't be concerned, as it is only muscle change and will go away in a few days. Your job is to take good care of your spine. It is important to both of us so please take care of it for me."

Visit No. 2 — WHAT HAPPENED IS GOOD

"Come on in, Mrs. Jones. I am anxious to see how you did and whether you took good care of your spine as I told you. You did a good job [after checking] and you must have felt more relaxed or slept better." (Note: If the patient exhibits nerve pressure again, say:) "I see it is back out of alignment. It was in alignment when you left yesterday, so you should have felt more relaxed and slept better last night." The doctor should thank the patient for efforts made to take care of her spine if results are good, and also tell her that he appreciates her doing so.

Visit No. 3 — DALE CARNEGIE VISIT

Get to know the patient. Ask him questions about his family, hobbies, work, etc. Show interest in them. Examples: "Do you have any grandchildren? [They always do!] May I see the pictures you have of them?" and "How did you meet your wife? How did you come to live in this town?"

Visit No. 4 — BACK TO BUSINESS

"Have you noticed any changes — good or bad — with any of the following problems?" The doctor goes through the patient's case history and asks about each condition. He takes notes and shows interest.

Visit No. 5 — ACKNOWLEDGE A CHANGE

"I was just noticing, Mr. Brown, that some of the tension in the muscles of your back is leaving. You should have been able to bend down and around better [doctor explains statement by bending his body down and around to illustrate]. Yes . . . something good must be going on."

Visit No. 6 — GOOD DISCIPLE

"Mr. Brown, it's test time. Do you remember what I told you was causing your condition? That's right, pinched nerves. Only by correcting the underlying cause are we able to help you. I want you to remember this, because someone might ask you what we are doing for you. I want you to know how to explain it to someone else. Thank you for being a GOOD disciple for chiropractic."

Visit No. 7 — THANKING YOU

"I want to thank you today for the good things you said about us the other day." The doctor here assumes that the patient *has* said something good about his chiropractic care; if the patient hasn't, at least he will get the message. However, if the patient says that he doesn't remember to whom he spoke well of the doctor, the latter will respond: "I don't remember who told me — I just noticed that you said something good." Note: You'll be surprised how many have by now said something good. It's what folks say behind your back that counts!

Visit No. 8 — GET THE FAMILY

Ask questions about the sick people in the family of a patient. (See "Family Health History Questionnaire.") Take an interest! Tell your patients: "I would like to help your loved ones."

Visit No. 9 — THANK THE REFERRER

"Mrs. Jones, I was just thinking of the interest Mrs. Brown has in you. She went out of her way to tell you about chiropractic. She put herself out on a limb for you and, now that you feel better, why don't you call her — now or this evening — and thank her for sharing chiropractic with you?"

Visit No. 10 — THANK THEM

Thank your patients for their cooperation, for keeping appointments, for getting better, for being such nice people, etc., etc.

Condition Regimen Program

Make it a point to tell all your patients about the nine main conditions that a chiropractor treats. Commit yourself that by rote you will discuss one of these conditions each visit for the nine visits (see Practice Expansion Wheel). This procedure produces results.

Treatment Regimen

Touch and Tell

This is a very simple method of increasing your practice and educating your patients. This has been effectively used in chiropractic for seventy years.

Explain to your patient the neurological ramifications of each vertebrae you adjust. For example, if you are going to adjust the T-5 vertebra, explain to the patient that this vertebra controls the nerves to the stomach and, when out of alignment, pinches the nerves, causing stomach ulcers. Further explain that the adjusting of these vertebrae helps patients with ulcer problems. Naturally, the patient didn't know that you took care of ulcer problems, and so you've taught him something new about chiropractic. Now he can send his friends who have ulcers to you.

When touching the patient at different tender or troubled areas, tell him where the nerves go from this area and the problems that can be caused by this nerve pressure. Example: "Do you feel that tender spot, Mr. Jones? This is where you have an important nerve pinched into the colon. When this nerve is pinched, it can cause such conditions as nausea, duodenal ulcers, burning sensations, improper digestion, heartburn and gas. It is important that we fix this nerve right now to prevent such problems from occurring. By fixing this area of your spine, chiropractors are able to help people with such problems. If you know anyone with similar problems, you should tell them about chiropractic." By explaining the principle of chiropractic as it relates to each adjustment, you are telling the whole story of chiropractic, telling what you are preventing, telling of various other conditions that you can treat, and making nerve pressure and chiropractic important in the patient's mind.

When you adjust the kidney area, tell the patient that this is the area that causes kidney problems, etc. When you adjust the lower back, explain that this area causes bladder problems and sciatica, etc. If a patient comes to you fifteen times, you will have explained how chiropractic can take care of fifteen different conditions if you follow this procedure. Naturally, this gives your patients a broader base from which to refer to you. The old-timers built their practices strictly by using this "touch and tell" method. It was very effective then — and it still is today!

Pamphlet Regimen Program

Utilizing health tracts on a pre-planned basis. I know a doctor who has the numbers 1 through 30 stamped on his file folders. Each of these numbers corresponds to a particular health tract that he has in his adjusting rooms. These numbers also correspond with the patient's office visit. Whenever the patient comes into the office, say for his sixth visit, the doctor gives him No. 6 Health Tract, and scratches off the No. 6 on his file folder. If done systematically, and with persistence, good results will follow.

C.A. Regimen Program

In addition to the regimen for doctors, there is also a regimen program for your C.A.'s to follow. The following is a listing of the C.A.'s Regimen abbreviations and their meanings:

1. FEC — First Experience with Chiropractor
2. OAT — Office Assistance To
3. RDP — Reassure Disappointed Patients
4. HHD — How [Patient] Heard About Doctor
5. WAF — Ask What Area From
6. EFT — Explain Frequent Treatment
7. MDH — Make Our Day Happy
8. BS — Boy Scout
9. RC — Referral Cards

Visit No. 1 — FIRST EXPERIENCE WITH CHIROPRACTOR
Tell the patients that they are in for a wonderful experience as their doctor is such a great doctor.

Visit No. 2 — OFFICE ASSISTANCE TO
Offer your help in any way you can. Offer to answer any questions the patients might have, or explain anything they don't understand.

Visit No. 3 — REASSURE DISAPPOINTED PATIENTS
Chiropractic is not an exact science and as various patients respond differently to care, some may feel that they are not getting well quickly enough. Reassure them that the doctor has treated many patients with problems similar to theirs and that he will do his utmost to bring them back to full recovery as quickly as humanly possible.

126

Visit No. 4 — HOW [PATIENT] HEARD ABOUT DOCTOR

Ask the patient how he heard about the doctor as you are amazed how people hear about his great successes with headaches (or his particular condition).

Visit No. 5 — ASK WHAT AREA FROM

Ask the patient what area he is from as you are amazed how many people travel considerable distances to see your doctor.

Visit No. 6 — EXPLAIN FREQUENT TREATMENT

Explain the necessity of frequent chiropractic adjustments in order to retrain ligaments, muscles, etc., to hold the vertebrae in normal alignment.

Visit No. 7 — MAKE OUR DAY HAPPY

Say: "Do me a favor and make my day happy. Send us a patient. Would you do that please?" Further state: "You know that we are here to help sick people get well, and usually by this time our new patients have sent us one of their relatives or friends. So, please do me a favor and send us someone we can help."

Visit No. 8 — BOY SCOUT

Ask: "Have you told someone about chiropractic care?" If the patient has told someone about your care, ask him what is wrong with the prospective patient, and compliment him for telling his friends about your doctor. If he hasn't told anyone, your referral hint may stimulate him to do so.

Visit No. 9 — REFERRAL CARDS

Hand your doctor's cards to your patients. Say: "I sure would appreciate it if you would pass these out to your friends and send somebody in to see the doctor."

Do the Regimen Programs Work?

Do they take guts to do? Does it take dedication to make these programs work? Is it hard work? The answer to all these questions is — absolutely YES! But then, no one ever said building a practice was easy! Use the regimen programs and there won't be any limit to your practice growth.

One of the easiest methods for stimulating referrals from your present patients is by developing a Reaction Program. This program is basically a series of pre-planned reactions (responses) to your patients' most common questions or statements. However, with a Reaction Program, you will be using your patients' questions or statements as a "springboard" to give your "reaction" (referral stimuli).

The following are some of the most common questions or statements made by patients to a doctor or C.A., and the Reaction Program responses.

Statement: "You sure are busy."

Reaction: "Yes, I am, thanks to people like you who are referring their friends to me. Thank you for helping your friends get well by referring them to my office. I appreciate you. Remember, we always have room for one more patient and if you have a friend who needs us, please call us and tell us you referred him. We'll definitely work one of your friends into our schedule."

Question: "May I bring my husband/wife in to watch how you treat me?"

Reaction: "Certainly, on one condition: I would like the opportunity to check your spouse's spine and see if he/she is developing nerve pressure (a spinal problem, etc.). What is your spouse's name?"

Statement: "I'm feeling better."

Reaction: "I'm delighted to hear that. Have you told anyone else about how good you are feeling? It's amazing how many other persons have your same problem. Do you know anyone who is learning to live with a problem such as yours? What is his name?"

Statement: "I really enjoy coming to your office."

Reaction: "I'm happy you noticed how hard we work to please our patients and to get them well. Why don't you send me someone so I can help him too?"

Question: "Can chiropractic help (condition)?"

Reaction: "Absolutely! Better than any other health profession! Who do you know who has this same problem?"

Statement: "I shouldn't have waited so long."

Reaction: "Most people wait, hoping their health problems will go away. Many people wait so long that they develop degeneration which can't be reversed. Tell your friends not to wait too long before getting treatment, or they may end up suffering the rest of their lives. Who do you know who could be helped by chiropractic?"

Statement: "I didn't think you would be able to help me."

Reaction: "Most people don't when they first come in. I'm sure you know other people who have the same condition as you have. Why don't you tell them about chiropractic?"

Statement: "I didn't know chiropractic would work so well."

Reaction: "The tragedy is that most people don't know that chiropractic can help them. Do you know somebody who should be in here for care?"

Statement: (Of a patient who was in an automobile accident) "There were three of us in the car."

Reaction: "The tragic thing about automobile accidents is that it sometimes takes so long for symptoms to occur. I make it a definite rule to examine everyone after an automobile accident. Most people, after having been in an automobile accident, will get their car checked over thoroughly before driving it again, but will never think about having themselves checked over thoroughly. They seem to put more value on their automobiles than they do their own bodies! And many times, problems that have their cause in automobile accidents, don't really show up for days, weeks, or even years later. The only way you can tell if a patient has been injured or not is to examine him. Why don't you make an appointment to get your friends in here for me to check them?"

Statement: "I have a friend who is seeing another doctor for [condition]."

Reaction: "Is this a personal friend? Have you talked to him about chiropractic care? Is he being helped? Why don't you tell him to come see me? What did you say his name was?"

Statement: "I wish my friend would get in to see a chiropractor."

Reaction: "What is your friend's health problem? What are you doing to encourage him to come to our office? Why don't you make an appointment to bring him in? I'll be happy to check him over to determine if chiropractic can help his problem. What is your friend's name?"

During the course of a day, you should take advantage of any opportunity to turn your patients' questions and statements into referral requests.

Be constantly aware of opportunities to plug for referrals. Let your patients know that you will welcome the opportunity to help their family and friends. Tell them you welcome their assistance in helping build your practice. Promise yourself that, as an automatic reflex, you will respond to your patients' questions and statements with referral requests. *Follow the Reaction Program and build a large rewarding practice.*

Recapture Procedure

Attempt to recapture your active patients. If you don't attempt to recapture a patient on the day that he misses his appointment, in many cases you will lose him. Strong rescheduling procedures will greatly increase your practice volume and income.

Recall Active Patients

Telephone all your present patients within two weeks of their missed appointments. The sooner you can reach a patient after he has dismissed himself from your care, the better chance you will have of reactivating that patient.

Reactivation Telephone Program

Your C.A. is to fill out Audit Cards on all your patients. The Audit Cards are then sorted into Zip Codes and a mailing list is typed, keeping the Zip Codes separate. Here is a sample Audit Card, with some of the information you may want to include:

AUDIT CARD

NAME _____

ADDRESS _____

ZIP _____

C/C	(chief complaint)	Tel.Res.	(residence phone)
DFV	(date of first visit)	Tel.Bus.	(business phone)
DLV	(date of last visit)	Age	(patient's age)
A/R	(account receivable?)	B/D	(birth date)
DLP	(date of last payment)		
INS	(insurance: type - auto, med. work comp.?)		

These Audit Cards will give you the information necessary for the recall system.

The Pot of Gold. Recently, in the *Wall Street Journal*, there was a full-page advertisement, with the heading: "You're Sitting

On A Pot Of Gold And You Don't Know It!" The ad went on to explain that most businesses and industries lose millions of dollars by neglecting and forgetting about their old customers. In a survey, consumers were asked how many business establishments had bothered to call to ask about any problems they had with their products, or if they were satisfied with the product sold to them. It was demonstrated that a very, very small percentage of business and industrial establishments did any recalling at all.

I can illustrate this point in the following manner. Have you ever had an appliance salesman call you six months after the sale to see if you were satisfied? Probably not. In all the years I have bought furniture, cars, appliances, etc., I don't recall a single instance when a salesman bothered to call back. If one salesman had shown this interest, whom do you think I would think of when I needed a replacement or additional items? How about you? Can you say the same? Has anyone ever called you back?

The *Wall Street Journal* ad was placed by a firm which specializes in helping businesses increase their profits by re-establishing contact with their own established customers, to help capture that missing "pot of gold."

The Bell System has run a series of TV commercials promoting recall on old accounts. Statistics are available to show the effectiveness of this program, and they are quite impressive.

The single most effective method of increasing a professional's practice is telephoning former patients. A good telephone recall system will not only prompt the return of many former patients, but it will also stimulate new patient referrals.

On the average, a good telephone recall system will prompt two former patients to return for care out of every ten calls made.

There are two major approaches to a telephone recall system. The first method is to update your patient records. The following procedure should be followed when doing a recall of former patients on this basis. Your secretary calls each patient to explain that you are in the process of updating all your files and that she is calling to see how the patient is doing since you haven't heard from him for quite some time. From here, the conversation may go in several different directions. How to handle each situation is discussed later.

The second method involves the addition of another ingredient to your recall system which should double the expected results from two out of ten, to four out of ten. This extra ingredient simply is the offering of some free service, such as x-ray or examination. Everyone likes to get something free. The results are worth it.

The following "Free X-ray, Free Examination" recall system can be ethically done in order to quadruple your practice without giving the impression that you are using a "gimmick." Your free x-ray and free examination recall program will last sixty to ninety days. The following points should be thoroughly understood before beginning any recall program.

1. When making the recalls, don't talk with anyone other than the patient.

2. Don't call at mealtimes, at night, or on Sunday, as this may promote hostility and the patient might feel that you are bothering him.

3. The doctor who expresses a genuine interest in the patient is the doctor who gets that patient. Be sincere!

4. Remember, that you are interested in serving the patient, not in making money. If you give a service, you'll be paid for it.

5. Patients appreciate a doctor who is genuinely interested in protecting their health.

6. Recall procedures are for the patient's benefit, not yours. You are not a salesman selling something, you are a doctor reminding patients of problems that might develop if neglected. Discuss the importance of periodic check-ups. Telling patients of the long-term effects of non-treatment is the obligation and responsibility of every doctor. It is your obligation to at least give the patient the opportunity to know about his condition and the chance to accept or reject your recommendation.

7. Put yourself in the right frame of mind prior to making these calls. One day you may be successful in zero out of ten calls, and the next day be successful in nine out of ten! Stick with the program in a positive frame of mind, realizing that your advice to a patient of his need for further chiropractic care is for his own benefit.

8. Remember, your object is to get the patient back in for needed care and to create good will.

9. Your goal for rescheduling former patients is: Six returning fomer patients per day.

10. Don't be timid. Your reactivation phone calls will succeed by being forceful, firm in your convictions, with urgency in your voice, and not by being domineering.

11. If you want to use this program when you have taken over another doctor's practice, you must realize that these patients are not your patients yet. You don't know them, and they don't know you. However, you do have their x-rays and case histories which you should review before making any call. Explain that you can tell from a patient's case history that he has weak ligaments

and that it sometimes hurts when he gets up from a chair, when he stretches or bends over, etc. Also, tell him that this type of spinal condition has a tendency to return if untreated, and can cause real problems. A periodic examination and treatment will prevent it from recurring.

12. Remember that the patient will only be interested in returning for care when you talk to him about a specific complaint or x-ray finding. We are a self-centered society. Talk with the patient about his problem, what will develop in his body if not treated, and what you can do for him. A caring attitude is what brings about successful recalls.

13. Review the patient's x-rays and examinations. Study them and become intimate with them prior to calling. Know what the specific problem areas are of each patient you call.

14. When reviewing patients' x-rays, examinations and case histories, pick out the things that will gradually worsen without proper care, such as scoliosis, disc degeneration, subluxations, congenital abnormalities which may lead to other problems, arthritis, kyphosis, lordosis, etc. When you talk about these problems, you will have a common bond with that patient. All patients are concerned with their own health problems. Remember, when you talk about things you know, you speak from a command position.

15. The following could help your recall procedure: "When you were last x-rayed [examined, etc.], there was some evidence of early arthritic development [disc degeneration, etc.] in your spine. A follow-up x-ray evaluation of this condition is indicated at this time to see if it has been stopped or is continuing to degenerate. Unchecked, it could lead to serious future problems, such as . . . ."

16. When you talk with the patient on the phone, ask him how his condition is doing. His response will follow one of the following patterns:

(a) If his condition is bothering him again, tell him about the availability of free x-rays and free examinations that you are offering right now. Tell him that you want him to come in at a certain time [make specific date and time for appointment] to be x-rayed and examined in order to determine why his condition has returned. Make the appointment.

(b) If his condition is bothering him slightly, tell him you are not surprised as this type of problem often returns without periodic care. Also, tell him that his previous x-rays, examinations, etc., indicate that he has a problem which usually will worsen or degenerate without periodic check-ups. Tell him he hasn't had a check-up in [state number of months, years, etc.]. Explain the research project and make an appointment.

(c) If the condition is not bothering him, tell him how pleased you are to hear that. Tell him that his previous x-rays and examinations revealed a problem that will degenerate or worsen without periodic care. Stress that he should not let the degeneration go too far or there may not be anything you can do to fix it. Explain the research project and the value of periodic check-ups.

(d) If he says that he was never told about the chance of his problem recurring, simply tell him that obviously the main concern at the time of his office visits was the pain he was in rather than the other problem that was developing. Tell the patient that he needs to be checked now.

(e) If the condition has not returned, it possibly was only minor in nature and did not require much initial care. Ask the patient about his current health status. Ask how his health is now, and whether any new problems have arisen in the last few years. Should he mention a health problem, tell him that you are not surprised to hear about it as his x-rays and examinations showed that he had a problem in a certain area. Further explain that this type of spinal problem frequently pinches the nerves into [state area of his complaint] and that it could cause considerably more trouble if not taken care of immediately.

17. If you get a definite "No" answer to your call, tell the patient that it has been a pleasure talking with him again, and that when he is in the neighborhood, invite him to stop in the office to see the new equipment you have brought into the practice, etc. Advise him that the research project also applies to his family and friends and if he knows of someone who could benefit from chiropractic services, to have them come to your office during this sixty-day period of time in order to save them the expenses of x-rays, etc. Be friendly, cordial, concerned, and a good neighbor. Remember, you are building up good will.

18. Do not be discouraged by patients turning down your offer. The patients who say "No" to your call will, nevertheless, appreciate your thoughtfulness in calling. This builds up good will in the community and is the most effective personal contact a doctor can make as it shows that he cares about his patients' health.

19. When you receive a "No" answer, use this opportunity to go after family and friend referrals. If you are successful in four out of ten, you are doing an excellent job. The patients whom you don't reactivate will, at least, realize that there is a doctor in town who cares about them.

20. Don't let the negative few bother you. Remember that the fortunate patients who are reactivated will get well because of your telephone call, and are now back within your "sphere of influence." This also gives you the opportunity for new referrals.

21. If a serious confrontation occurs, dismiss the patient as a loss and remove him from your mailing list. However, be polite.

22. Impress upon the patients that comparative x-rays and examinations to check on potential problems is essential for a complete health care program.

23. When you are ready to start calling, stick with it until all former patients have been contacted. Be methodical. Do not call on a "hit-or-miss" basis.

24. Be sure to have your appointment book in front of you when making these calls, so that a firm appointment can be scheduled at the time of your call.

25. The most important factor in making an appointment is telling the patient when you want to see him.

26. If the patient is evasive or unable to commit himself to an appointment time, due to vacations, etc., tell him you will call back in a month to set a definite date. Put his name and telephone number in the memo space in your appointment book for one month from the date of your recall. Call him back at that time. Don't forget him.

Don't be discouraged with a poor rescheduling rate when making a telephone recall. If you recall patients alphabetically, you will notice quite a few patients of the same letter of the alphabet returning for care within two or three weeks of being recalled. Many of them are startled when they hear the C.A. unexpectedly talk to them when doing a recall. They automatically say they are feeling fine, but when they think about your telephone call, they will recognize the need for care and call your office for an appointment.

Reception room sign to consider with your telephone recall program. Place a sign in your reception room:

ALL X-RAYS AND EXAMINATIONS
WILL BE *FREE*
From MARCH 15 thru MAY 15
as we are participating in a research project.
The research organization is providing x-rays at no
charge to us, and we are providing the examinations.
TELL YOUR FRIENDS AND RELATIVES
that this will be an excellent opportunity to begin
Chiropractic Care at a Substantial Savings!

A slip of paper should also be printed and handed out to all patients. On it should be printed the same information except for this added sentence:

We are anxious to x-ray and examine as many people as possible to help us with our statistics. Thank You.

The doctor or the C.A. should give one of these slips of paper to each patient and enthusiastically talk to them about the research project and the opportunity to x-ray and examine many people. Push for referrals! Don't be afraid of asking! The worst that can happen is that the patient will not refer; the best that can happen is that your practice will grow!

Almost all doctors' offices follow the same basic procedures and generally have similar traffic patterns. What, then, makes the difference between doctors' practices? It has been found that the successful practitioner does all that other doctors do, and more. It is this something extra that increases referrals and builds the larger practices of the more successful practitioners. The following are some of the extra touches that make a difference in practice growth.

Have your outside sign break the plane of people's visions by hanging it at an angle. (See illustration below.) Try to have a sign that is truly set off from the rest of the signs in your neighborhood. Make sure it is big enough for people to see and doesn't have unreadable, fancy lettering. Make it look professional and make it easy to read so people can spot your office.

Does your office have poor visibility? Is your sign too small? Is your building obscured by large bushes, trees, etc.? If so, cut down the shrubs and purchase a large, well-lit, professional sign. Increase your visibility and you will increase your practice!

Does the outside of your building need repair, paint, etc.? If so, have it done as quickly as possible. Don't chase patients away with a tacky-looking building — people judge you by your surroundings. Make it look good! A growing practice needs good visibility.

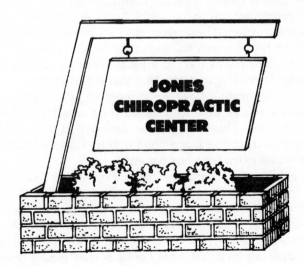

137

Is your office in a good location? If not, move! People will go to well-located offices and will avoid patronizing offices in a remote location. The doctor with a large practice pays particular attention to his office location. A well-located office could result in a twenty-to-fifty-patient visit-per-week difference in a practice! If you have any questions regarding the accessibility of your office location, I recommend you purchase the book, *How To Start A Profitable Practice From Scratch*, which I wrote and published in 1980, in which office location is discussed in more detail. (Available through the author.)

Is the inside of your office meticulously clean? Patients will not refer friends of their same or higher socioeconomic levels to an office that will embarrass them. By cleaning and beautifying your office and adding more lighting, you will increase the referrals to your office.

Your reception room should always be impeccably clean. This is the first impression a new patient has of your office. Make it a good one!

Is your equipment ripped, damaged, or in need of upholstering? If so, fix it immediately. The achievers in our profession do not have anything that is worn, tattered, frayed, etc., in their offices. They know that people go to establishments that are clean, neat, modern, and up-to-date. They stay away from low-class, tacky surroundings.

Have chiropractic magazines in the reception room. This is an excellent opportunity to educate your patients. Let them read about the miracle of chiropractic. Capitalize on it!

Place reproductions of a 1909 Sears & Roebuck catalog in your reception room. These catalogs spark interest among patients. They love to flip through the pages to compare prices of the early 1900's with the present day. If a patient has to wait for a doctor, at least provide reading material that will entertain him.

Place a "Physician's Desk Reference" in your reception room. Your patients will be able to look up the side effects of their prescribed medicines. This book will become one of the most popular in your reception room. It is a good public relations' tool and provides something extra for your patients.

Place a "Peoples' Pharmacy" or a "Physician's Desk Reference for Non-Prescription Drugs" in your reception room. These books allow patients to look up their non-prescription drugs to determine their side effects, etc. These books will be the most popular reading material in your reception room. A word of caution: Purchase multiple copies of all these books as they have a tendency to disappear!

Display a copy of "Our Patients Speak" in the reception room. This book is a three-ring binder that has testimonials from patients about your care. Take a Polaroid picture of your patient and include it, along with his testimonial describing how you helped him, in the book. Make the book look as professional as possible. Have your receptionist type up the patient's testimonial and have the patient sign it. Group the patients' testimonials according to their conditions, such as back problems, disc problems, headaches, sciatica, whiplash, etc. Index the book so that patients can flip through the pages to find testimonials from people with similar problems to theirs, those who have responded well to your care. When a patient becomes discouraged, reading about other patients with problems similar to theirs who have recovered, encourages him to stay under your care long enough for you to produce results. You'll be surprised at the enthusiasm this will generate.

Have a lending library. If you are an avid reader and like to read the latest books, buy them for display in your office so that they become tax deductions. Read the books yourself, then place them on an attractive book display rack in your reception room. Have your receptionist run the lending library. Lend a book to a patient for two weeks. At the end of the two weeks, the patient should bring the book back to the office. Obviously, some of your patients will forget to return books. However, there is no real loss since you've already read the books. You have received a tax break that you didn't have before and you have made your patients happy. This is good public relations and the patients love it!

Place a large, cork-backed map of your community on your reception room wall. Purchase fancy yellow, red and blue stickpins. These pins have yellow, red and blue balls on the ends. The red pins should be placed on the map over the residences of your patients who have not yet referred new patients to your office. To create extra excitement, have the patients place the pins into their own addresses. The blue pins would be for patients who have referred five or more patients. The yellow pins would be for patients who have referred ten or more new patients. After all the patient pins have been placed on the map, can you imagine the conversations that will take place when the patients ask you or your C.A. what the different colored pins designate?

Try this idea. You'll like it. It is effective. The distribution of the pins will also let you know the sections of your community which need more of your attention for referral-boosting.

Don't place a desk between you and the patient in your consultation room. If you do, it will present a physical as well as a psychological barrier between you and the patient. Place a desk against a wall, with the patient's chair alongside the desk. Then, when you talk with the patient, you will be facing each other. This relaxed, "homey" atmosphere is more conducive to good consultations. Some practitioners of larger practices have totally eliminated desks in their consultation rooms and have replaced them with small, round tables surrounded by comfortable chairs. This produces a very workable arrangement.

Have a private section of the receptionist's office. This is necessary for her to discuss delicate financial matters with patients. Remember, the financial situation of one patient is no business of another patient. Respect each patient's right to privacy.

Use a referral board in your practice. These are little boards (approximately 16x24 inches) that are normally seen in restaurants, on which small stick-on letters are used to make signs, names, prices, etc. Your board should state: "Thank you for referring patients to our office." Then list the patients' names who have referred someone to you that month. The referring patients look forward to seeing their names on the board.

A variation of this approach works as follows: The top part of the board is numbered 1, 2, 3, 4. The first number is for your No. 1 referrer, the second number is for your No. 2 referrer, and so on. Patients will usually ask: "Who is the man at the top of the list? What does that mean? When am I going to be in the No. 1 slot?" You reply: "That man has sent me a hundred patients so far. When you send me a hundred and one, you will be on the top of the list, just like he is now."

Who benefits from this procedure? The patient who does the referring will benefit, because he is serving others. The patients who come in for care will benefit, because they will get well. You will benefit, because you'll have the extra patients in your practice to care for. Everybody benefits from a referral board!

Have a bulletin board in your office. Change the material on the bulletin board at least once a month. Articles explaining what chiropractic does for certain conditions should be featured. Take these articles out of our professional journals. If there are articles on health in your newspaper that are pro-chiropractic, put these articles on the board. Have pictures of your younger patients placed on the bulletin board. Most patients don't realize that chiropractic is good for children. However, if your patients see children's pictures on your bulletin board, they will refer their children and grandchildren to you.

Tips on How To Make Your
Bulletin Board "Sizzle":

- Mention that over five hundred insurance companies cover chiropractic care.

- Make up a sign saying: "In case of automobile accident, be sure to have your spine and nervous system examined. Whiplashes are dangerous. ALL INSURANCE POLICIES COVER CHIROPRACTIC CARE FOR AUTOMOBILE ACCIDENTS!"

- Have a HERO COLUMN. This column contains names of patients who have referred new patients to you.

- Boost your own service — chiropractic. Do not knock the M.D.'s, medication, shots, etc. Be for natural health, not against drugs which are accepted by the masses.

- Recognize "families" that are under chiropractic care.

- Include testimonials. Place a brief case history of a patient's outstanding recovery.

Have a message board in the reception room. Place on the message board weekly messages such as: "Why keep suffering when chiropractic can help you?" etc.

Have bulletin boards and blackboards for office personnel only. Place your goals, tasks to be performed, projects to be carried out, etc., on these boards. You'll be surprised how much more quickly you will do these jobs when they are posted. The more you can accomplish, the larger your practice will be.

Have literature display racks placed throughout your office. Not only should you place literature display racks in your reception room, but also in all dressing rooms, adjusting rooms, and in the bathrooms. Statistics show that patients take more literature out of dressing rooms and bathrooms than from any other room. No one wants to be embarrassed by getting up in front of a group of people, walking over to a literature display rack and picking up literature on menopause or hemorrhoids. However, if the racks are in the dressing rooms, bathrooms or adjusting rooms, the patient won't be embarrassed about taking literature on sensitive subjects. Have plenty of literature display racks filled with a great variety of pamphlets, etc., to give to your patients. The more conditions that patients know chiropractic can help, the more people they will refer to your office.

Have good quality coat hangers in the adjusting and/or dressing rooms, as well as hooks to hang clothes on. Fastidious patients don't like to hang their clothes on hooks as they may mark or crease the material. Patients appreciate the extra touch and consideration of coat hangers.

Place a referral sign near the receptionist's desk. This sign should state: "Please telephone our office when referring a new patient so we can reserve sufficient time for consultation and thorough examination. We appreciate your caring." This sign is a constant, subliminal referral reminder. It also reminds patients that you will give their friends and relatives quality care.

Have referral or educational signs placed throughout your office. These signs, professionally done, should prompt your patients to refer, and also educate them on certain aspects of chiropractic, i.e., Workmen's Compensation, auto accidents, etc. Either way, referrals or patient education will be the result.

Have a music device that plays music into the telephone when a patient is put on hold. This lets the patient know that yours is a professional office because of this extra touch. This is a small but very important point.

Have more than one telephone line if warranted. Call your telephone company and ask them to do a free survey on your telephone to determine how many busy signals you get in a day. If you have more than ten busy signals per day, this indicates that you need a second line. You will increase your business by getting a second line because more patients will be able to contact you.

Have a good quality carbon ribbon typewriter. An I.B.M. typewriter is most highly recommended. However, do not use a regular ribboned typewriter, as doctors and C.A.'s have a tendency to use the ribbon too long, which results in poor printing of the typed word. Don't sacrifice quality.

Have good quality stationery and business cards with raised lettering and without flamboyant messages. We are judged by our business cards and what we mail out from our offices. Poor quality stationery with name and address imprinted on it by rubber stamp describes graphically the quality of the doctor who sent the letter. The price difference between 100 sheets of quality vs. tasteless stationery is approximately one cent per page. Don't jeopardize your chiropractic reputation for one cent!

You can't sell what you don't have. This pertains to products you would normally have in stock in your office, i.e.: vitamins, orthopedic supports, heel lifts, laboratory reagents, etc. Can you imagine a patient going to a drug store with a prescription for an antibiotic and observing the pharmacist stumbling around his store trying to locate the product and having to report that he is out of antibiotics, and then asking the patient to come back in ten days when he expects a new shipment to come in? That is a very embarrassing situation for him to be in. Do you think that the patient would ever return to that pharmacy? I wouldn't!

Be certain to keep your office well-stocked with extras, and have them arranged in an organized, accessible manner.

Send plants to your patients. Whenever patients go to the hospital, are sick at home, when a new baby is born, or on any occasion that you would normally send flowers, send a plant instead. Flowers die in two or three days, but a plant lives for months, sometimes years. Whenever a patient sees your plant, he or she will remember your kindness. It is the enthusiastic, appreciative patients who send you new patients.

Use Thank-You checks. These are special checks made up to look like actual checks. They are only good for "One Big Thanks" for a special favor someone has done for you. They are used in a manner similar to Thank-U-Grams.

Have giveaways for children and adult patients. These giveaways could be small toys, balloons, etc. for the children and disposable raincoats, stick-on roses, smiley faces, calendars, etc. for adults. Patients like the extras you add to your practice. It adds warmth and personality to a normally impersonal professional practice.

Have an unusual Christmas card. At the end of this chapter are copies of two unusual Christmas cards. The first card offers free x-rays to patients of a clinic. This Christmas card produced fifty-four new patients in two weeks! The second card created so much excitement that the doctor had to disconnect his office phone because the volume of incoming calls totally paralyzed his front desk!

Take the yellow paper that surrounds x-ray film and put it on a clipboard for children to draw on. After a child has drawn on the paper, have him sign it and place it on your bulletin board. Then, every time that child comes into your office, he will look for his drawing that you placed on your bulletin board. The parents will also notice their children's drawings and will be proud that you placed them on your bulletin board. Proud parents become good boosters!

Give a flower to female patients on certain dates. There are many occasions when the giving of a single flower would be a good touch, i.e.: birthdays, anniversaries, Mother's Day, Secretary's Day, Valentine's Day, Easter, Christmas, Thanksgiving, etc., etc. These flowers don't have to be expensive. Remember, it is the personal touch and thought that counts.

Send your secretaries and C.A.'s flowers for Secretary's Week. Don't forget this one! A little appreciation goes a long way. You can imagine what would happen to your C.A.'s attitude if she should learn that another C.A. received flowers, and she didn't!

Give yourself and your staff large birthday cakes on birthdays. Slice the cake in your office, and serve it to your patients with punch, coffee, etc. This creates excitement in the office for your staff as well as for the patients. Excitement results in enthusiastic patients. At the same time, remember to give flowers or plants to your C.A.'s on their birthdays. A good C.A. is invaluable. Show your appreciation.

Have a New Patient checklist. This is a checklist of all business transactions that are necessary to process a new patient, i.e.: pre-history questionnaire filled out, urine containers given, blood samples taken, x-rays taken, report of findings packet made up, requests to bring spouses to the report of findings, etc. With this checklist, your office will be orderly and businesslike. Patients like to go to professional offices that are efficiently run. They reason that if the business portion of an office is orderly and planned, then the care rendered by that office will be well thought out and planned.

Have a Patient Update History form. Whenever a former patient returns for care, have him fill out an Update form in order to determine if his address is the same, if he is returning for the same condition he originally was treated for, or if he is returning with a new condition. This form will also identify whether or not he has been involved in an accident. This form impresses the patient with the doctor's thoroughness; allows the doctor to ask for referrals in cases of automobile accidents; keeps his business files up-to-date with proper address, etc., and helps the doctor with an updated case history.

Thank You for Payment. Have your receptionist write, "Thank you" on the front of a patient's check. This should be written at an angle and in red ink. At the end of the month, when a patient balances his checkbook, he will see "Thank you" written in red ink and he will be reminded of your office. Remember, it is the little things that make big differences in practice-building.

Have the patients address their own appointment reminder cards. Whenever a patient is coming to your office on an every-two-week schedule, or less frequently, have him address an appointment reminder postcard. The C.A. will then put the patient's appointment time and date on this postcard and file it in her tickler file for four to five days prior to that patient's next appointment. When this date comes up, the C.A. will mail the card to the patient, in addition to giving him a telephone reminder call. This reduces the number of "no-shows."

The doctor or the C.A. should not write dunning remarks on statements to patients who have overdue accounts. Use stickers instead. The patient who owes an overdue balance may be reluctant to come back into the office to face the person who wrote those nasty comments. Using a sticker personalizes it less, and the patient is not as reluctant to return. The collection stickers say everything you could say and they don't have negative, interpersonal overtones.

Credit your accounts receivable at Christmastime. Whenever you have destitute patients who owe you money, at Christmastime send them Christmas cards with a handwritten statement on each: "We have credited your account the amount due. You now have an '0' balance. Merry Christmas." This procedure is good for your heart as well as your practice.

Call active patients when they return from vacation. This is extremely important. Normally, when a patient is going on a vacation, he will say to the C.A., "I'm going to be gone for a month. I'll give you a call when I get back." When the C.A. tries to schedule him for one month hence, the patient usually says something like: "I don't know exactly when I'll get back, so I'll have to call you." When the patient returns, he is usually too busy settling back into his daily routine to remember to call you. Therefore, whenever a patient says, "I'll see you in a month," the C.A. should write a note in the memo column of the appointment book for one week after that patient is due to return from vacation. Then, if he hasn't come into the office for his adjustment, your C.A. can call him to schedule his next appointment. He will appreciate it. He will stay under your care. He'll stay healthier — and so will your practice!

Have your telephone covered twenty-four hours a day. Do this by using either an answering device or an answering service. Don't miss your regular patients or new patients calling for appointments. Many important incoming phone calls are placed prior to your office opening in the morning, during lunchtime hours, or in the evening. An answering service or device will result in four to five extra office visits per week. The more calls you pick up, the larger your practice will be. Keep your telephone covered!

Get your staff involved. Your office staff must also be involved in referral stimulation. Have them read chiropractic testimonial magazines. Hold question-and-answer sessions on chiropractic and health. Keep your staff enthusiastic about chiropractic and your work. Have them talk about chiropractic and pass out your cards to family, friends, and anyone they meet. Have them pass out literature about chiropractic.

145

Have your C.A. call patients when you move your office. If you are relocating, have your receptionist call your former patients to tell them that you have moved and to give them your new location. They will appreciate this extra kindness and many of them will be motivated to return to your new office for care. Follow this up with mailed announcements of relocation.

Have a photograph of your office on your office checks. This is an excellent attention-getter. Once someone notices your unusual checks, he will also notice that you are a chiropractor, and this may prompt discussion about an ailment. However, be sure to keep your checks professional in appearance.

Look at your fee schedule. Is it in line with the other progressive D.C.'s in your area? Call other chiropractors in your community and determine whether or not your fee schedule is too high or too low. If it is too high, you are financially keeping people out of your practice. If it is too low, you are rendering services and not being paid enough for them. Either way, when you correct the deficiencies, you will increase your practice.

Utilize modern office procedures. People like to go to modern, up-to-date offices. Therefore, modernizing your office procedures will attract new patients to you.

Take good care of vitamin salesmen and detail men. These people, if they like you, will sing your praises to other doctors in your state. Whenever these doctors have patients moving to your locality, they will refer them to you. Remember — one-third of our population moves each year!

Have sensible office hours. Do not practice odd-ball hours that your patients won't be able to remember, i.e.: Monday-Thursday & Friday, 9 A.M. to 1 P.M., 4 P.M. to 7 P.M., and Wednesday, 3 P.M. to 5 P.M. If you told your patients that you practice 9 A.M. to 5 P.M., Monday through Friday, imagine how many more new patients and drop-in patients you could see!

Vary the treatment of patients. Does this occur in your practice?: A patient comes in and is examined, x-rayed, and is placed on a treatment program that lasts forever and ever. He receives the same adjustment — given in the same manner — each and every visit. If this is the case, that patient will soon feel that he is not going to a doctor's office but rather to a glorified masseur. He also feels that the treatments are not to his benefit, but only to the benefit of his doctor's wallet. To prove this point regarding patients' attitudes, note the current tendency for patients to say, "Chiropractors keep you coming to them forever." Therefore, if you normally adjust the cervicals first on a patient, adjust them last on the next visit. If you normally adjust a patient

146

face down on the adjusting table, stand him against the wall next time and give him an anterior thoracic adjustment. If you normally adjust lumbars first, do the lumbars last. If you normally use one particular type of therapy on a patient, switch therapies so the patient doesn't think he is just getting an automatic function every time he comes into the office. Remember, vary it! Make the patients think that you are thinking about their condition on each and every visit they make. The sameness of treatment, over and over again, ruins a patient's enthusiasm for his doctor and, therefore, will decrease the size of that doctor's practice. Vary your treatment to increase your patient retention, patient enthusiasm, and patient referrals.

Don't give too gentle an adjustment. You don't want your patients thinking that you are giving them glorified massages. They didn't come to you for massages, they came to you for chiropractic care! You should trade off adjustments with two or three of your local chiropractors. Critique each other's adjustments. Have your friends tell you if your adjustments are too hard, unsteady, too rough, or too gentle. Have them tell you honestly, because it is very difficult to judge your own adjustments. Only another D.C. can really judge your adjustments. If you are too gentle or too unsure when you give an adjustment, the patient will pick up on it as insecurity or lack of knowledge, and you will lose that patient.

Don't give a rough, painful adjustment. If it is possible for a doctor to give a painless adjustment, why do some doctors hurt their patients? Obviously, if one doctor can perfect his technique so that it is painless, all other doctors can do the same. The only reason a doctor would give a painful adjustment is indifference! He either doesn't have his mind on the patient at the time of the adjustment, or he never cared enough to perfect his adjusting technique in the first place. I have known D.C.'s who felt that one rough adjustment did the work of three easy adjustments. These misguided doctors, in an effort to cure a patient quickly, actually drove away patients. The doctor's "cure" was worse than the patient's problem. If your patients, friends or relatives complain about your painful adjustments, do something about it.

Use instrumentation to impress patients. Show the patient, at the time of his first adjustment, the instrument you will use each visit, how it works, and what it tells you. If you don't use instrumentation, use orthopedic testing or kinesiology. A non-partisan third part (instrumentation) will impress the patient with the accuracy of your care. The more the patient is impressed with you and the caliber of your care, the more he will refer.

147

Use instrumentation to retain patients. Many times a patient will indicate that he is going to terminate your care prematurely for various reasons. If the doctor has trained the patient as to the importance of his instrumentation, he should say, "Let's see what the instrument shows." After the doctor has utilized his instrumentation, he should say, "It shows you are doing better, and also shows that you need a little more care to correct your condition." This technique has saved many patients for chiropractic and, in doing so, helped people back to health. And they referred!

Explain the function of each piece of therapy equipment to your patient. If the patient understands why you are using a certain therapy, he won't be concerned about the cost. It is only when a patient doesn't understand what a doctor is doing, or what a doctor's therapy equipment is doing, that a doctor-patient relationship falls apart. Make sure the patient understands everything that you do on each and every visit. The more the patient understands, the longer he will stay under your care, and the more he will talk to others about chiropractic.

Place a typed or printed sign on each piece of equipment explaining its function. When a patient understands the purpose of the equipment placed upon him, he will appreciate its value. If the doctor doesn't explain why he is using a piece of equipment, or doesn't have a sign on it explaining its function, that patient will not appreciate its value and will soon cease care with the doctor. Patients must be constantly reminded of a therapy's or a treatment's value. If they are not, they will think the use of the equipment is unnecessary.

Use charts to explain chiropractic. A picture is worth a thousand words! Every adjusting room should be equipped with anatomy charts and spinal charts for explaining to the patient where and what his problem is. Patients, once they know what is wrong with them and what you are doing to help them, will stay under your care, and they will refer.

Use charts to overcome patients' objections. This author has developed a chart which shows the onward progression of disc degeneration, spinal arthritis and nerve pressure, along with the time in years that it takes for this degeneration to occur. This chart was developed from the research of Dr. Clarence Gonstead (disc degeneration), Dr. Carl Cleveland II (nerve atrophy due to nerve pressure), and medical research denoting the time intervals for a disc to degenerate. When a patient states that he has just developed a problem and I show him the comparison of his lateral x-ray with the wall chart, he can see that his problem originally occurred many years before. Once he realizes that his present problem is an aggravation of a pre-existing problem, he will give you the time necessary to treat his condition. If he thinks his condition just happened, he won't. (See chart on following page.)

Handling the "T'ain't nothing" patient. When a patient returns with a seemingly "T'ain't nothing" problem, the doctor should do a short case history and a cursory examination. He should then explain that the patient's present problem is different from his original problem (if it is) and that he wants to carry out a few small tests to determine what is wrong. The doctor should then proceed to do an indepth examination (promise a little and give a lot). After the examination, he should explain to the patient that it looks like only a minor problem but will necessitate a few spot x-rays rather than the number of x-rays that were taken when he originally initiated care. Once the x-rays are studied, combined with the examination findings, a report of findings can be made as to needed care. This method is like catching a chicken by placing a row of corn on the ground. The chicken eats each piece of corn until he has walked himself into the chicken coop! By leading the patient step by step into the x-ray room, you are using good procedures and not high-pressuring or running off patients.

As a standard procedure, take each patient's blood pressure during the first examination. Recheck it during the course of treatment two or three weeks later. If this is a non-blood pressure patient and you notice an improvement in his blood pressure on re-examination, tell him that you are not surprised because chiropractic care works effectively on blood pressure problems. This is an excellent time to suggest that the patient refer his parents and elderly relatives to you for blood pressure checkups.

MECHANICS OF SP

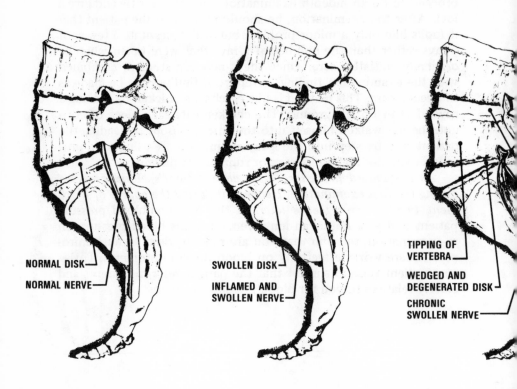

·NORMAL·

·ACUTELY SWOLLEN DISK·

DEGENERATIO

NORMAL DISK
NORMAL NERVE

SWOLLEN DISK
INFLAMED AND
SWOLLEN NERVE

TIPPING OF
VERTEBRA
WEDGED AND
DEGENERATED DISK
CHRONIC
SWOLLEN NERVE

'O'YEARS

IMMEDIATE

7-1

NAL MISALICNMENT

F DISK · · EXTREME DECENERATION · · FUSION ·

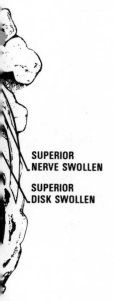

SUPERIOR
NERVE SWOLLEN

SUPERIOR
DISK SWOLLEN

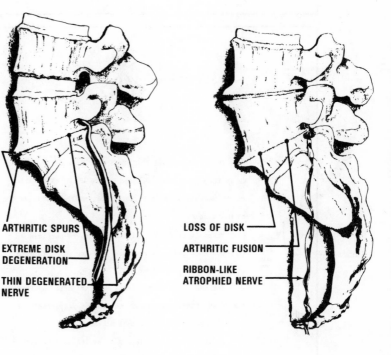

ARTHRITIC SPURS

EXTREME DISK
DEGENERATION

THIN DEGENERATED
NERVE

LOSS OF DISK

ARTHRITIC FUSION

RIBBON-LIKE
ATROPHIED NERVE

EARS **15-20 YEARS** **25 YEARS**

©S P YANDEK 1980
Clearwater, FL 33517

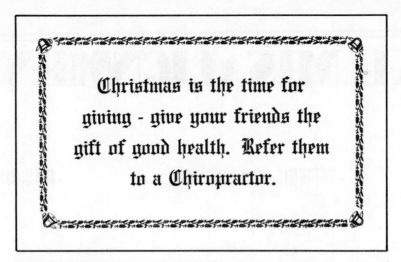

> **Christmas is the time for giving - give your friends the gift of good health. Refer them to a Chiropractor.**

 Merry Christmas

This is a special CHRISTMAS GIFT from me to you. We at the Clinic have wondered how we could thank all of our wonderful patients for referring their friends to our clinic.

Since it is financially impossible to purchase a gift for each individual patient, we are going to make a present of our services.

For you - our good friends - we are offering FREE X-RAYS AND EXAMINATIONS for you, your family, and your friends, during this Christmas month.

In this way we can give good health as a Christmas gift and thank you at the same time.

Merry Christmas,

God Bless You,

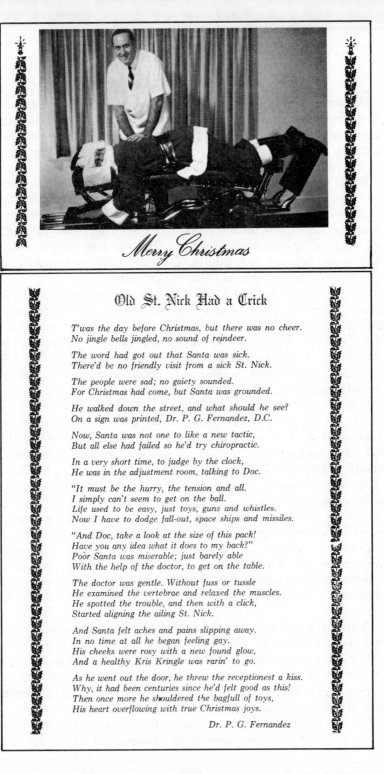

Merry Christmas

Old St. Nick Had a Crick

T'was the day before Christmas, but there was no cheer.
No jingle bells jingled, no sound of reindeer.

The word had got out that Santa was sick.
There'd be no friendly visit from a sick St. Nick.

The people were sad; no gaiety sounded.
For Christmas had come, but Santa was grounded.

He walked down the street, and what should he see?
On a sign was printed, Dr. P. G. Fernandez, D.C.

Now, Santa was not one to like a new tactic,
But all else had failed so he'd try chiropractic.

In a very short time, to judge by the clock,
He was in the adjustment room, talking to Doc.

"It must be the hurry, the tension and all.
I simply can't seem to get on the ball.
Life used to be easy, just toys, guns and whistles.
Now I have to dodge fall-out, space ships and missiles.

"And Doc, take a look at the size of this pack!
Have you any idea what it does to my back?"
Poor Santa was miserable; just barely able
With the help of the doctor, to get on the table.

The doctor was gentle. Without fuss or tussle
He examined the vertebrae and relaxed the muscles.
He spotted the trouble, and then with a click,
Started aligning the ailing St. Nick.

And Santa felt aches and pains slipping away.
In no time at all he began feeling gay.
His cheeks were rosy with a new found glow,
And a healthy Kris Kringle was rarin' to go.

As he went out the door, he threw the receptionest a kiss.
Why, it had been centuries since he'd felt good as this!
Then once more he shouldered the bagfull of toys,
His heart overflowing with true Christmas joys.

Dr. P. G. Fernandez

If asked to relate the No. 1 idea on how to build a large and productive chiropractic practice, I would instruct every new practitioner to start developing the pediatric practice the day he opens his doors. Concentrate on the pediatric practice, and in the future you will have a large and rewarding adult practice.

When I opened my practice in St. Petersburg, Florida, many years ago, it was my privilege to take care of a high school football team. I worked with the students, examined them prior to football season, treated them on the field, and when they were injured, I took care of them in my practice. The children that I treated many years ago are now adults. They are still my patients and their spouses and children are also my patients.

If you wish to build a good, solid practice, concentrate on the pediatric portion of your practice and five, seven, or ten years later, you'll have a full practice of adults who you have educated from day one. There's a saying in chiropractic: "There are no home runs." But I would say, there is an exception to this rule, i.e.: If you concentrate in your early years of practice on building a pediatric practice, it will become a "home run" later on.

One of the drawbacks of building a pediatric practice is that children often disturb the doctor with their noise, yelling and screaming, etc. As a father of seven children, I can attest to that fact! In a chiropractic practice, it is the chiropractic assistant's responsibility and duty to keep the little kids under control. Now, if you take an overview of your practice, you can easily see that children running back and forth, screaming, yelling, crying, etc., can get on the nerves of the patients who are in the reception room. Remember, these patients are already sick; they're already tense; they're already in pain; and children, with the high noise level they create, will aggravate these people and may cause them to tense up even more than they already are. This makes their adjustment take longer and makes it more uncomfortable for them.

Another point to consider is that if you have patients who bring their children in with them when they're being treated, if their children misbehave, this tenses up the parent and makes him/her less receptive to treatment. The parent tightens up and the treatment may be uncomfortable to the patient. It is an uncomfortable and unpleasant experience for everyone concerned.

Let's extend the *noise level* even further to the C.A.'s. How can they concentrate on answering phones, talking to patients, relating with patients, etc., when the children are running up and down the halls of the office, screaming, yelling, and so on? The same is true of the doctor. The doctor's concentration has to center completely on the patient he's attending. When the noise level in his office gets extremely loud, it's almost impossible for him to really concentrate on taking care of that patient. Therefore, it's the C.A.'s responsibility and duty to control the children, to keep them quiet, keep them occupied — to help the sick parent who is in the office for care, to help the doctor concentrate on the patient, and to help her do her own work. Children love having close scrutiny, they react well to discipline, so make it your C.A.'s prime responsibility to control the children in your practice.

The following are some ideas on how to entertain children when they come to your office; how the C.A. can best handle the baby-sitting department; how to keep the little "critters" out of mischief and out of your staff's hair. These are a few pointers to help the reception room become a happier place for the little children. Remember, any practice that is made up of a large portion of children is a large, growing practice, and will be a larger practice in the future.

If space permits, you'd be better off to have a *separate reception room* for children. If you can't do this, maybe you could have a separate portion of your reception room as a child's play corner. In this separate area or separate reception room, you could have scaled-down chairs (little chairs for little children), tables, shelves, books, paintings on the walls of clowns, and so on. This gives the children a feeling of belonging. It's their own private place in an adult world. You can put all kinds of toys and books in this small area, this little child's private reception room. It would encourage good behavior among the children because there's something for them to do. Whenever a child is rambunctious and makes a noise, it's because he's bored. If you give him something to do that he's really interested in, he'll concentrate on it and be quiet.

In this small children's reception room, or in the children's corner of your reception room, you could have a *small TV set* with the controls of the volume out of reach of the children. They can sit and watch their favorite kiddy programs while waiting to see the doctor or while their parents are seeing the doctor. The children should be made to understand that they are in a doctor's office where there are sick people, so they must be quiet. Having a TV set in a small reception room will keep the kids busy for a long period of time and will prevent toys from being scattered all over the office.

Another idea is to have a *bulletin board* in the reception room with "The Chiropractic Kids" on it. You can get an inexpensive Polaroid camera, take the *pictures of the children* as they come in to be treated, put the pictures up on the bulletin board with their names underneath, and maybe even give them pads to draw pictures and have them sign them and put them up on the bulletin board next to their pictures. Every time a child comes in, he'll run to the bulletin board to see if his picture or drawing is still there, and he'll point it out to different people, saying, "See, that's me!" The children will be pleased and happy to come to your office.

Some practitioners use a *scrapbook* and call it "Our Chiropractic Children." In this scrapbook are pictures of the children who are patients of that doctor and perhaps a little case history of what was wrong with the child and what the doctor was able to do to help him get well. This is a very good idea, and I would suggest that it be placed in the adult reception room so that adults can flip through and see what chiropractic can do for children. For every adult who's out in the reception room, there's usually one or two children at home, and those children are prospective patients.

Another thing to consider as far as the C.A. is concerned is that when the adults see a *separate children's reception room* or separate portion of the adult reception room set up for children, they automatically know, of course, that the doctor does take care of children in his chiropractic practice. This is important as most adults don't realize that children can be chiropractic patients as well. Most adults feel that one doesn't go to a chiropractor until one is older, and we all know that this is not true. Therefore, when your adult patients see a children's bulletin board, a child's scrapbook, and a children's reception room, they are more apt to bring their own children in to see you, because they've seen that you are someone who cares about children.

In this separate reception area or room you could get some large, bulky *toys*, like a giant stuffed panda or a big teddy bear for the kids to play with. Usually, if it's big enough, the children can't move it too far and it won't get in the way of the normal traffic in a chiropractic office.

Another good idea to use in the chiropractic office is to get a small-sized table for the child's reception room and place on it an old *typewriter*. You can get some of the yellow paper that comes in the x-ray boxes for wrapping the x-ray film, and put it in the typewriter. Kids will be delighted to pound on that typewriter all day long. You don't have to get an expensive one, an old, used one will do. It can be bought at a flea market, a garage sale, etc., for five to six dollars only. It is something that kids just love.

Another idea is to put a *hobby horse or rocking horse* in the child's reception room.

Some doctors even have *ant farms.* Naturally, if you have an ant farm — with a glass front so the children can see the work the ants are doing and the little caves they've dug — make sure that it can't be tipped over!

A small *pinball game* could be purchased for the children's reception room. There are some models that don't make very much noise and, naturally, this is the type you'd want for your office. You wouldn't want the normal pinball machine, because of the racket it would make.

For the older children, get a spill-free *fish tank.* Actually, the adult patients would like this as much as the children, but children are particularly fascinated watching the tiny fish swimming around in a fish tank. It would have to be of a type that is adequately secured, just like the ant farm, to prevent tipping.

There are some *smaller toys* that can be purchased for the children's reception room. These are all tremendously entertaining for small children. How about a *Vista Viewer,* with stereo slides of Disney World or the Grand Canyon? Or you could get an *Etch-A-Sketch* or magic slates. There is also a whole new group of *water toys* you could purchase. These are all very inexpensive, and the children will play with them for hours on end.

You could purchase children's *picture or coloring books* that aren't very expensive. Also, get some *chiropractic comic books.* These are always entertaining for children in the reception room.

Another good idea is to take the *yellow paper* that is wrapped around the x-rays, and put it in place on a clipboard and have the children draw on it with *washable crayons.* Then place the child's name on the paper and post it on the bulletin board.

Large *building blocks* would be all right for a private reception area for children. Don't get the small ones, else they'll be all over the office floor and patients might trip on them.

Little *noiseless pull toys* would be fine, too. Also, *soft dolls, trucks, airplanes, toy cars, little doll collections, trains, etc.*, are all excellent for a small child's private reception room.

The durability of the toy is really of prime importance. You must remember that you're not going to have only one child playing with a toy. Most of the C.A.'s reading this chapter will have children at home and know that there is almost nothing indestructible as far as a child is concerned! Remember too, in your practice you'll have many children playing with the same toy, so it should be a very durable, tough toy. Little children kick, bite, pound, chew, throw toys, so make sure whatever you purchase for your children's reception room is practically indestructible.

Another important point is to make sure that any dolls you might have for the little girls to play with are made of washable rubber or plastic. Make sure each doll is in one piece instead of having moveable arms and legs, as a child can dismantle a doll in thirty seconds! Make sure, then, that it is in one piece — the head can't come off, the eyes can't come out, the hair can't be pulled out, etc. However, make sure that any clothes on a doll are easy to take on and off, because there's nothing worse than a child being frustrated trying to undress or dress a doll and screaming at the top of her voice. Good material, workmanship and durability all cost a couple of pennies more, but it's well worth it. Don't try to economize with cheap toys.

Another point which is of prime importance as far as toys are concerned is the *safety* of the toys. They must be perfectly safe when children pick them up, drop them, sit on them, lay on them, throw them around, etc. No toy should have sharp edges or corners or anything protruding from the side that might stick in a child's eye. Also make sure that the toys are not painted with a lead-based paint, as this is poisonous.

Have your C.A. check the toys periodically to see if any of the eyes are coming out of the stuffed toys or the dolls. If there is something wrong with a doll or toy, don't fix it — throw it out. If a child has broken something loose, and you repair it, that toy will most likely be broken again, and could hurt a child. Get a new toy — don't try to repair the old one. Remember, as far as the safety of toys is concerned, you want the children to leave your office in better shape than when they came in, and if you have an unsafe toy, they may leave in worse shape!

There are certain toys which you should NOT have in your office. Obviously toys that make noise are out of the question for a chiropractic office. For example, a fire engine with a siren should never be in the reception room. Little pull toys which make noise when pulled should not be in the chiropractic office. Bugles, drums, things of that nature, should never be in a chiropractic office. You can imagine the havoc created hearing little Junior strutting up and down the hall pounding on a drum, and screaming at the same time!

Keep the toys in your office down to medium sizes. You don't have room for a large doll carriage going up and down the hall. Other toys which you should not have in your office are: erector sets, puzzles comprising many pieces (the main piece *always* gets lost!), jigsaw puzzles, construction sets, games requiring a long time to finish (the child may only be in the reception room for ten to thirty minutes, and if he is in the middle of a forty-minute game when he has to leave, he'll want to stay, and this will upset the parents), games that have small marbles as playing pieces, as the children might put the marbles in their mouths, and so the list goes on.

Many offices give *rewards* for good behavior. In some dentists' offices they have miniature toothbrushes that they give their young patients who behaved well when the dentist was filling their cavities, etc. One of the ideas we've used in our office, and one which we've heard is used successfully in other chiropractic offices, is the *treasure chest*, which is a box built exactly like what we imagine a treasure chest looks like, and inside are small plastic dolls, cradles, toy aluminum tea sets, small cars, wind-up cars, little tiny games, puzzles, toy military vehicles, toy boats, toy soldiers, balloons, balls, etc. — in fact, any tiny inexpensive toy to delight a child. When a child has behaved himself in our office, he is allowed to reach into the treasure chest and pick out a reward to take home with him. This makes the visit to the doctor of chiropractic an enjoyable and exciting experience for a child, and not something to be dreaded.

You'd be surprised at the *good comments* the parents of these children give their friends at their P.T.A. meetings or at their social clubs regarding the excellent care given their children at their chiropractor's office. Just remember one very important point: It's not only satisfied patients who build your practice, it's *enthusiastic* and satisfied patients! When you take good care of a mother, and good care of that mother's children, you'll have an enthusiastic mother, and a booster, and referrals, and a larger practice.

Give your patients *"warm fuzzies."* These are special little things that you give people over and above the call of duty. The same applies to "warm fuzzies" for children. I'm referring to the buttons and badges that are always popular with children. We've all seen them — smiley face buttons, roses, little hearts that say "My Chiropractor Loves Me!," etc. Children love to walk around wearing these little buttons. I remember when Avis was trying to become the largest rental car agency. They had buttons saying, "We Try Harder," that many adults wore. Children will wear the roses and the smiley faces and the "My Chiropractor Loves Me" buttons. This also serves as a valuable reminder to your patients, to the people in your community, and their sphere of influence that this child goes to a chiropractor. When neighbors ask, "Who gave your child that smiley face button?" your patient will credit you. The next thing you know, your patients are talking about your office and your office gets referrals.

Some doctors have totally pediatric practices. They have their adjusting tables re-upholstered to look like teddy bears, polar bears, dolphins, and so on. It takes only a little originality as far as the upholsterer is concerned to modify an adjusting table to look like a stuffed animal. Children love to climb up on the panda bear adjusting table to be treated by the doctor, and they can't wait to get back to him to be treated again on the panda bear. So, if you're really serious about building a pediatric practice, see if you can modify one of your adjusting rooms into a pediatric adjusting room. Use Walt Disney characters on the walls, little chairs in the dressing room, mirrors placed low enough on the walls to adapt to the children's height, etc.

Send out *birthday cards* or *birthday gifts* to the little children in your practice. You know children always get a letter or card from their grandmother or grandfather, and usually a present from their relatives, but they don't usually get anything from anybody else. So this would be a little extra something nice for a child to get a birthday card from his doctor. Make it a card suitable for children, i.e., Walt Disney characters, Mickey Mouse, etc. The children will love them, and they'll remember their doctor. But, more important, the parents of the children will remember the doctor for remembering their children!

Another excellent example of how to build a pediatric practice is the *questionnaire* that you should give every new patient. It is a *family health history questionnaire* and the reason you should do this, naturally, is to determine if there are any congenital or hereditary problems that run in their families. So you should ask the patient about the health of his mother, his father, his brother, sister, children, and so on. Once you find out that the patient has a child, and you see something on an x-ray which might be transmitted from parent to child, simply tell the parent that studies have shown that these type conditions can be inherited and you would like to examine his child to see if he inherited the same weakness. There isn't a mother or father who's not going to take better care of their children than they will themselves. This is something a C.A. can do: if the mother has a chronic neck problem, for instance, ask her to bring her children in so that the children's necks can be checked to see if they inherited the mother's neck trouble.

It is important to hand out family health history questionnaires to all your patients. When you find out that they have children, ask them to bring their children in to see if they have inherited any of the problems that the parents are suffering from at that time.

Another use of these questionnaires is to enable you to learn if a patient has a child who has a condition other than the parent's condition. Then you could explain to the patient that you know this is a condition that chiropractic might be able to help. Ask him to bring his child in for an examination. There are two ways you can use the family health history questionnaire to build your pediatric practice.

Remember, people like to talk about themselves and their families, so when they fill out these questionnaires, they'll be happy to do so and to elaborate on their children. However, remember to use proper timing in giving a patient one of these family health histories. If the patient is bent over in pain, that is obviously not the time!

Do you have a *family plan* in your office? Do you give a reduction of fees for more than one member of a family coming to you? Many doctors have family plans where the adult members of the family are charged a certain amount and the children are charged a lesser amount. Some doctors charge the first adult in a family the standard rate, the second adult a little less, and the children half the adult fee. If you have a family plan, tell the patients in your practice about it. Put up signs in your office. You can buy them from any office procedure course. Don't rely on the patient to ask you about the family plan — do something about it. Tell the patient what the family plan is all about. Ask him, "Have you heard what our family plan is? Do you know how we charge families here in the office?" Explain to your patient that you have many families coming to you for chiropractic care. Talk it up! They won't know unless you tell them! Give them brochures on your family plan. If you don't have any, get them made up or buy one of the standard family plan brochures available at the many office procedure seminars and symposiums.

Give every man and woman who walks out of your office a family plan brochure and explain it to them. Make it a point to go out of your way to tell them what the family plan is, and give them something to take home to show their spouses. If you want more business . . . if you want pediatric business — go get it! Mail out to your entire mailing list your family plan brochures. Do it as a one-shot deal where the entire mailing list is given one of these family plans.

Another alternative to mailing a family plan brochure to everyone on your mailing list is to get an extra hundred family plan brochures and go through past patient files to find those patients who have children — patients who you know have had excellent results

161

under your care. Mail these patients the family plan brochures. Mail out these brochures to people you feel would be most likely to bring their children under chiropractic care.

Inquire about other members of their families. You are never going to get the business unless you ask for it. Ask patients how the various members of their families are doing. When someone comes into your office, instead of the usual opening remark, such as, "How are you feeling today?" simply say, "How's your family, John?" or "How's your little boy/girl?" Make notes on the patient's file folder about his children, if any. Tell the parents that if they have children aged eight, nine, ten or eleven, you know that the child should be checked at least every six months to find out if he has symptoms of any of the developmental diseases prone to children in those age groups. This lets the parents know that their doctor has an interest in this area. Explain what the value of chiropractic is to growing children. You know that adolescent children and teenagers are prone to certain developmental problems that chiropractic takes care of very effectively. First talk it up, tell the people that chiropractic can take care of the children and, secondly, explain the family plan. The next thing that will happen is you will have a new patient. Remember, if you have a child as a new patient, that child will later become an adult, whose spouse will be a patient, and whose children will be patients. That's how big practices are born.

All doctors should give *preschool examinations*. In Florida, every child entering second or third grade must have a complete examination by a physician. This examination must certify that the child is free of certain developmental problems, such as scoliosis. The medical professions are very busy during the summer months each year, because they are examining children prior to the fall classes. This is an excellent opportunity for chiropractic doctors to examine children and get them ready to return to school in the fall. It takes only a few minutes to examine a child, and he is usually very cooperative and likes to go to a doctor who doesn't give injections, etc. You should put a *sign* up in your reception room, in each of your dressing rooms, and in each of the adjusting rooms, stating: "Please schedule your children prior to August 1, for back-to-school examinations." If you post these signs where patients will notice them, they will be more likely to make appointments for their children to get these examinations. You can, when examining a child and finding a problem, report it to the mother and, the next thing you know, you've got a new patient who is a child, who will become an adult, who will have children, who will fill your practice in the future.

When there are children who are involved in athletics, you should constantly remind their parents that their children should be checked at least every ninety days to find out if any of the many falls, slips, accidents that children have in athletics, have knocked their spines out of alignment, subluxated their spines and pinched their nerves, etc., etc. It's extremely important that children are checked regularly throughout football, volleyball, wrestling, basketball, track, and other athletic seasons. The parent will not mind. In fact, he'll be very appreciative of your concern that you want to make sure his child doesn't develop a minor problem which could become a major problem when he grows up. Impress upon your patients your concern for their children. They'll love you for it; they'll refer to you; and you will increase your practice.

Have a special *spinal checkup program* for all family members. This is a program which we have had in our office in St. Petersburg for many years. Any member of a patient's family can come to our office and get a chiropractic examination to see if he has nerve pressure. This is at no cost to the patient and at no obligation. I can report that at least thirty percent of the people who are examined under this program show no nerve pressure. They are fine. They don't need care. We just examine them and, if we don't find pressure, we tell them everything looks good, and then we ask them to check back with us in about a year. The other seventy percent most definitely do have nerve pressure. We show them on the graph that they have nerve pressure and recommend that they schedule themselves for complete orthopedic and neurological examinations and x-rays to get started on the road back to better health. They wouldn't know about our free spinal checkups to family members unless we told them. This is the point I'm trying to make — tell the people, stressing that there is no initial charge for family members. Tell them to schedule their children, their mothers, fathers, brothers, sisters, spouses, etc., etc.

Send letters out to all your patients, i.e.: *"Chiropractic Bulletin — family checkup*. We have found that usually, by the time a patient gets under care and starts getting relief of his symptoms, he has considered the possibility of bringing other members of his family under chiropractic care. Perhaps family members have problems that need chiropractic attention. Perhaps there are problems that until now have gone undetected or unnoticed. Spinal deviations, spinal misalignments, often exist without the person being aware of them, or until they have become advanced, become chronic — at which point it is extremely difficult to correct.

Place this sign throughout your office: "In cooperation with the President's Program on *Physical Fitness*, it is the policy of this office to give spinal checkups to all members of a family at no charge and at no obligation, strictly to find out if nerve pressure or spinal defects are present and if they can be corrected. This applies to all children, of any age, even through college, without obligation. We encourage patients to call our office and make appointments for family members. We are happy to examine them to determine if they do, in fact, need chiropractic care."

Send letters to this effect to your patients. They'll appreciate it. No one can be offended by their chiropractic doctor wanting to help his patients' families.

Make sure this is a program in which you want to help the other person and not just to get another patient. If you do it with the right motivation, you'll get the new patient, who will refer other new patients, and your practice will grow.

Have special *scoliosis examination* programs in your office. Talk to all parents who come into your office and who have children between the ages of eleven and eighteen. Tell the patients that you're concerned about their children. Tell them that you recently read some statistics which stated that fifty-eight percent of the children in that age bracket are developing scoliosis or excessively curved spines, and these scoliosis or curved spines are going to cause extreme amounts of back pain, deformity, disability, and heart problems in the future. Tell them that they should bring their children into your office to be examined without delay. Talk to them about the seriousness of this problem. All children in this age bracket should be examined and x-rayed by the chiropractic doctor to determine if they are developing scoliosis. It's very alarming when you consider that fifty-eight percent of children are now developing this deformity. It can be corrected, however, through chiropractic measures. Why let a child become a spinal cripple when you could prevent it by simply telling the parents? Accept the responsibility of being a doctor — tell your patients to bring their children under chiropractic care.

It is not enough to just talk about the scoliosis program — you should hand out *scoliosis brochures* to every parent and grandparent in your practice. Tell them of the alarming incidence of fifty-eight percent of children developing this problem. Tell them to get their children and grandchildren under chiropractic care or at least arrange for an examination in order to determine if their children or grandchildren are developing scoliosis. Remember to tell them that there is no charge for these examinations. Point out that if, however, there *is* a problem, detailed examinations and x-rays would be at a charge. But, under no circumstances, make the patient obligate himself to you in any way.

Mail the scoliosis brochures to your *entire patient list*. Let them know what you are doing about this problem. Let them know about your concern for this problem. You'll be surprised at the number of parents who will bring their children to you after receiving these brochures, who will put their children under your care, or at least under examination, in order to determine if they are, in fact, developing a scoliosis.

Show pictures of children at your *patient lectures*. The majority of patients don't know that the doctor of chiropractic can take care of children. They assume that he is an older person's doctor. To counteract this, during the course of a chiropractic lecture, show slides of children getting their chiropractic adjustments. This would let the patient know professionally that the chiropractic doctor does in fact take care of children. Then, tell the people in the audience what chiropractic does for children. When you do this, it encourages the people who are attending the lectures to send their children to you.

Place a scoliosis x-ray of a child on a viewbox. Throw the light on so whenever a patient goes into the room, he will see the x-ray of the curved spine of that child. He will probably say, "What's wrong with that child?" This gives you the chance to say that it is a little boy/girl, tell him what the problem is, why the mother brought the child to you, what you are doing for the child and how the child is responding. Then ask the patient, "Do you have any children of a similar age?" If the patient does, then you should say, "Do get your children in for scoliosis examinations to prevent them from being as bad as this little child." It's a great way to get new patients, while at the same time providing a service to your patients.

Show children's *before-and-after full spine x-rays*. Put them on lighted viewboxes and, of course, block out the patients' names. A patient will say, after seeing these x-rays, "Wow, what a difference in x-rays! What did you do to help that child?" Then you can tell the story of that case, how the child responded, and how grateful the mother is. If the patient looking at these x-rays has any children of his own, you can encourage him to bring his children in for at least an examination. Just follow the same procedures as you did with the individual scoliosis x-ray, and the next thing you know, you have new patients. This reminds all your patients that you take care of children. It also reminds them that they should have their children under chiropractic care.

Whenever a patient mentions, "I didn't know that Dr. So-and-So takes care of children," that gives your C.A. her entree to

165

explain what chiropractic does for children and what you have done for each one of these little children whose pictures are on the bulletin board. It's a good conversation piece in the office and the next thing you know, they, in fact, will send their children in and you have helped another person on the road back to better health.

Many chiropractic doctors have *testimonial books* in their reception rooms. Some of the titles of these books are: "Chiropractic Patients Speak," "Chiropractic Speaks Out," etc. In these testimonial books are shown three or four pictures of children who have been under chiropractic care, together with descriptions of what was done for them. Naturally, these testimonials were written by the parents, but the children's pictures and the fact that chiropractic took excellent care of them, are all recorded in the books. Everyone reading these books are taught the benefits of chiropractic for children. In other words, if you acquire such a testimonial book to place in your reception room, the "uninformed" patient will be educated to the fact that you do, indeed, take care of children very well. Then that patient will refer his adult friends *and* their children to you. You may double the size of your practice if you have a testimonial book in your reception room.

Have a specific *picture album devoted only to young patients* in your office. You can put Mickey Mouse pictures on the front, or Bozo the Clown, or whatever kind of child's storybook characters you'd like. But it should be entitled, "Our Young Patients Speak." Ask for testimonials of the children under your care. Of course, these will be written by the parents, but you may be surprised how many parents, or grandparents, will love to flip the pages of the book to see the little children who are under your care, and to learn what was wrong with them and how they responded to your care.

Send out literature pertaining to the pediatric aspect of chiropractic practice. There are many pieces of literature that explain how chiropractic helps the *bed-wetting* problem in young children. As a doctor of chiropractic, I can tell you of outstanding results I've had in my practice with bed-wetters. I really feel sorry for the thousands upon thousands of children who have this bed-wetting problem; how embarrassed they are every time they have an "accident." The pathetic thing is that these children respond extremely well to chiropractic, and they probably would be over their problem of bed-wetting within sixty days of initiating chiropractic care if someone took the time to tell the parents that chiropractic can help children with bed-wetting problems. Ask your C.A. if she knows of any patients who have children with bed-wetting problems. If she does, ask her to mail out the bed-wetting literature to them. She could also enclose a little note, i.e.: "Mary, I thought that maybe this would apply to some of your children, if they have this problem. — Joan." You'll be surprised at the results you will get from this.

Try *sponsoring a good posture contest*. You could have a good posture contest for young adults, or for little children under the age of ten. Maybe two or three doctors in your area could get together and put on a good posture contest for children. It has been done in the past, and very successfully. Contact the various civic clubs in your area. You can find their addresses and the names of their chairmen through your local Chamber of Commerce.

Notify all the civic clubs that you are helping to sponsor a good posture contest and that if they would like a speaker to explain what the contest is about, you'd be happy to speak. This is an excellent opening to let your community know that you care about — and can treat — young children.

Another idea which has helped to develop pediatric practices in the past, and which would help you expand your pediatric practice, is for you to have an agreement between yourself and a local *photographic studio*. Whenever a child is born in your community, you should send the parents a letter congratulating them on the birth of their child, and include a coupon from the photography studio for one free picture of their baby. You'll find that many of the people who receive the coupons will, in fact, go to have their babies' pictures taken at the photography studio. They will thank you; they will refer patients to you; and many of the little children who have their pictures taken at no charge, eventually will become patients of yours.

BUILDING THE PERSONAL INJURY / WORKMEN'S COMPENSATION PRACTICE

One of the most frequent questions asked of a chiropractic consultant is: "How do I build a Personal Injury (P.I.) / Workmen's Compensation (W.C.) practice?" Before discussing how to develop a P.I. / W.C. practice, certain elements should be explained so that you can be sure that this is the type practice you wish to pursue.

Complaints, fears, dangers, falacies, procedural differences, paperwork, bottlenecks, courtroom testimony, fire-breathing defense attorneys, etc., should be thoroughly understood prior to deciding whether or not you wish to enter the Personal Injury field.

Complaints About A
Personal Injury / Workmen's Compensation Practice

One of the most common complaints about a Personal Injury practice is that it entails too much paperwork — which it does! However, the doctor is very well paid for the time he spends on paperwork.

Another complaint is that it is a credit practice rather than a cash practice. This is true. However, a cash practice is harder to build than a credit practice. Can you imagine what would happen to this country if all houses and automobiles were sold for cash only? There would be very few houses built and everyone would be walking because they wouldn't be able to afford automobiles or other necessities of life so taken for granted by the American people. Because of credit, people can buy cars and houses and end up having some equity. The same is true of a chiropractor building a practice. By having a well-controlled credit practice, a doctor can have more people under his care and, in doing so, can build a larger practice. It is true that some people will not pay their bills (two percent). However, ninety-eight percent of people are honest. This author would rather have ninety-eight percent of fifty thousand dollars a month than have a hundred percent of two thousand dollars a month! Think about it!

One advantage of a Personal Injury / Workmen's Compensation practice is that it is a no-loss practice. Some doctors fear that if they lose a trial in court, all services rendered to that patient will be for nothing. This is not the case. When a doctor takes care of a patient, that patient is responsible for the bill, regardless of whether or not the trial is won in court. Another factor to consider is that less than five percent of P.I./W.C. cases go to court.

Does a P.I./W.C. practice create havoc with patient scheduling, especially when a doctor has to go to court? Not necessarily. If the D.C. develops a good rapport with the plaintiff attorney, he can request that he be called as the last witness before lunch. By doing this, he may only miss one hour in the morning of his office practice. Plaintiff attorneys, wanting a good rapport with a plaintiff doctor and wanting a calm, cool, and *winning* doctor, will go along with his request for a late-morning testimony time. The last thing a plaintiff attorney wants is an aggravated, antagonistic doctor. He will usually cooperate with the doctor, for everyone's benefit.

Fears About A Personal Injury / Workmen's Compensation Practice

Many doctors have a fear of going to court. They fear that the defense attorney will make fools of them. Sometimes this happens. In order to eliminate much of this embarrassment, a doctor should take some of the training that is available throughout the country on courtroom testimony. The chiropractic doctor will soon find that he is just as qualified as anyone else at testifying in court. As soon as he learns how to properly answer the trick questions an attorney might pose, he will not have trouble with courtroom testimony.

Many doctors feel unqualified when pitted against an orthopedic surgeon. If this is the case with a D.C., perhaps he should sharpen his skills! An orthopedic surgeon is more qualified as far as surgery is concerned, but not as far as treatment is concerned, diagnostically the chiropractic doctor and the orthopedic doctor are about equal. If a doctor feels less capable of diagnosing than an orthopedic surgeon, he should take some orthopedic courses, available through the American Chiropractic Association, or college and state association extension courses. Remember, we are treating doctors and they are surgical doctors. We both have expertise, but in different areas.

If a doctor feels that he is not qualified to read x-rays as well as a radiologist, then he should take some of the excellent courses in x-ray interpretation, available through the A.C.A. or college extension courses.

The Dangers of Building a P.I./W.C. Practice

One of the true risks of having a P.I./W.C. practice is being overloaded with Personal Injury cases. A successful practice is a balanced practice. A balanced practice is fifty percent P.I. and W.C. and fifty percent private pay or insurance. A practice must be multi-faceted or the doctor will become bored in his work. If a doctor becomes overloaded with P.I./W.C. patients, his main objective shifts from a desire to get sick people well to a desire for monetary gain, and it will show. He will soon get the reputation of being interested only in money.

There are three basic types of practice: (1) The Private Pay practice, with little W.C. and P.I.; (2) the Private Pay with W.C., but only a little P.I.; (3) The P.I./W.C. and Private Pay practice.

The first type practice is usually found in a more expensive area of town, where the W.C. patient will hesitate to go because the office is too plush, etc. The second type practice, the private pay with W.C., usually has little P.I. because it is located in the workmen's part of town. The last type of practice is a mixture of both. Much of the success of this type practice depends on where the office is located. It usually is located in the middle-class area of town where the doctor can take care of the working man, the rich man, and the P.I. patient.

The most successful practices in the country are twenty-five percent private pay patients, twenty-five percent P.I., twenty-five percent W.C., and twenty-five percent medical insurance patients. A doctor should not sacrifice his private pay patients in order to build a P.I. practice. Oftentimes, a doctor will substitute one type of practice for another, and end up with the same income, which defeats all objectives. A doctor has to maintain what he is presently doing and add the P.I. and W.C. patients to his practice. He shouldn't lose sight of what he already has. He should simply establish additional goals.

Falacies of the P.I./W.C. Practice

Many doctors who enter the P.I. field, feel that they have to convert insurance companies, attorneys, judges, and juries to chiropractic. This is not the case. A doctor should go to court to present his findings as a doctor, to assist in winning the case, NOT to convert. Doctors who have practiced P.I. know that they can attract more patients to them by winning cases than they can by trying to convert others to chiropractic.

170

Procedural Differences in P.I./W.C. Practices

All four types of cases (private pay, major medical, P.I., and W.C.) must be handled differently. The differences are not the techniques of adjusting, but in the paperwork and fee schedules. Some doctors may say that a different fee schedule for P.I., W.C., and private pay patients is a double standard, but it is not. This is the system that insurance companies have set up, and we must work within that system. If a doctor visits an insurance company, he will see one adjuster for major medical insurance, another for W.C., and another for P.I.

Each of these adjusters works with different fee structures and parameters, because all three areas are so totally different. The same thing is also true with a doctor's practice, since he is going to have these same three departments in his office. They don't have to be separate rooms, but separate procedures are necessary.

Examination and x-rays. P.I. and W.C. cases necessitate more complete orthopedic and neurological examinations and x-rays than do private pay cases.

If a doctor does not do a thorough orthopedic, neurological, and x-ray examination, an insurance company may be held liable for something in the future that they should not be. For example, a patient was involved in an at-home accident and suffered a compression fracture of a mid-thoracic vertebrae, but his doctor only examined and x-rayed the lumbo sacral spine. A few years later, the patient was involved in an automobile accident and now blames the compression fracture on the automobile injury. The automobile insurance company may be held responsible. However, if the doctor had performed an indepth x-ray examination at the time of the first accident, he would have spotted the compression fracture. Then, when the patient reported the compression fracture to the automobile insurance company, trying to make it the insurance company's responsibility, all that the insurance company had to do was contact all doctors that the patient had seen in the past in order to determine that the compression fracture occurred years prior to the automobile accident. If the doctor had been thorough in his examination at the time of the first accident, he would have saved the insurance company a considerable amount of money. The insurance companies demand, and rightly so, that doctors be thorough in their examinations, for their own and the patient's sake.

Re-x-rays and examination. The doctor should re-x-ray his patients approximately every three months, or as needed, but he should be consistent. If it is the doctor's policy to re-examine

171

every ten visits, then he should stick to that policy. If it is his policy to re-x-ray every thirty visits, then he should not change it. Consistency is very important in P.I. and W.C. cases.

Procedural differences in paperwork. Some states require authorization for the doctor to treat W.C. cases. If so, get it signed. The C.A. has to make sure that all assignments and liens, etc., are signed by the patient in order to protect the doctor.

Assignments/liens. In any P.I. case, where the doctor extends credit to the patient, he must have the patient sign an assignment or lien form. This document instructs the insurance carrier, the patient's attorney, etc., to pay the doctor out of any proceeds of the patient's case. A word of caution here: an "authorization to pay physician" is NOT an assignment of benefits or a lien, and the doctor's services are not protected.

Attorney liens. This is a form that the patient's attorney must sign guaranteeing payment of the doctor's bill. A policy that many doctors follow is that if an attorney requests a narrative report and he has not signed an attorney lien form, they refuse to send him a report until it is signed.

Another word of caution: If a patient changes attorneys, the lien and/or assignment form that has been signed by the first attorney, does not obligate the second attorney to pay the doctor. A new assignment/lien form is necessary to protect the doctor's bill.

Monthly supplemental reports. The doctor should send progress reports on a monthly basis to the attorney or the insurance company — whoever is ultimately responsible for paying his bill or reimbursing the patient. However, there is an exception to this rule. If an attorney sends the doctor a letter telling him that he cannot send statements, bills, reports, etc., to anyone other than the attorney, the doctor must follow his dictates. The attorney, along with this letter, will have a signed letter from the patient instructing the doctor to follow the attorney's instructions.

Monthly billings. A doctor should build credibility and respect with the legal and insurance community in his area by billing his patients every month. If he doesn't bill his patients monthly and waits until the end of care for the attorney and/or insurance company to pay his bills, he will give the appearance of being in collusion with the attorney or having a vested interest in the outcome of the patient's case. This results in a lack of credibility for the doctor with the legal and insurance community.

History. One especially important aspect in a P.I./W.C. practice is the taking of thorough recent and past histories. Some doctors with busy practices do a consultation on the immediate problem, then have a top-flight C.A. do an indepth history and past history. The doctor, of course, reviews this history and past history with the patient.

Some of the questions a doctor or C.A. should ask in consultation are: How did the accident occur? Was the patient a driver or a passenger? If a passenger, where in the car was he prior to the accident and after the accident? (Many times a passenger in the front seat of a car prior to an accident ends up in the back seat after the accident if he was not using safety belts at the time.) Is he the owner of the car? If not, who is? Did he strike anything in the car, i.e., did his chest hit the steering wheel, did his head hit the windshield, did his shoulder hit the door, did his knee hit the dashboard, etc., etc.? Did he go to hospital or to an emergency room? Was he x-rayed? By whom and with what result? Was he treated by anyone at the hospital or at a doctor's office prior to seeing you, and what were the results? What other symptoms has he developed since the accident? Has he lost any time from work and for what reason? Who told him to take time off work and for how long? Is he back at work? If so, part-time or full-time? Who told him to return to work? Is he taking medication? If so, what kind and what for? If the patient is a woman, can she perform all her household chores? Or does she have to hire someone to come in and help because of pain? The doctor should also ascertain the kind of physical effort necessary in the patient's employment and whether this physical effort aggravates his pain.

Past history and surgery. The doctor should obtain a good past history on the patient, including surgery and illnesses. Was he ever involved in another automobile accident or injury to his back or neck? If he received care previously, was an insurance report filed?

A point should be made to tell the patient that whether or not he was injured before is not important to his present case. All a previous injury does is make a patient more susceptible to a new injury. However, emphasize to him that if he does not tell you of a previous injury or accident, he could lose the entire case because he withheld information.

Daily office notes. The office visit on a P.I. or W.C. case, by necessity, should take no longer than a private pay patient, because of office notes, etc. Remember, when a doctor takes care of a patient under Workmen's Compensation or personal injury, the insurance company wants to know everything that is wrong with that patient each visit.

Notes should be made when the patient is off work, is allowed to return to light work, and when he may return to regular work. If the patient states that he can't take off work for financial reasons — such as feeding a family — notes should be made in the

173

patient's file outlining this fact, because an attorney will surely ask the doctor why the patient didn't take off work if he was injured so badly. The doctor's office notes should state in such a case: "The patient said that he had to work, against my instructions, so he could feed his family."

Aggravating factors. Any and all aggravating factors should be noted on the patient's file, i.e.: if he lifted something and it aggravated his condition; if he slept in an incorrect position and it aggravated his condition, etc.

The doctor should make very clear instructions to the patient when placing him in cervical supports, lumbo sacral supports, over-the-door traction devices, etc. For example: "I want you to wear this support all day, except when you are bathing or sleeping." Notes of these instructions should be made on the patient's file at the same time.

Disability questionnaires. Have the patient fill out a disability questionnaire at the time of his first office visit and again every six weeks during care. These forms will record any improvement in his condition. In a P.I./W.C. practice, a doctor has to justify his care. By filling out questionnaires, a patient documents, in his own handwriting, the results obtained, thus justifying his doctor's care.

Bottlenecks and Problems in P.I./W.C. Practices

Writing of narrative reports. One of the biggest bottlenecks a doctor has in a P.I. practice is the writing of narrative reports. A standardized narrative report aids the doctor in getting the important paperwork done quickly. With experience and training, it takes about three minutes to write a narrative report, and ten to fifteen minutes to type it.

Progress reports. Another bottleneck is the writing of monthly progress reports. This problem can be eliminated quite easily by the use of a checklist progress report. The doctor simply checks off how the patient is progressing, his prognosis, and his plans for examinations in the future, etc.

Predeposition and pretrial conferences will keep the doctor out of trouble. Whenever there is a pending deposition or trial, a predeposition conference or pretrial conference is mandatory. If the plaintiff attorney doesn't particularly want to grant you such a conference, refuse to give him the deposition or refuse to go to court. A plaintiff attorney doesn't want to go to court or into a deposition with an antagonistic plaintiff doctor. Insist on pretrial and predeposition conferences.

If you have never had a deposition or have never been to court, you should tell the plaintiff attorney. The attorney will then explain how he wants you to testify. This will be time well spent and will better prepare you for future courtwork.

Courtroom dress and demeanor. Most plaintiff attorneys advise doctors to have standard go-to-court "uniforms." This usually consists of a dark blue suit, white cotton shirt, black socks and shoes, dark maroon tie, with very little jewelry, except maybe wedding band and a moderately-priced watch. People are sometimes jealous of the fact that doctors are monetarily successful, and whatever a "flashy" doctor says in court will sometimes be discounted by a jury for this reason. Therefore, wear the proper dress, which is extremely conservative. The initial impression you make with the jury will have a bearing on how much weight your testimony will bear.

The same is true of the doctor's body language. A doctor who fidgets or is nervous on the stand will have less credibility than one who has a relaxed, professional demeanor.

Inexperienced? If you are inexperienced in courtroom testimony, one of the simplest methods of learning courtroom procedure is to go and watch several trials. This will enable you to know what to expect from defense attorneys, judges, and juries.

Another possibility is to get together with a trial attorney for a rehearsal of courtroom procedures. Most attorneys are willing to teach you how to testify. This is not only for your benefit, but theirs as well, since they will be presenting a more capable witness in court.

Courtroom testimony. Shakespeare once said, "All the world's a stage, and all the men and women merely players." The same is true of courtroom testimony. The courtroom is the stage, the jury is the audience, and you are one of the major actors. The main goal in the performance is to win the academy award or, in this case, the settlement.

You can win the trial in court by being prepared. Your testimony should come easily, without undue hesitation. When an expert is unprepared and has to stumble through his testimony, it has a devastating effect on the jury. The witnesses (actors) are playing to the jury, not to the attorneys.

The doctor, when giving an affirmative response to a question, and when addressing the jury, should nod his head. Chances are that at least one of the members of the jury will nod his head with him. From that point on, all the doctor's answers should be directed to that sympathetic person in the jury.

At the beginning of the doctor's testimony, the plaintiff

175

attorney, the one who represents the patient, will qualify him. Usually he will ask the doctor his name, address, education, societies he belongs to, etc. He will usually also ask the doctor to define chiropractic and tell how many patients he treats each week.

It is also an excellent idea for the plaintiff attorney to ask any of the negative questions which the defense attorney would normally ask, but to bring them out in a positive way. For example: "Do you have hospital privileges?" "Are you licensed to prescribe harmful drugs?" "Are you licensed to do surgery?" etc. The defense attorney most definitely will ask these questions in a derogatory manner in order to give the jury a demeaning view of the doctor or of our profession. The plaintiff attorney should "beat him to the punch."

It is best to stay away from controversial issues, such as the diagnostic value of 14x36" x-rays, subluxation terminology, and any procedures which are not generally utilized by other professionals.

When asked for his examination findings, the doctor should go to his narrative report and read off the answers in order to explain to the jury what happened during the course of the patient's examination.

If asked to explain an examination procedure, the doctor should use arm and body motions to explain the tests, such as, cervical compression test, adson test, etc. By reading the doctor's body language the jury can better understand the tests that the doctor used, how they were performed, and what the results were.

It must be remembered that although the technical knowledge of an expert is critically important, it is even more important that he has developed the proper communication skills necessary to convey his knowledge to the jury, in such a manner to make him more believable than any other witness.

The defense attorney will often use the testimony of an orthopedic surgeon to refute the testimony of a chiropractor. The qualifications of the orthopedic doctor are usually elaborated upon to the point of making him appear to be a super-examining and treating doctor. At the same time, the defense attorney often tries to minimize or undermine the chiropractor's qualifications. In order to counteract this, the plaintiff attorney should simply ask the orthopedic doctor how many patients he saw in a given week. When the orthopedic doctor gives his answer, the plaintiff attorney should ask him how many of those patients were in his office solely for examinations. The plaintiff attorney should then ask the orthopedic doctor to subtract the number of patients he examined from the total number of patients he saw that week.

The jury will find that he treated very few people and that, generally, he simply examines patients. The plaintiff attorney, who has already asked the plaintiff doctor how many patients he treated that week, will remind the jury that the orthopedic doctor treats very few people. This makes the plaintiff doctor (the chiropractor) a treating specialist. The jury will then understand exactly the differences between a treating doctor and an examining doctor and will thus be more inclined to give equal weight to both doctors' testimony. This makes a tremendous impression.

Another trick question usually asked by the defense attorney is, "How much are you being paid for your testimony?" To counteract this question, the plaintiff doctor should state that he is not being paid for his testimony but only being reimbursed for the time spent away from his practice.

The Cardinal Rules of Courtroom Testimony

✓ Be polite, courteous, and give a good impression at all times.

✓ Take your time in answering questions.

✓ Never testify to anything unless you can substantiate it in your office records.

✓ Never mention insurance or an insurance company during a trial.

✓ Avoid displaying an "ivory tower" or conceited attitude when testifying. This antagonizes the jury.

✓ Think ahead and try to anticipate where the attorney's questions are leading.

✓ If you don't know the answer, tell the attorney so. There isn't anything wrong with not knowing an answer. No one is expected to know everything. Don't guess if you don't know. Never stick your neck out!

✓ Never let the defense attorney get you angry, confused, or rattled. Defense attorneys will use different tactics, according to their personalities. Some attorneys are desk-pounders, some are sneaky, others try to discredit you or your profession or try to make you feel inferior.

Generally, the real confrontation begins with the cross-examination. The defense attorney will try to rattle you or ridicule you in order to demean you in the eyes of the jury. Don't worry about this; he sees that as his job. Maintain your calm and answer questions directly. The first one to lose his temper will likely lose the case.

Many doctors get upset when asked damaging questions or when slanderous remarks are made about their profession. After the trial, however, the plaintiff attorney and the defense attorney will often go out and have drinks together. Attorneys don't take the courtroom scene personally. Neither should the doctor!

If it comforts the chiropractic doctor, the general practitioner, M.D. also detests going to court, perhaps more so than the chiropractic doctor. The courtroom is not a natural environment for anyone except the judge and the attorneys.

Never try to pull a case out. The doctor testifies in court as to what he found wrong with the patient and what he did to help that patient. He is not trying to win the case for the patient. That is the attorney's job, NOT the doctor's! Don't lie or exaggerate on the witness stand for the patient or the attorney. Don't try to help anyone do anything. The doctor is only a reporter of facts.

Don't jeopardize your credibility for one trial, because once your credibility is questioned in the legal-chiropractic community, it is very difficult — if not impossible — to re-establish it.

Courtroom work does not have to be a horrifying experience. It can be a very gratifying experience when you do it in the right way. It also may be very lucrative. The better known you become as an expert witness, the more often attorneys will request your services. The best way to become a good expert witness is to work at it. Prepare carefully and win! The more exposure you get in court and the more "wins" you have to your credit, the more attorneys will refer cases to you for treatment and/or impairment ratings.

How much should you be paid? You can determine how much you should be paid for testimony very simply. Total up your average income per day, divide it by the normal amount of hours you practice per day, and you will have the total amount of money per hour that you generate. Then, charge the court or the patient or the attorney for the time spent out of your office. This time is figured from the minute you leave your office until the minute you get back. This is called Portal to Portal. If you are out of your office for two hours and you average one hundred dollars an hour in practice, then the courts or the attorney should reimburse you two hundred dollars.

How does a doctor attract P.I. and W.C. cases? The answer to this question is very simple. P.I. and W.C. cases are already within your practice. Your patients are people, and people drive cars, and people work for their livings. These same people have automobile accidents, and hurt themselves at work. Tell your patients that you have begun treating quite a few automobile accident cases and

Workmen's Compensation cases. Oftentimes a doctor will attempt to get attorneys to refer injury cases to him. This usually doesn't work because it is a rare patient who consults an attorney about an injury who hasn't already consulted a doctor.

The No. 1 step to take in establishing a P.I./W.C. practice is to make a firm commitment to do it! That's all it takes. It doesn't happen overnight. A doctor has to make up his mind to do it and then slowly start to develop this type practice. He shouldn't wait until he has taken all the courses, learned how to perform the proper examinations, had management courses to teach him how to testify in court, before starting a P.I./W.C. practice. He should simply MAKE A COMMITMENT — and STICK TO IT!

The following are some tried and true methods of attracting P.I./W.C. business:

1. Have lunch with attorneys. Tell them that you specialize in personal injury and Workmen's Compensation cases. Give them one of the books on chiropractic/legal matters.

2. Advertise on TV, radio and newspapers for P.I. and W.C. patients. This will soon attract the attention of personal injury attorneys. They will know that you have this type of business because of your advertising. They may then feel that you could be a good person to know and to refer their clients to. They will also know that you, in turn, may refer your patients to them.

3. Open house for attorneys. Show the attorneys what a modern chiropractic office is like. Explain to them what each piece of equipment is for and how it benefits their clients — your patients.

4. Send out letters offering a tour of your office. This is the same basic idea as an Open House, but instead of attracting attorneys to be shown your office at one time, you could show them through your office individually.

5. Form a legal-chiropractic group. This is a great method of acquainting attorneys with chiropractic and of making yourself better known. Once the attorneys find a doctor whom they can rely upon, they will refer to that doctor. The longer these inter-professional relationships continue, the more productive it can be for all parties concerned.

6. Teach examination procedures to attorneys. Most of them know law but not anatomy. By having small get-togethers and teaching them what your examination procedures are and how to interpret them, you will be educating these attorneys as to how much you know. You definitely will increase your chances of getting their referrals.

7. Letters to employers about Workmen's Compensation: offer

to treat their employees after working hours in order to help him keep his employees on the job and to keep his insurance premiums at a minimum.

8. Send letters to attorneys offering to participate in P.I. and W.C. cases. Whenever this type of letter is sent to attorneys, referrals and inquiries result.

9. Advertise to your patients for P.I. and W.C. cases. They won't know you handle these cases until you tell them.

10. Have signs in your office stating that you take care of P.I. and W.C. cases. The more you inform the public that you treat these type cases, the larger your practice will become.

11. Send pamphlets to your patients on what to do in case of automobile accidents. This pamphlet describes the steps to be taken when someone is involved in an automobile accident. Tell your patients to keep the pamphlets in the glove compartments of their cars.

12. Speak to civic clubs regarding whiplash. The more people who know that you treat P.I. and W.C. cases, the larger your practice will become.

13. Tell your patients that you specialize. Every patient who comes into your office should be told by you or your C.A. that you have had extensive training in the treatment of automobile accidents and on-the-job injuries. The more you "talk it up," the more P.I. and W.C. patients you will attract.

14. Telephone employers. After examination and x-rays have been done on a Workmen's Compensation patient, telephone that patient's employer and explain the details. Inform him that by following your recommendations you will prevent his employee (your patient) from aggravating an already severely strained condition. Also explain to him that by following your recommendations, the employee will be in as good condition as he was prior to his injury.

15. Conduct safety clinics. Notify employers that you are available to conduct training classes on "How To Lift" and "How To Prevent Back Injuries," etc.

16. Advertise in legal publications. The American Bar Association and the American Trial Lawyers Association have excellent magazines in which to advertise your specialty of P.I. and W.C. Also, consider a local bar publication.

I hope this chapter challenges your imagination and points you toward success is a Personal Injury / Workmen's Compensation practitioner. It's a great field with very few "stars." The "star" in your community could be you!

A word of caution: Unless you plan to be the very best in courtroom testimony, examination procedures, etc., don't enter this field. A chiropractor who has not had careful training in this area is usually embarrassed in the courtroom. His credibility in the legal community is damaged but, worst of all, the credibility of our profession will have been hurt by an incompetently testifying chiropractor. If you decide to enter this field, study it carefully and — be the best!

THE ERA OF THE
MULTIPLE DOCTOR PRACTICE

How would you like to earn fifty percent to a hundred percent more income with little more work? How would you like to help two, three, or four times as many people get well without the extra work? How would you like, while you are on a two-week vacation, to have a full, bustling practice, a full office from early in the morning till late at night? You can do this with a multiple doctor practice.

Most doctors' practices are stymied only by the amount of effort the doctor is willing to expend in order to run his practice. Basically, most doctors restrict their own practices because they don't want to work any harder. They want more income yet don't want to do the work to earn it! This is natural and normal. I would challenge the doctor to work *smarter*, not harder, in order to raise the "lid" off his practice!

To see how a doctor places a lid on his own practice, consider the following examples:

A) Have you ever had a tremendous influx of new patients (six to ten in a week) and found yourself overworked as a result? You would automatically stretch out prematurely the care of your regular patients in order to ease up your schedule and to take the work load off of you. If you have ever found yourself in such a position, you are putting a lid on your practice!

B) Have you ever turned down a new patient or a regular patient for an illogical reason? The new patient may have been slightly outside your scope of practice. The regular patient may have started to give you a little static and, because you were busy, you decided you didn't want to take care of that patient any more. Can you remember back in the early years of your practice when you took care of everybody regardless of whether they gave you static or not, or when you took care of all new patients because you wanted to give them a chance at getting well? Now, you may find yourself in the position where you turn down patients because they don't fit into your mold. If this applies to you, then this is the lid you have placed on your practice!

If your practice is solo and you only have one assistant, of course you've put a lid on your practice. But wouldn't it be wiser to take care of twice as many people (provided you don't have to do twice the work), bring in additional income, and serve humanity to a fuller extent? Also, since you own the facility, wouldn't it be wiser to use it to its maximum capacity? Do you realize that you utilize your space less than one-third of a twenty-four-hour period?

Why not open up your schedule, start earlier in the morning, cover the lunch hour, and stay later at night? You could convert that extra storage room into an adjusting room. If you have a room that is of sufficient size for an adjusting room but it is full of your accumulated junk, you could hang storage cabinets from the ceiling, around the walls of your present room, and thereby open up another room for patient care. You could put another doctor into that new adjusting room!

CRITERIA FOR HIRING AN ASSOCIATE

1. 120/140 patient visits a week.
2. Case average of over $400 per case.
3. Average of $20.00 per visit.
4. Average of 15 office visits per patient.
5. 30-35 new patients per month.
6. Can comfortably give 12-15 new patients to associate.
7. Overhead at 55%.
8. Adequate facilities.
9. Adequate, efficient staff.
10. A community that can support another D.C.
11. Willingness to work harder to train new D.C.
12. Willingness to risk losing a few new patients in training the new D.C.

The first doctor that you hire should be an examining doctor. He takes the load off you, as well as increases your income. Frequently we find ourselves, when we have placed that lid on our practice, failing to re-examine our regular patients, failing to do further X-rays or additional lab work, when we really should. Our excuse usually is because we are too busy!

Have you ever had a patient say to you, "Doctor, you are supposed to re-examine me today," and you say, "Yes — let's schedule it for the next visit"? As you know, the next visit often doesn't come! The patient gets discouraged and quits coming because he's not re-examined, or re-X-rayed, as promised. Many doctors would like to give fuller service to their patients, but just don't have the time to do it.

If you have an examining doctor working for you — just doing your examinations and following your instructions — you will be able to double and triple and quadruple the amount of examinations and X-rays that you normally would give, but you don't because you are too busy. This will free your time to adjust more patients, thus doubling your income. This is what an examining doctor will do for you! Any doctor who has an examining doctor with him, can tell you that he gives better service than ever before, makes more money than ever before, and has more free time than ever before.

The question often arises: Where do I find associate doctors? Have you ever known a chiropractor who was shy, or a great chiropractor who had a great education, great mind, but no personality on which to build a practice? Have you ever known a chiropractor who just didn't have taste as far as dress was concerned, but who had good hands? Have you ever known a chiropractor who was a good adjustor, but just didn't have the confidence in his ability to get sick people well? Have you ever known a good chiropractor who just didn't make it in practice because he didn't have capital behind him to sustain himself through the first couple of years? Sure — we all know those kinds of doctors! They're out there — some of them selling shoes, some are teaching at college, some of them are practicing — and they're probably just barely existing. *These doctors are your associate doctors!* Why don't you select this type of chiropractor, put him to work for you and, at the same time, help more people get well and make yourself more money?

These doctors, under your influence and guidance, can help you have a larger practice in your office. You will make a percentage on their efforts, and you'll be doing them a favor by building them a practice at the same time. You would also be doing the people of your community a favor by getting them healed and providing extra services. You would be doing your family a favor because you'll have more time off to rest, be with them, and yet still have additional income. In other words, it is a situation where everyone wins!

There are many advantages to being an associate doctor. The owner/operator is the one who has all the responsibilities of meeting the mortgage payments, the lease payments, etc. He has the responsibility of hiring and firing the staff. If the practice is down, it is his responsibility to pick it back up. He is the motivator. It is a round-the-clock job being the owner/operator. It is a lot of stress. But all the associate has to do is show up, smile, adjust backbones, examine patients, etc.

The owner/operator may not have made a net profit in the first two years of his practice. The associate, however, makes a net profit in his *first week* of practice! He gets a regular take-home salary. He doesn't have to worry about hiring and firing. He doesn't have to worry about whether the practice is up or down. All he has to do is take care of what the owner/operator tells him to take care of.

There are many associates in this country who are making thirty or forty thousand dollars a year, and upwards, as associates with little responsibilities. How would you like to find yourself in such a position? One of the great benefits is that the associate doesn't have any of his own money tied up in the practice. How would you like someone to give you a hundred-thousand-dollar-a-year practice for free? All you would have to do is take care of it. There would be no investment on your part. You wouldn't have to buy any equipment . . . you wouldn't have to buy an x-ray machine . . . you wouldn't have to train a CA or take the CA to special training sessions. In fact, the position of an associate is a position to be envied. If an owner/operator has a lot to offer, he should not have any trouble finding the right man for his practice.

HOW MUCH SHOULD YOU PAY AN ASSOCIATE?

Many doctors have heard of fifty-fifty deals where someone pays the owner/operator fifty percent of his income in return for the use of his office. Have you ever wondered why these types of operations rarely work out? We all know doctors who have started with this type of arrangement. We also know that very few of them could make a fifty-fifty arrangement last more than a year, or two at the most. The reason for this failure rate is simple: Any growing practice worth its salt will have a fifty-five percent to sixty percent overhead or higher. If the overhead is below this, it usually means that the practice has levelled off, that the doctor has paid off his equipment, and that he is coasting. But he is losing money and doesn't even know it!

If the owner/operator has a sixty percent overhead and he pays his associate fifty percent of his associate's income, he is absolutely pulling ten percent out of his own pocket to subsidize his associate doctor. Normally, the owner/operator doesn't figure this out until the end of the year when he finds he has less spendable income. In such case, the fifty-fifty partnership usually splits up.

There are many deals in our profession where a doctor will invite another doctor into his practice as an associate to supposedly share the overhead fifty-fifty. Actually, this is not an associate position. It is a shared-expense position. However, if the overhead of this practice is so high and the practice is so low, how could it possibly support the additional overhead of another doctor? If the practice is bordering on becoming a failing business, bringing in another doctor will surely result in bringing that failing position only closer. Shared-expense agreements rarely work. They are usually put together by beginners and rarely last over one or two years.

While the fifty-fifty income or overhead splits do not work successfully, it is still definitely financially advantageous for the owner/operator to bring in associate doctors under him and feed them new patients until each associate has a full practice. At this point, the owner/operator will make ten to twenty percent profit on the labor of his associate doctors, and the associates themselves will make similar amounts. This is enough for the owner/operator to relax and take more time off. After all, he deserves it. He has probably spent fifteen to twenty years building his practice — and now, with the help of associate doctors, he is able to take time off and enjoy his family or hobbies.

Another advantage of an associate-doctor practice is seen in the event of death of the owner/operator. How much is his practice worth? If he has a solo practice, it is worth the value of his office building and the depreciated value of his office equipment — if he owns them. If the building or equipment belongs to a bank, of course the building and equipment are worth no more than the value of his equity. If he leases his equipment and/or office, these items will revert back to the leasing company upon his demise. Within a month after the chiropractor's death, his patients will have scattered, and so the value of the *good will* of his practice is minimal.

If a two-hundred-thousand-dollar-a-year doctor with leased office space and equipment passes away and his widow takes six weeks to sell his practice, how much is it worth? Most of his patients would have already transferred to other doctors and the equipment and building is owned by lending agencies. Therefore, that lucrative practice would be worth absolutely nothing to the widow within thirty to forty-five days of her husband's death!

However, if the owner/operator has an associate doctor practice and the owner/operator passes away, the associate doctors would simply continue the practice as before. Now the widow can work out arrangements with the associates to sell the practice. How much would the practice be worth? Obviously, it is worth $200,000 or more. Fortunately, the owner/operator realized that he should have some protection for his family in the event of his death.

Another advantage of a multiple doctor practice is that the owner/operator has a sounding board for professional ideas. The doctor must be mentally stimulated. He goes through chiropractic college being constantly stimulated and learning his subjects. When he gets out into practice, he is mentally stimulated by building his practice. Once he has built his practice, the mental stimulation lessens. And, at this point, his practice may start to plateau or go into a slow decline because he is bored.

With an associate doctor practice, the owner/operator has other doctors he can train, that he can work with, that he can give the benefits of his expertise. The associate doctors in turn can give him the benefits of the education they received at their different chiropractice institutions. They also have the added benefits of more up-to-date information. A multiple doctor practice keeps all doctors mentally stimulated!

Another advantage of a multiple doctor practice is the ability to specialize: one doctor could be excellent with low back problems, another on cervical problems, a third on shoulder problems, and another might be excellent with laboratory methods, etc. They can teach each other their specialties. We all practice, more or less, what is naturally right for us. Wouldn't it be a treat to have an office with five or six doctors whose natural specialties were in different areas? Think of the benefits for the patients. Such a practice is possible for every doctor.

A tandem association works especially well. In this type operation, the owner/operator provides the majority of the new patients for the associates. Since the owner/operator has been established for a longer period in the community than has his associates, he attracts new patients to himself. He assigns these new patients to his associates. The classic example of a tandem-type practice is found in the medical profession, in the OB/GYN clinics. Usually, in these clinics, all patients are seen by all doctors. Sometimes individual selection of the doctor by the patient is allowed. These clinics are usually started by one doctor who, once filled to capacity with patients, brings in an associate to take his overflow of patients. When that doctor is also filled to capacity with patients, the owner/operator hires a second associate, and so on. He pays his associates a salary plus a percentage. Usually it is split twenty percent to the owner/operator and twenty percent to the associate. However, most doctors put the associate on a guaranteed weekly salary, plus a sliding scale of percentage or gross receipts that is applied toward the guaranteed salary.

Some associate doctors may feel that a sliding scale remuneration schedule that gives the associate doctor fifteen to twenty-five percent of gross receipts is unfair. However, he should think of other businesses, such as the music business, where the entire markup on wares is ten percent. They have to borrow money from a bank to floor-plan everything they buy at fifteen to twenty percent interest just to have the items in their stores so that they can sell them! The payments on the floor-plan notes, building leases, salaries, utilities, etc., come out of the ten percent markup. The ten percent profit of a music store allows the owner to have adequate income to support himself, his family, his employees, and their families. When you compare this example with a doctor who earns twenty to twenty-five percent, then you can see that the doctor is really in excellent shape. The man who owns the music store gets rich on his five to ten percent profit margin. So can the D.C.!

This author knows an associate doctor, a millionaire, who made it entirely by working as an associate doctor. His income as an associate is over forty thousand dollars a year! The owner/operator invests this man's overage and has put him into the million-dollar category. He has never had a financial stake in that practice. He has never put up one penny for overhead. He has never put up one penny for salary, equipment, etc. Yet . . . he is a millionaire! He is an associate doctor, and he wouldn't change it for anything in the world! And, can you blame him?

BEWARE OF PITFALLS:

A. If an associate is paid too much, this will lower his motivation and incentive. Yours, too!

B. If an associate is paid too little, he'll starve!

C. Have a "no competition agreement" drawn up by an attorney. Without it, you will not be motivated to *fill up* the associate. It is to the associate's benefit that a "no competition" clause be added to the contract. He wants unrestricted referrals from you.

D. Overhead always rises with production. Don't assume that the overhead will remain the same. *It won't!* Telephone the associate doctor practices around the country. The owner/operators will verify this statement.

E. An examining doctor should increase your practice by thirty percent before he starts treating patients.

F. The associate doctor must produce three times his salary to justify his employment.

G. Don't reduce the size of *your* practice until twelve to fourteen months have elapsed after hiring an associate doctor.

H. You shouldn't plan on making money during the first six to twelve months of your associate's practice. You will lose money for the first six months because of decreased patient visits and time spent training your associate. However, money spent on this investment is money well spent.

One of the problems that a solo doctor encounters is that if he has comfortably treated a hundred and twenty patients a week for the past ten years, his income most definitely would have gone up every year, because obviously he will have raised his fees to keep pace with the cost of living. The man who made fifteen thousand dollars a year ten years ago, is now making forty thousand. However, this same man has found that he has much less buying power than he did ten years ago, and doesn't know why. The reason why is that our partner in practice — Uncle Sam — has a rule that charges a higher percentage of tax as a man's income increases, therefore, a higher percentage of his income is taken as taxes. A doctor raises his fees and, at the same time, raises his tax bracket. Uncle Sam takes a larger percentage of his income and, therefore, leaves him with less spendable income. This, combined with inflation, which raises the cost of everything he buys, is the reason he finds himself in tight straights with a successful practice.

Unless a practice is growing twenty-five to thirty percent a year, it is actually slipping backwards. At the present time, we have a twenty percent inflation rate in this country. If you add an additional ten percent, due to a change in tax brackets, you can see that a doctor has to grow thirty percent a year to stay even. Talk to your accountant about this. He will explain it fully.

The successful solo doctor has a choice of doing one of three things: (1) he can raise his prices to an excessive level. This, however, could price him out of the market as his patients might not be able to afford him; (2) he could work twice as hard trying to keep up with the rate of inflation (but who wants to work twice as hard?); or (3) he could increase his practice and his income with little extra work and without chasing his patients away. How? By adding additional doctors to his staff and have them take care of his additional patients. He will then be making a percentage of his associate doctors' income as he increases his practice. He will increase his service to his patients, thus making additional income for himself. Everyone comes out better this way. Which of these alternatives is best for you?

Some doctors will say, "There are not enough patients to

justify an associate." Once you realize that the chiropractic profession takes care of three or four percent of the population in this country, then you'll realize that ninety-six to ninety-seven percent of the people in this country are potential patients at this time. I think that we all have room to grow! The patients are out there — we just need to sell our professional services!

PRACTICE-BUILDING MOTIVATORS

A chiropractic doctor should have very little time in his office for anything other than his main purpose in life: the treatment of humanity through chiropractic methods and principles. Those important hours (office hours) have been set aside solely for the purpose of treating humanity's ailments.

While this idea is often realized in larger, thriving practices, in the smaller practice, the doctor frequently has more free time than patient-time. Therefore, he should be using his free office time to devise ways to fill his slack office hours with new patients.

Make this a rule in your office: Office time not already occupied by treatment of patients is for office work. Never do anything in these slack hours other than practice-building work. Never read anything in your office other than chiropractic or health-related material. Use every minute of practice time wisely. Every hour you are in your office should be directed towards practice growth. When you find that you have a few minutes of idle time, perform some of the "Busy Acts" designed to make the public more aware of your practice.

In the smaller practice, the doctor cannot begin treating patients until he has attracted these patients. This is what the chapter in this book, entitled "Bird-Dogging and Busy Acts" is for, so follow its guidelines carefully. Once your practice has increased, referrals will generally keep you busy, and you will have few slack hours left in your practice's working day.

Experience has shown that it is during this period of building a practice that a doctor either sets habit patterns of success or he becomes a victim of negative, failure concepts. Either he used his free time to solidify his desire, drive, and philosophy of success, or he fell prey to the crepe-hangers of the world who sold him on the idea that it "can't be done."

Therefore, the following motivators should be engraved in your mind in the same way a scupltor would etch his thoughts into granite. Whenever idle time comes your way, read this section over and over until it becomes part of your thinking process. Then you will become the doctor you want to be!

Practice-Building Motivators:

1. Keep up with the ever-changing techniques within the profession. Remember that a new technique enables you to be of better service to your patients.

2. Attend progressive seminars.

3. Establish a listening, innate, or meditation time and utilize it daily.

4. Occupy your mind with new patients, lifetime patients, results, etc.

5. Read good books and put good books in your office.

6. Build character by keeping your word — *always.*

7. Think abundance and prosperity. You don't have to be smart to think this way, and the positive determination will guide your success. You have to think anyway, so why not think abundance?

8. Associate with successful people. Be certain to select friends of good character, those who have positive outlooks.

9. Remember, you control your thoughts. Keep an eternal vigilance on your attitude.

10. Motivate yourself with logic, reason, and fact. Motivate others with emotion.

11. Either be the Best Chiropractor or be the Best Something Else, but don't try to be everything to everybody.

12. Have office hours and keep them. Start on time, but finish only after the last patient has been seen.

13. Don't call other chiropractors to see how business is going unless you know their business is better than yours.

14. Don't take advice from a failure or one who doesn't produce or practice what he preaches.

15. Don't vacillate in your thinking. It is important to think, but it is ten times more important to control that thinking and to be firm in the positions you take.

16. Don't become emotionally involved with problems outside your office over which you have little control.

17. Don't fail to appreciate people and to show your faith in them.

18. Always have a positive attitude when dealing with the public. People are automatically attracted to a positive, enthusiastic individual. Remember, you are selling yourself and your profession.

19. Don't forget to love your patients, your practice, and your profession of chiropractic.

20. Don't fail to have a mirror in your office. Constantly check your appearance. Remember, first impressions count.

21. Don't fail to act and to think in terms of what you can do for others.

22. Don't fail to be energetic. Enthusiasm is the yeast that raises the dough; little low, no dough!

23. Don't set foot in your office on a Monday — or on any day — until you have a cause, a vision, and an organized desire.

24. Make sure your telephone is covered 24 hours a day.

25. W.O.C. means "Whip Out Cards" — *Fast!* Always carry an abundant, easily reached supply of business cards to avoid groping.

26. Make "lemonade" out of the "lemons" you receive in life. That is what "lemons" are for!

27. Do not chat idly with your receptionist or spouse whenever you have a break in your schedule. Use the time productively.

28. Do talk about and show your enthusiasm for Noble Causes, i.e., saving lives and restoring health.

29. Be 100% convinced about every service you render. Don't do something just for show or because you were taught to.

30. To give the best service, you must feel that you are the best chiropractor anywhere. If you don't feel this way, change yourself *NOW!*

31. Do give patients instructions and make certain they are followed.

32. If you are a recent graduate, it is advisable to obtain experience with a successful D.C.

33. Do something newsworthy!

34. Don't give a report of findings to a patient without the patient's spouse being present.

35. Be as well-dressed as your best-dressed patient.

36. Be more positive than your most negative patient.

37. Be available when patients need you.

38. Building a practice in your community requires intense desires and convictions.

39. Get to know and love your community. Share its assets with everyone; let them know how you feel.

40. You are always a doctor, so wherever you go, dress like one. You never know when the unexpected might happen.

41. Set goals and keep raising them.

42. The blood, sweat, and tears of determination and effort you expend today will affect your success for years to come.

43. Experience has shown that if a doctor doesn't "make it" in the first ninety days, he won't make it. If he does make it later on, it was because he changed his attitudes, his motivations, etc. If you find your practice growth stymied and you have been in practice longer than ninety days, attend progressive seminars, etc., to change your concepts and thus your practice.

44. "Image" new patients coming to you.

45. Spend "non-busy" time contacting people by personal notes.

46. Make it a point to say something good and inspiring to everyone you meet. Have the whole community speaking well of you.

47. Be enthusiastic.

48. Do that which you dare to do.

49. Use your idle time to eliminate your idle time!

50. Thought alone is only thought. Actions make the thoughts a reality.

51. The successful doctor does what the failure doctor fails to do.

52. Nothing happens unless someone makes it happen.

53. Use the "Law of the Vacuum": A vacuum always seeks to be filled. If there is no vacuum, there is no force to fill. The doctor who fills his time with idle reading, telephone conversations, etc., will never use the Law of the Vacuum in his favor. Finding idle time in your office should create some restlessness within you. You should never be content with an empty office, but should have an ever-continuing desire — backed by a willingness to work — to fill your office with patients. Never accept anything other than a full office.

54. Success and achievement are based on knowledge and action.

55. It is wise to spend a little more money and get quality business cards. Quality cards denote a quality doctor.

56. Every time you leave your office, you should try to meet three new people.

57. Educate those who have open minds to the benefits of chiropractic. This is best carried out by giving a testimonial. If you yourself have been helped by chiropractic, this could be your best method.

58. Patronize local businesses in your area. When doing business with your neighbors, you are insuring their business with you.

59. Contact as many people as possible with the attitude: "I love this town. I love the people in this town. I feel good about this town."

60. Give service for the sake of giving service.

61. Everything that you have ever wanted is achievable. But you must totally commit yourself to that achievement.

62. Seek advice, even when you feel you know the answers.

63. As you become better known in the community, your practice will grow in size and prestige.

64. Become involved in some activity to make your name known.

65. If someone tells you, "I'll tell some of my friends about

you, Doc," you should send him three of your business cards. This will remind him of his offer and will make it easier for him to tell his friends about you.

66. If you want a referral practice, you must commit yourself to teaching the scope of chiropractic to your patients. friends and relatives.

67. Send Thank-U-Grams to everyone for everything. Write legibly — especially your name.

68. "The sooner you get the dollar out of your mind — the sooner you will get it in your pocket" — according to Edward L. Kramer.

69. Don't allow the patient's wallet or the way he dresses determine what services you will render. Give everyone first class care, and the finances will take care of themselves.

70. The Golden Rule (and doing it one better): "Do unto others as you would have them do unto your very own mother or father, as you would prefer more for them than for yourself."

71. Read this chapter and the one on "Bird-Dogging and Busy Acts" daily, and see what can be done to build your practice. There is always something to get out in the mail, some calls to make, and some people to meet.

SUCCESS IS EASY IF YOU KNOW THE ROAD TO SUCCESS.
This book is your road . . . follow it!

POTPOURRI OF
PRACTICE-BUILDING IDEAS

This section of the book is a potpourri of articles written previously by this author on practice building and practice management. I am sure that even though the figures in these articles are "dated," the principles are still the same and will definitely contribute to practice growth. My special thanks to Doctors Jim and Karl Parker of the Parker School for Professional Success and *Share International Magazine*, and to Mr. William Luckey of *Chiropractic Economics Magazine*, for their gracious permission in reproducing these articles.

HOW TO "BREAK THE BARRIER" AND
HANDLE MORE PATIENTS PER DAY

Stack-A-Day

Expanding a chiropractic practice is many times simply a matter of breaking barriers. If a doctor is treating fifteen to eighteen patients a day and has many times tried unsuccessfully to see twenty patients a day, the "twenty-patients-a-day" concept can become a barrier. If another D.C. tries unsuccessfully to build his practice to a thirty-patient level, it could be the "thirty-patients-a-day" that becomes this doctor's barrier.

Many times we set our goals at a certain level but, at the same time, we do not really believe it is possible to attain these goals. A doctor who sees fifteen patients per day is usually completely busy with these fifteen patients. Therefore, no matter how many times he says to himself, "I want to see twenty per day," his subconscious mind is actually telling him, "Who am I kidding? I am totally busy seeing fifteen. I couldn't possibly see twenty patients in one day's time."

Barriers in practice growth are simply mental barriers, and if we can change our mental concepts, the mental barriers will be eliminated. The easiest way to overcome our mental barriers is to *do what we think we cannot do.*

I have a very simple procedure that has helped me build my practice and overcome any mental barriers that creep into my mind. I simply research my appointment book records to determine the largest number of patients I saw on each day of the week. These figures will look something like this:

M	T	W	Th	F	S
25	18	22	16	27	18

At this point, I systematically set out to break each day's record. If my goal for a certain day is thirty patients, I pick that day two weeks in the future and tell my C.A. that by scheduling everyone we can think of, we are going to see forty patients on that day. If I have a patient on a once-a-month, once-a-week, or once-every-two-weeks basis, he is scheduled on that day.

After a two-month period of time, I have shattered each day's record and, in doing so, have doubled my practice. I proved to my subconscious mind that I absolutely could see thirty patients a day, thus breaking my mental barrier.

I have shared this little trick with thousands of D.C.'s around the country, and they have reported to me that they have had the same success in their practices.

Many D.C.'s reading this article will undoubtedly tell themselves that this "stacking-a-day" might work fine for a small practice, but wouldn't work for their larger practices. Not true! Many years ago, I found myself at a forty-patients-per-day barrier. I tried everything I knew to break this barrier . . . everything but my "stack-a-day" trick.

As I always do when I find myself with a practice problem, I hopped on the next jet for a practice management seminar. Throughout the seminar, I talked with our largest practitioners, searching for the answer to my problem. Finally, I talked with the sage, Dr. Earl Bush of California, telling him my sad story.

Earl looked up at me and said, "Pete, do you really want to get over your forty-per-day barrier? Really? If so, you simply have to STACK A DAY, and you will overcome your mental barrier."

I had overlooked the one simple method that had elevated my practice to its present status. To make a long story short, I returned home, "stacked a day," and was immediately seeing sixty patients a day.

Try it! You'll like it!

PRACTICE BUILDING DURING
AN ELECTION YEAR

It is frequently said: "If you want to double your practice, double the people who know you."

Here is an ethical, surefire way to double the number of people who know you and, at the same time, contribute to the electoral process that has made our country great.

The first step is to contact the political party of your preference, volunteering to help elect your party's candidates.

The next step is to meet with the election chairman, explaining that being busy in your practice, you have only limited time to devote to your candidates and, therefore, would like:

1. A list of names and addresses of all your political party's members *around your office.*

2. Enough literature on all your party's candidates to cover the list of party members around your office.

3. Permission to contact personally each party member on the mailing list, and

4. The opportunity to meet the candidates to ask pertinent questions as to how they feel about some important issues.

Set up a schedule of your Saturdays and other days off to walk the precinct around your office, meeting the people on the mailing list, handing out electoral literature, and extolling the virtues of your candidates. Here is the procedure to follow:

"Hello, I'm Dr. Smith. I'm a local chiropractor. My office is at [address]. I'm here on behalf of the Republican/Democrat Party [hand the person one of your business cards to identify yourself]. I'd like to give you some literature on *our* party's candidates, recommend these candidates to you, and answer any questions you may have regarding these candidates, as I know them personally." (You met them — remember?)

Hand out the literature, discuss the candidates, and answer any questions. End the conversation with, "Thank you very much, neighbor. It's nice meeting you. Let's try to get out and vote for our candidates."

Then move on to the next name on your list and repeat the process.

It's entirely possible that you will meet fifty to seventy-five of your neighbors each day that you walk the precinct. If you do this for ten days, you'll meet five hundred to seven hundred and fifty new people. They'll know who you are, what you are, where you practice, and that you're a good guy because you belong to the same party that they do.

Will they ask you questions about chiropractic? You bet they will! Will you get new patients from this procedure? You bet — lots of them! Because, if twice as many people know who you are, your practice will be twice as big. It's as simple as that.

What about the candidates whom you helped get elected? Will they appreciate all the footwork you have exerted on their behalf, getting them elected? You bet they will! And when chiropractic legislation is in question, all you'll have to do is call the candidates and ask for their support. They'll gladly give it to you.

One thing to remember: the candidates *never* forget the people who helped them get elected; it is those people to whom they owe their allegiance.

This is a much-tested practice building aid. The D.C.'s in St. Petersburg, Florida, have gladly donated their time, efforts, and shoe leather to getting their candidates elected and, therefore, have reaped the benefits of larger practices and an appreciative legislative delegation.

Try this idea, doctors. You'll be glad you did.

Thousands of Dollars of Free Publicity Received . . .
HOW TO CONDUCT A
FOOTBALL TRAINING CLINIC

It's football time again! The chiropractors of St. Petersburg, Florida, reaped thousands of dollars of publicity, made hundreds of good personal contacts, and provided the public with a much-needed service, and all of this was accomplished with the investment of only a few hours' time and about two hundred dollars. How? We sponsored a football "Training Clinic."

Training Clinic? What's that? No, we didn't train boys to play football. We taught the coaches how to treat athletic injuries . . . taught them to be football "trainers."

The theme of our clinic was "How to prevent minor injuries from becoming major injuries." Understandably, this theme is the reason our clinic was an instant success.

The biggest problem the coaches encounter is not in getting good players, but keeping the players healthy. The largest need of high school coaches is to learn how to prevent needless injuries and to hold down staggering insurance costs, through proper "training" methods. By sponsoring this clinic, we filled a need and reaped the benefits.

Major injuries cost professional football five million dollars per year. The majority of these injuries were simply an aggravation of

199

minor injuries. Imagine how these figures are compounded in high school athletics when the players are not in superb physical condition or do not have available the outstanding trainers and facilities of the professional ranks.

Here is How to Present a Football Training Clinic In Your Area

Have a well-known college trainer conduct the clinic for you. The key to this clinic is the fact that the chiropractic profession only sponsors the clinic; the professional trainer does the teaching.

This trainer should be from one of your state universities and be well known and respected by all the high school coaches and news writers in your area. HE is the reason your clinic will be a success; the coaches will turn out to hear HIM. If you don't know a good trainer, ask three or four local coaches or the local sports editors, and you will soon find out whom they respect.

Proper Timing

The ideal date for this type seminar is one week before spring football practice starts, usually the first week in August. At this point, the coaches are very enthusiastic about the upcoming season, while still having time to attend your "Training Clinic."

Proper Advance Notice to the Coaches

Here is how to notify the coaches. First, compile a list of coaches. This can be done by calling the Board of Education, parochial schools, and private schools for the names and addresses of all their coaches.

Engraved announcements are sent to all coaches telling them that your Chiropractic Society is sponsoring a football training clinic, telling them who will be teaching it, and what the theme will be. Emphasize that the purpose of the seminar is to teach the coaches how to prevent minor athletic injuries from becoming major injuries, not only preventing pain and discomfort to the players, but actually keeping them in the game. The coaches' prime interest is to keep the boys playing.

The announcement is to be mailed at the beginning of July and is followed by a typewritten letter reminding them of the seminar, informing them where it will be held, and telling them they are welcome. This letter is mailed in mid-July. Next, telephone the coaches two or three days prior to the clinic, reminding them for the third time what the seminar will consist of and that they are welcome.

How to Obtain Public Relations

This is the simplest part of the plan. With football season coming up, all sports writers at this time are enthusiastic and anxious to write anything about it.

Contact all TV stations in your area, as they, too, are looking for any news about sports. Tell them who you are, what the seminar will be, who will teach it, and that you would like them to mention it on the air or, if possible, have you as a guest on a program to explain what the seminar is about. They will be happy to do so. I personally was on TV twice, explaining that the seminar was a public service of the chiropractic profession, and at the same time I was plugging chiropractic.

The trainer who teaches your seminar will be happy to go on TV and explain what the seminar pertains to. If you tell the TV announcer that the trainer will be happy to speak, he will jump at the chance to have him on his show. Actually, in sports circles, the trainers are big celebrities.

Also, invite the TV stations to take pictures of the "Training Clinic," showing how hard the coaches study to prevent their athletes from being injured. They will do it because it is a good public interest story.

Then to the newspapers. Introduce yourself to the sports editors. Tell them what the county society is doing, and ask them for as much free publicity as they can possibly give you so the seminar will be a success. They are happy to do this. Our training clinic was mentioned in two or three newspapers on numerous occasions, encouraging the coaches to go to the seminar. Also, welcome the newspapers to take pictures of the seminar if they so desire, and they will do so.

Contact the radio stations and tell them the same thing. They will give you free publicity. All publicity should start about two weeks prior to the seminar.

Length of the Clinic

The clinic consists of one Saturday's instruction — a morning session of two hours, and an afternoon session of three hours. This is all the time the trainer will need to teach this course.

Handling injuries of the upper extremity should be taught in the morning session, and the lower extremity injuries in the afternoon session. Don't let the coaches know when the lower extremity will be taught. If the coaches know this, some of them will attend only the afternoon session, because they are primarily concerned with knee injuries.

Participation of the Chiropractors

At the beginning of the clinic, the president of your society should welcome the coaches, tell them who is sponsoring the seminar, the purpose of the seminar, and introduce the trainer who will conduct the clinic. After this, the chiropractors just mingle with the coaches, getting acquainted with them.

Midway through the morning session, the president of the local society tells the coaches that the Doctors of Chiropractic are licensed physicians and are qualified to run physical examinations on the boys, to play football or any other sport. He also tells them that the county society has examining teams of chiropractors who will be happy to examine the boys free of charge.

In my opinion, all county societies should have these examining teams; this also is great for public relations.

Necessary Supplies

Make sure that you have a high school boy who is willing to be taped; you must have a live figure for the trainer to show his art. Athletic injury literature can be obtained from the ACA or ICA, and should be available. Training supplies can be obtained free of charge from Johnson and Johnson, Bike Tape Co., or any other tape manufacturer. The trainer will give you a list of necessary supplies.

Finances

The trainer will usually charge two to three hundred dollars, plus traveling expenses and overnight accommodation, usually approximately six hundred dollars. Printing expenses and literature will run about seventy-five dollars. Facilities for the clinic are usually donated by a local motel or hotel. Total cost is approximately seven hundred dollars.

Follow Up

After the seminar is over, a letter is mailed to all the coaches, thanking them for attending the seminar and inviting them to next year's seminar. Include in this letter a piece of literature on athletic injuries.

Have county society examining teams. A team of three doctors can examine thirty boys in one and a half hours, and these examinations can be scheduled at the doctors' convenience. One year in St. Petersburg, Florida, a three-doctor team examined a hundred and fifty boys for football, basketball, wrestling, and track.

This year we plan to initiate a program that will cover all high school athletes, approximately one thousand. All of this can be done with no loss of office hours. It's a lot of fun and we have a chance to meet many coaches, teachers, principals, players, and parents.

Make sure that all high schools have a chiropractor as a team physician and that he attends each football game. This brings chiropractic to the attention of thousands of fans. It also acquaints the boys with chiropractic care, because later they will become your patients.

This is one of the easiest county society functions you can sponsor. The rewards are outstanding. Not only are the coaches and players informed about chiropractic, but the rewards received from public relations are tremendous. I recommend it highly.

HOW I'VE MASTERED THE MOST IMPORTANT FUNDAMENTAL OF OFFICE PROCEDURE . . . *CONSULTATION*

Patient drop-out after only three or four visits is one of the biggest problems the average chiropractor encounters. I have found that early patient drop-out is usually due to his lack of confidence in the doctor and/or in the doctor's knowledge of a particular problem. At what point does the doctor instill confidence in the patient and at the same time gain the knowledge of the patient's problem? The obvious answer to this question is in the consultation.

It is my opinion that the most important time you will ever spend with a patient is during your initial contact with him while in consultation. An examination performed on a patient who has no confidence in the doctor is ineffective.

A report of findings given after an unimpressive consultation will also be ineffective. Therefore, since the consultation is where we make our first and lasting impression upon a patient, it behooves us to make our first impression a good one.

This article will center on how to conduct a proper consultation. I realize that many of the readers will consider this article very fundamental. You bet it is! The doctor who masters the fundamentals is the doctor who masters success.

All of us remember the late Vince Lombardi, the great coach of the Green Bay Packers football team. He won many world championships on just simple fundamentals. His teams were characterized by their repertoire of only a few dozen plays, while most other professional football teams had hundreds of plays.

How, then, did he win his games? The other teams surely knew what his plays were, and how to set their defenses against them. The answer is simple. His players mastered the fundamentals of these few plays so well that when these plays were executed, they were done in so perfect a manner that the other teams were powerless to stop them.

The same is true of a physician's practice, when he masters the fundamentals, all defenses and objections will be overcome.

After conducting thousands of consultations and attending many seminars, I have subdivided my consultations into six stages.

Stage I: *Greet the patient with a smile and a warm handshake.*

Stage II: *Establish a common bond.*

This procedure is obvious to all who read this article. This is done merely by talking briefly and enthusiastically with the patient about the person who referred him, mutual membership in a civic club, etc.

Stage III: *Strive to understand the patient's problem — as he understands it.*

Ask the obvious questions: "Tell me, Mrs. Jones, what seems to be your problem?" It is important to have the patient thoroughly explain his/her health problem to you.

Once the patient has fully disclosed his problem, the doctor then follows this very important procedure. The doctor *parrots* the patient's history back to him. This is accompanied in the following manner: The doctor states, "Now, let's see if I understand your problem correctly. Please correct me if I'm wrong." Then he proceeds to repeat the patient's history to him, verbatim, if possible.

This accomplishes two things: It determines if the doctor has completely understood what the patient has told him, and it impresses the patient with the fact that the doctor understands his problem as he understands it.

This last point is highly important. The patient probably quit his previous doctor — not because he didn't think he was a good doctor, but because he felt that the doctor didn't really understand his particular problem at that time.

Stage IV: *Interrogate the patient and qualify the problem as to area of origin.*

This is the area I feel most doctors do not pursue in depth. If this stage of the consultation is properly pursued, there is a possibility that the doctor will be able to make an accurate, tentative diagnosis prior to examination. The following x-rays and examination merely substantiate the tentative diagnosis the doctor has made during consultation.

When I say "interrogate" the patient, that is precisely what I mean! Visualize yourself as a captain in the Army who has just captured an enemy general — one who is willing to tell everything he knows. How would you interrogate him? Would you be thorough in questioning him, trying to pry every bit of knowledge out of him? You bet you would! This is the same thoroughness that you should use when interrogating a patient about his health problems.

The following is a list of topics that pertain solely to spinal injuries and the possible rationale, designated by parentheses, which I use in regard to these questions.

Lumbar Questions

1. Are you aware when and how this happened? (Mechanics of the injury.)

2. Did you feel a tearing or ripping? (This may indicate spasm or disc injury.)

3. Does this interfere with your work or living habits? (This pinpoints mechanics of pain production.)

4. How do you feel upon arising in the morning? (If gradual onset of pain, this may indicate a possible strain or sprain. If immediate pain upon assuming the erect posture, this may indicate a nerve root pressure.)

5. What time of day is pain worse? (See above.)

6. What posture aggravates the pain? What position eases the pain? (When forward bending aggravates the pain, this may indicate a disc involvement. When backward bending aggravates the pain, this may indicate a facet inflammation or nerve root pressure.)

7. Do you have difficulty sleeping? What position is most comfortable? (In sciatica and disc injury, the patient is more comfortable lying on one side, and is unable to assume another position. A patient with a strain or sprain is more comfortable on his back.)

8. Does heat or cold affect the pain? (Heat usually eases a muscle involvement and aggravates a nerve involvement.)

9. Does the patient suddenly wake up at night in pain? (This indicates possible malignancy.)

10. Does the pain move up or down the spine? (This may indicate muscle spasms.)

11. Does aspirin relieve the pain? (Aspirin may relieve a muscular problem but rarely a disc and/or nerve involvement.)

12. Does coughing, sneezing, or straining to move the bowels produce pain? (This indicates a disc injury.)

13. Is there numbness or tingling in the feet or legs? (This indicates possible discogenic nerve involvement.)

14. Is there continuous or intermittent radiating pain? (Intermittent pain may indicate disc injury. Constant pain may indicate inflamed nerve trunk.)

15. Does the pain go down your leg? (This indicates discogenic nerve involvement.)

16. Is there impaired sexual activity? (If not due to pain, this may indicate a possible sacral plexus nerve involvement.)

17. Does pain radiate into the abdomen? (This indicates possible nerve paralysis.)

18. Is there impairment of bowel or urinary function? (This may indicate autonomic nervous system involvement.)

19. TYPES OF PAIN: Stabbing (nerve pain); Throbbing (presence of edema or hemorrhaging into tissues); Sharp (nerve pain); Dull (muscle pain); Grabbing (muscle spasm); Shooting (nerve radiation); Cramping (anoxeria); Toothache (constant nerve root irritation); Dull ache (muscular strain).

Cervical Questions

Most questions that apply to the lumbar region are also applicable to the cervical region.

1. Do you hear grating sounds? (Cartilage of joint is affected.)

2. Is there arm and shoulder pain? (This indicates a possible radicular involvement.)

3. Do you have difficulty in turning your head? (This indicates muscle spasm, inflammation of facets, or disc injury.)

4. Is there numbness of the hands or fingers? (Numbness in a few fingers [dermatome level] may indicate nerve involvement. Numbness in all fingers may indicate impaired circulation.)

5. Are there headaches? (Some types are due to ischemia of the brain or nerve involvement.)

6. Is there pain and pressure behind the eyes? (Superior occipital nerves are involved, or a sinus involvement.)

7. Is there nausea? (Autonomic nervous system is involved or a cerebral concussion.)

8. Is there difficulty in swallowing? (This indicates nerve paralysis.)

9. Is there chest pain? (This may indicate autonomic nervous system involvement, a heart problem, or nerve root pressure, etc.)

10. Is there increased nervousness and irritability? (This indicates autonomic nervous system involvement.)

11. Is there a neck injury that affects vision, hearing, balance, or causes a ringing in the ears? (This may indicate autonomic nervous system involvement.)

12. Do you sleep with or without a pillow? (Not using a pillow

may aggravate a facet injury.)

13. Do you read in bed or lie down to watch TV? (This may aggravate a facet injury.)

This is a partial list of questions used in qualifying a patient's problem. Once you are through asking these and similar questions, you should have made a tentative diagnosis of a muscle, nerve, joint, or disc injury. I'm sure that the reader will have many additional questions that he would like to add to this list. Use them all! The patient will be impressed at the thoroughness of your interrogation, and you will have qualified the injury.

Stage V: *Dig for chronicity.*

Questions similar to the following will aid you in this quest.

1. Have you ever had this problem before?
2. Think back — back to when you were a child. Did you have it then?
3. Does anyone in your family have this type of problem?
4. Have you had former treatments for this type of problem?
5. Have you ever had a bad fall?
6. Have you ever been in an automobile accident?
7. Have you ever had surgery?
8. Have you ever been hospitalized?
9. Did you ever play football, etc.?

Stage VI: *Descriptive close.*

After I establish chronicity, I usually end the consultation by proceeding into the descriptive close by saying, "Why don't you slip on a gown [remove your shirt] and let's see what is causing your problem?" I feel that this is the most logical method to bring a consultation to a conclusion.

If the reader will follow these simple steps in consultation, I am sure that early patient drop-out will be greatly eliminated. The patient will be impressed by the doctor's understanding of his problem as he understands it, and will be amazed at how thorough the doctor was in his interrogation. If you are a winner with your consultation, you will be a winner throughout the care of your patient.

Let me relate a personal experience that I encountered with a consultation that I had on a health problem.

Many years ago I had an elusive urinary problem. Many urologists were consulted and many varying opinions were set forth, all incorrect. One day I consulted my fifth or sixth urologist.

The doctor entered the consultation room with a big smile and gave me a warm, friendly handshake, making me feel welcome. Immediately he mentioned the D.C. who referred me to him, and how much he thought of this man (common bond).

He then asked me what my problem was. After I purged myself of my problem, he then repeated my problem to me to see if he understood it correctly. Then he asked a series of qualifying questions to zero in on the problem. When he finished interrogating me, he knew exactly what my problem was and, more importantly, I knew that he KNEW what my problem was!

Was I impressed? You bet! After four or five doctors had failed miserably on my health problem, this doctor, by using only proper consultation methods, was able to determine my problem accurately. I salute this physician for his thoroughness.

I feel that if the real professionals are extremely thorough in their consultations, this behooves me to be as thorough and to recommend these methods to you. Remember: the last objective of a consultation is to have the patient say to himself upon leaving the office, "I'm glad I went to this doctor." If you will use the above described procedures, this is exactly the impression HE will have.

An Enlarged Appointment Book
Increased My Daily Patient Visits by Fifteen!
HERE'S HOW AND WHY

I'm a doctor who likes gimmicks. When I refer to a "gimmick" I am not talking about a trinket or a toy that will increase my practice. I'm referring to a gimmick that will trigger my imagination and enthusiasm and thus move me up-scale to success.

One of my favorite gimmicks is how I motivate my Innate to obtain new patients.

Whenever my new patient volume is down, or whenever I need new patients for some particular reason, I move into action in this manner:

1. All x-rays are immediately developed, dried, analyzed, posted, labeled, and filed.

2. Any unfiled x-rays are immediately marked and filed.

3. Patients' folders, not in their proper place, are immediately filed.

4. All insurance forms are filled out and mailed.

5. My desk is cleaned off and polished.

6. My C.A.'s desk receives the same treatment.

7. Old magazines are thrown out and new ones are put in.

8. Pre-history questionnaires are placed in clipboards, ready to use.

SAMPLE APPOINTMENT SHEETS

With Scratch-Outs

9		
15	Parker	Taylor
30	Bates	Taylor
45	Wilson	~~Allen~~
10	~~Horth~~ Squires	Squires
15	Runnels	Hiants
30	Brown	~~Lorno~~ Wall
45	~~Larson~~	Fenton
11	Vetter	Phillips
15	Shankes	Woodward
30	Bloomberg	
45	Sherif	Evans
2	Waters	Fernandez
15	~~Holly~~	Jones Smith
30	Edwards	
45	Flori	Doe

With Erasures

9		
15	Parker	Taylor
30	Bates	Taylor
45	Wilson	
10		Squires
15	Runnels	Treble
30	Brown	
45		Wall
11	Vetter	Fenton
15	Shankes	Phillips
30	Bloomberg	
45	Sherif	Evans
2	Waters	Fernandez
15	Edwards	Jones
30	Flori	
45		Doe

9. The x-ray solutions are stirred vigorously, rinse water is cleaned, and hangers put in their proper places.

Now I'm set! Innate has received the message that I am ready for new patients, and the new patients will start flowing.

How or why this gimmick works is simply by letting Innate know you are ready for, and expecting new patients. It drives this message home with the enthusiasm obtained from the action steps of preparation for these new patients. It is easy.

Thought + Action + Enthusiasm = Results!

How do I know that new patients can be obtained in this manner? I once was a heavy advertiser. I found that every time I mailed out any literature, my biggest influx of new patients was three or four days *prior* to the actual mailing, with no exceptions! Actually, the largest new patient influx was while I was in the process of addressing the mailouts. Naturally, it is at this point that our enthusiasm was the highest and we had an expectation of receiving these patients. This method of new patient procurement is borne out by experience, not just idle philosophy.

How to Use Your Appointment Book for Growth and Practice Stability

Another workable "gimmick" I use in my office is the proper use of my appointment book.

Always have an appointment book that has many more spaces for appointments than patients you are presently seeing. If you now serve thirty patients per day, you should have a fifty-patient-per-day appointment book. If you see fifty per day, you should have a hundred spaces per day in your appointment book.

Why more spaces than necessary? It's obvious! If your book has twenty-eight appointment spaces (as do most "complimentary" appointment books), and you have twenty appointments scheduled, forget about dreaming of fifty patients per day and don't even mark up your goals at fifty per day, because you will never reach it. Why?

Whenever you look at the book and see it full, automatically your Innate receives the message that "I'm full . . . can't see any more today . . . I don't need any more," and not "needing" any more patients, you won't get any! This not only cuts off your flow of new patients, but also that of former patients. This is an important point to remember. Now, think of the effect that this "full" appointment book has on your C.A. She is the one who controls the appointment book and your schedule. If she sees the schedule is "full," she will immediately turn off all the new and/

or former patients. This will happen every time, as she thinks: "The doctor just can't see any more patients." When I switched from the outmoded book I was using to an enlarged appointment book, I had a jump of *fifteen patients per day within a month*, from no other source than the new appointment book! My C.A. and I were amazed!

When writing on your appointment book, USE PENCIL ONLY. Why? Because whenever a patient reschedules his appointment, the C.A. can erase his name, leaving a vacant space. Important? You bet!

Look at the appointment sheets on Page 209. One appears full, the other has plenty of available appointment spaces. Both, however, have the same amount of available appointments. The appointment schedule on the left was filled out with pen. Whenever a patient rescheduled an appointment, the only way the C.A. could cancel the name was to scratch a line through it. Granted, this space is now officially open to another patient, but whenever the C.A. and/or you look at the page, it appears full and you will automatically schedule the patient for another day.

Imagine your C.A. writing a receipt for one patient, pulling a file on another patient, and making an appointment over the telephone, all at the same time! Do you think that at this rushed period in her schedule that she is going to carefully scrutinize the appointment schedule for an empty space? Heck no — she will just glance at it, and if it appears full, she will schedule the patient for another day.

You may say that it doesn't matter if the patient comes another day because you will still see him anyway. Not so! If a former patient calls you, he is not calling you just to come in to spend the time of day. He is hurting and needs you NOW! Your duty as a doctor is to see him, if possible. Also, whenever a former patient calls in and is hurting, it is not just a one-visit proposition. Putting him off one day may mean the difference of seeing him two or three visits that week.

I don't have to elaborate on putting off a new patient for one day. He may go to someone else, a distinct possibility if he is in pain.

If you put off one former patient per day throughout the year, you can figure on a loss of $3,750.00 that year. Quite silly, because you had the time; only the use of a pen on the appointment book prevented you from seeing that the time was available. Imagine the loss if this happened two, three, or four times per day! Get with it! Always write appointments with pencil.

How to Use the Appointment Book for
Practice Control

1. Add up the patients you see each day (excluding new patients) and post this number at the top of the page.

2. The next figure to be posted will be the number of new patients seen that day.

3. The third figure is how much money was taken in that day.

4. The fourth figure is how many patients missed appointments; add to this figure the number of patients who called and said they will call you later.

5. The last figure is how many former patients your C.A. called today and made new appointments for.

The figures at the top of each day's appointment schedule should look like this:

$$45 - 3 - 325 - 3 - 3$$

Do this each day and total at the end of the week.

Example: $170 - 10 - 2005 - 8 - 11$

Now transpose these figures to a master chart in your dark room.

For further elaboration and review of this Practice Control procedure, please refer to the following "Slip and Check" article.

By using these proven "gimmicks," you will be amazed, doctors, at the resultant increase in traffic in your office. They REALLY WORK!

HOW I USE A "SLIP AND CHECK" SYSTEM FOR PRACTICE CONTROL

How would you like to analyze your practice in regard to growth of patient volume, new patients, income, patient drop-out, and patient recall — and do it all in thirty seconds? Also, compare this week to last week, to last month, and to last year — all in the same thirty seconds. Interested? Read on!

The mark of a truly successful practitioner depends upon his capability not only of building a practice, but of maintaining it at a high level, and then to climb higher. If we look around at outstanding chiropractors, one factor we are sure to observe is their ability to eliminate fluctuations of cycling in their practices.

A practice which fluctuates between six thousand dollars one month, two thousand dollars the next, and five thousand dollars the next, is extremely frustrating to the practitioner. This cycling makes it impossible for him to know where he stands financially, plan investments, pay bills efficiently, or plan for vacations, etc.

Why do practitioners go through cycles? It's obvious the doctor doesn't usually know why his practice went up in the first place, or down in the second place. By the time he notices that there is a decline, it's too late, the cycle has started downward and it may take weeks to recover. This type of practice is like a game of chance: sometimes you win; sometimes you lose.

The object of my "slip and check" system for practice control is to be able to predict the start of a cycle at a glance. It shows when the cycle is on an upward trend in income and patient volume, enables me to determine why it is going up, so that I can pour on the coals to ride this upward wave and enlarge upon the upward trend. It also shows when the practice is starting a downward trend, helps me determine what has gone wrong and what appropriate steps should be taken to stop it.

Sound complicated? Not at all! As a matter of fact, this will be the easiest and cheapest office procedure you have ever initiated. Time consuming? No! This procedure takes no time from the doctor as the C.A. does all the work, and she can put the system into operation with only two or three minutes' time per day. Expensive? No! About five cents is all it will cost!

Here's what we do:

The C.A.:

1. Notes the missed appointments in the appointment book.

2. Notes the "reset" appointments that have been rescheduled.

3. Writes three figures at the top of page used in appointment book each day. These figures are simply: (a) Total regular patients seen that day; (b) Total new patients seen that day; and (c) Total cash received that day.

Example: 45 / 2 / $350

I believe all doctors already have a procedure similar to this. For, how are we going to know where we are going if we don't know where we have been?

The reason this is done daily is that we all should have daily goals. If we see that the first two days of the week are down in patient volume, new patients, or income, we can go like mad and not let the rest of the week be bad also, thus stopping a downward cycle before it gains momentum. If the first two days are excellent in all respects, great! Pour on the coals for a record week. Now you have spotted an upward trend and need to enhance it.

The second step of the procedure is for the C.A. to total the figures above at the end of the week — in this order:

1. Total regular patient volume.
2. Total new patients.
3. Total cash.
4. Total missed appointments.
5. Total rescheduled patients ("resets").

Example: 150 / 7 / $1250 / 6 / 4
This is entered just under Saturday's appointment schedule.

Looks confusing? Complicated? Too detailed? Absolutely not! It's simple and didn't take more than two or three minutes of the C.A.'s time.

Doctors, it's what you do with these figures that will determine whether or not you can break a downward cycle or enhance upon an upward cycle, thereby completely controlling all aspects of your practice by preventing fluctuations.

The C.A. takes this list of five figures and puts it on a chart that you may hang in the dark room. In my office, the chart is a piece of white paper, 44"x18". This sheet is divided into four parts for 1978, 1979, 1980, and 1981. Each year has five weekly columns and a sixth column for monthly totals. (See Page 218.)

Now stop reading this article for a second and look at the chart. Observe the total patients seen weekly. If this figure is going upward, wonderful! But don't just stop here.

Look at the other figures and see why you are increasing. Are the total patient visits declining? Bad news! Look at the other figures and see why. Are the total income figures going up or down? Look at the other figures and see why.

Here is the rationale I use in determining why each figure will vary from week to week.

Figure #1— Total Patient Volume

Reasons for increase in patient volume; Increased new patients, as explained in next section. . . . Going the extra mile with each patient, each visit. . . . Making recheck examinations and x-rays and giving a re-evaluation written report, keeping present patients coming for THEIR benefit. . . . Proper goals and consistency in driving toward them. . . . Constantly reviewing names of old patients, and using a dynamic, persistent recall system getting them back into the office. . . . Newsletters, a constant reminder of your services.

Reasons for a decrease in patient volume: Loss of new patients, as explained in the next section. . . . Improper communication

214

with patients. . . . Drop-out of patients due to a poor or no recall system. . . . Not talking about chiropractic results. . . . Taking short cuts with patients rather than going the extra mile. . . . Not re-examining disgruntled patients. . . . Independent ivory tower attitude. . . . Having patients come back too often. . . . Excessive fees due to greed . . . . Not driving constantly toward proper goals . . . . Lack of present time consciousness (PTC).

Figure #2 — Total New Patients

Reasons for increase of new patients: In my opinion, the most important factors in obtaining referrals from my patients are an excellent, thorough, impressive, well-planned consultation, examination, and written and verbal reports of findings.

Increased enthusiasm on the doctor's part in his contact with regular patients, stimulating them to refer new patients. . . . "You're better" procedures. . . . "Touch and Tell" procedures on each patient. . . . Telling the patients about similar and different cases that have responded to chiropractic. . . . "The case of the day" . . . . Going the extra mile with each patient. . . . Driving toward proper goals. . . . Proper patient communication. . . . Newsletters and good, solid referral concepts in which the doctor expects referrals.

If we take good care of our present patients, we'll never have to worry about the increase of new patients; they will always be there.

Reasons for a decline in new patients: Poor, sloppy consultation, unimpressive examination, no written report, poor verbal report, a lack of enthusiasm on the part of the doctor. . . . No referral concept. . . . No newsletters. . . . No touch and tell procedures. . . . Not talking of case histories and their results. . . . Not striving toward goals. . . . No "You're better" procedures. . . . In other words — NOTHING!

Figure #3 — Total Weekly Income

Reasons for a rise in income: A rise in income is due to a rise in the first two figures. Keep improving the first two figures and your income will rise steadily. Other methods of increasing your income are expanding your services, such as counseling, physiotherapy (if you are so inclined), nutrition, different x-ray studies, orthopedics, and adopting an improved collection system.

Reasons for loss of income: If the first two figures on the chart go down, naturally the income will follow. Correct the cause of a downward trend in new patients and patient volume, and the income will come up accordingly. A poor   collection system definitely will lead to poor income. A proper foolproof collection procedure is a Must!

Develop an expectant attitude in yourself in reference to payment for services rendered. My office is run on a ninety-seven percent collection record. It can be done!

Figure #4 — Total Patient Drop-Out

Reasons for an increase in patient drop-out: Bad, unimpressive consultation, examination, and reports. . . . Having the patient come back more often than necessary. . . . Poor service to patient. . . . Too rough an adjustment. . . . Poor explanation of chiropractic to the patient. . . . A poorly run appointment system (eliminate the long wait and you will increase your practice volume). . . . Letting your patients determine when they should come back (this is *your* job). . . . Not telephoning patients for appointments over two weeks hence. . . .

Not calling missed appointments immediately. . . . Not using patient reminder cards for missed appointments. . . . Not bringing out negatives of patient (a small negative now can become a big negative later). . . . Not re-examining patients when they are in trouble, failing to respond, or responding slowly. (The cheapest method of keeping a patient is re-examining and re-x-raying. This, many times, turns a disgruntled patient into one of your most enthusiastic supporters.) . . . An indifferent, stuffy "ivory tower" attitude, etc.

Reasons for a decrease in patient drop-out: A good recall system, for example, telephoning patient when appointment is more than two weeks away, calling patients after missed appointments, using reminder cards. (Why not take a lesson from dentists? They have a beautiful recall system.) . . . Talking chiropractic to the patient, teaching him what we do. . . . Telling the patients when to come back for their own benefit. . . . Re-examining the patients who are in trouble.

Improve your appointment system in order to eliminate long waits. Bring out negatives of all patients before they become big negatives and the patient quits. Think about the last patient who quit: think why he quit, and then never make that mistake again!

Figure #5 — Total Patient Recall

Reasons for an increase in recall figures: This is one of the most important aspects of good office procedure — PATIENT CONTROL. If you can stop patients from drifting out your back door, you won't need a tremendous amount of new patients coming in the front door to maintain your practice. Soon you will be all filled up.

The recall system is simple. When a patient has an appointment over two weeks away, a telephone call is made or a card is mailed, reminding him of his appointment time. If a patient misses a visit, he is called within fifteen minutes and rescheduled. If the patient can't be reached within fifteen minutes, a card is sent, scheduling a new appointment. A good recall system for inactive patients is to send them letters reminding them it is time for a check-up.

If a patient states, "I don't know when I can come back. I'll call you in three weeks," have the C.A. make a note on your appointment book and call the patient in three weeks, reminding him that he is due for a visit, and make an appointment.

Reasons for a decrease in recall figures: Obviously — NO recall procedures!

Now the most important aspect of my chart is a simple color code. I color in red the only figures that I consider acceptable, i.e., a minimum of three hundred patients per week, ten new patients per week, and eight thousand dollars per week. I color in green the only figures that I consider ideal, such as over four hundred patients per week, fifteen new patients per week, and a minimum of ten thousand dollars per week.

I simply color over the figures on the chart with a felt marker pen; red for acceptable figures, and green for ideal. It really is a pleasure to glance at your chart and watch your practice grow from no color to solid red, and then to solid green. Naturally, as your practice continues to grow, you will want to raise your standards higher and change the color code accordingly.

Doctors, no matter what income level you have now attained, the use of this chart system is rewarding. If you can stop fluctuations, you will improve your practice and income. Look where you have been, where you are now, and where you are going, and control it all the way. This system takes just a few minutes of time and a few pennies' investment to implement.

Don't let your practice control you. You control it!

1978

WEEK	Regular Patients	New Patients	Income	Drop Out	Recall	MONTH
1/2-1/7	294	15	7056	17	14	
1/9-1/14	291	14	6984	17	14	
1/16-1/21	291	17	6984	15	13	January
1/23-1/28	300	16	7200	12	10	$28,224.00
1/30-2/4	338	16	8112	17	10	
2/6-2/11	330	8	7920	21	10	February
2/13-2/18	316	12	7584	21	19	$39,288.00
2/20-2/25	332	20	7968	16	19	
2/27-3/4	321	17	7704	17	14	
3/6-3/11	313	16	7512	16	10	
3/13-3/18	286	11	6864	17	12	March
3/20-3/25	343	18	8232	21	18	$30,192.00
3/27-4/1	316	13	7584	14	13	
4/3-4/9	328	15	7872	16	12	
4/10-4/15	321	12	7704	23	13	April
4/17-4/22	304	16	7296	16	15	$30,600.00
4/24-4/29	322	11	7728	23	15	
5/1-5/6	311	15	7464	21	18	
5/8-5/13	328	16	7872	14	12	May
5/15-5/20	340	15	8160	13	12	$31,728.00
5/22-5/27	343	18	8232	16	14	

1979

WEEK	Regular Patients	New Patients	Income	Drop Out	Recall	MONTH
6/1-6/6	328	16	7872	18	16	
6/8-6/13	340	17	8160	18	15	June
6/15-6/20	338	18	8112	16	13	$32,376.00
6/22-6/27	343	15	8232	17	14	
6/29-7/3	341	17	8184	15	13	
7/5-7/10	338	18	8112	14	12	July
7/12-7/17	349	17	8376	14	13	$41,232.00
7/19-7/24	350	15	8400	13	13	
7/26-8/2	340	19	8160	11	10	
8/4-8/9	351	21	8424	16	14	August
8/11-8/16	349	18	8376	12	10	$33,672.00
8/18-8/23	355	17	8520	13	10	
8/25-8/30	348	17	8352	14	14	
9/1-9/6	349	21	8376	19	16	September
9/8-9/14	348	17	8352	17	16	$41,784.00
9/15-9/20	347	16	8328	13	13	
9/22-9/27	345	17	8280	12	13	
9/29-10/4	352	19	8448	13	10	
10/5-10/11	355	20	8520	15	13	October
10/13-10/18	353	19	8616	13	12	$34,008.00
10/20-10/25	353	20	8472	14	10	
10/27-11/1	350	21	8400	16	11	

HOW A SERIES OF THREE LETTERS
IN SIX WEEKS BROUGHT $1700

I have had excellent results with three mailings (shown below) which I made when I opened my office in St. Petersburg, Florida.

The first letter was mailed from Augusta, Georgia, and went to five thousand families in my community. The second letter, mailed to the same list, was from my office. It was a personal introduction and included a picture of my family and myself.

Boutwell Chiropractic Clinic

1916 Walton Way, Augusta, Georgia

Dear Friend,

It is with great pride that we introduce Dr. P. G. Fernandez, chiropractor, to your community. Due to the growing need of chiropractic services in the St. Petersburg area, he has decided to open his office there.

We know that his presence in your city, along with his desire to get sick people well, will bring forth great blessings to those in need of his services.

Dr. Fernandez comes to St. Petersburg well trained and well qualified in the chiropractic field as a spinal and structural specialist. During the last four years he has been Associate Director of the Boutwell Chiropractic Clinics throughout Georgia. Dr. Fernandez has specialized in:

Headaches — their cause and prevention!
Back pain — the treatment and correction!
Nervousness — and associated conditions!

His office is located at 4800-4th Street North, phone number 525-1141. If you have a health problem, call him for an appointment.

Remember, it's not true to say "Everything possible has been done," unless modern, scientific chiropractic is included.

Cordially,
DR. J. T. BOUTWELL, Director

Fernandez Chiropractic Clinic

GOOD MORNING!

We want to take this opportunity to thank you for your hospitality. Everyone has been so helpful and interested in getting us off to a fine start in our new offices!

As you may already know, I was invited to settle in your area after spending more than four years as Associate Director of one of the south's largest and finest clinics, the Boutwell Chiropractic Clinic in Augusta, Georgia.

During this time we have been of service to thousands of patients afflicted with a wide variety of conditions. Using this experience and aided by the latest in equipment and techniques, we have brought to your area modern, scientific chiropractic service.

Should you or a member of your family have a problem which has not yielded to usual methods of health care, please feel free to call me at 525-1141 and discuss your problem, or stop by and inspect our facilities at your convenience.

Yours very truly,
DR. P. G. FERNANDEZ

4800 Fourth Street, St. Petersburg, FL 33703

Fernandez Chiropractic Clinic

Good Morning, Friends:

My name is Dr. P. G. Fernandez. As a St. Petersburg chiropractor, I am a member of a Research Foundation that is conducting a "Public Safety" program. Research shows that in your profession the majority of time lost from work is due to on-the-job spinal injuries, such as back strain, slipped discs, and sacro-iliac injuries.

We have something that can reduce this time loss and cut insurance expenses. Due to the amount of lifting done by your employees, some spinal injury will no doubt occur; however, the enclosed "How to Lift" posters could help prevent many needless accidents. Protect the health of your employees and protect your interest, too.

Also, you may be interested to know that Florida State Workmen's Compensation Insurance fully covers chiropractic services for those on-the-job injuries.

We have taken the liberty of attaching an adhesive-backed sticker with our name, address, and telephone number. If any of your employees or clientele should need the services of a chiropractor, we'll be happy to be of service.

We hope that you can benefit from the use of these posters.

Sincerely,
DR. P. G. FERNANDEZ

4800 Fourth Street, St. Petersburg, FL 33703

Pictured below is the poster which was included in the mailing Dr. Fernandez made to the employers in his area. The actual size of this poster is 8½x11 inches.

Pictured below is a picture which appeared with an article in the newspaper. This publicity was the result of Dr. Fernandez introducing himself and his family to a local reporter. I refer you to Page 73 to see how this was accomplished. The article is reproduced on the following page.

Dr. and Mrs. Peter G. Fernandez and their two children are new residents in St. Petersburg. Originally from Fort Lauderdale, they moved here from Augusta, Ga. From left, Dr. Fernandez, Ray, 6, Lois, and Dianne, 2.

Reprint of picture, March, 1966

"We'd Like You To Meet..."

"FAMILY PROJECTS CITY'S YOUNG IMAGE"

By Jean Donald
Independent Reporter

They're a young, active and good-looking family, typical of those helping to change St. Petersburg's image.

Dr. and Mrs. Peter G. Fernandez and their two children, Raymond Peter, 6, and Dianne Michele, 2, moved to St. Petersburg last month from Augusta, Ga. Both Pete and Lois were raised in Fort Lauderdale, and were graduated from high schools there. Several years ago they moved to Augusta where Dr. Fernandez was associate director of the Boutwell Chiropractic Clinic. "But we wanted to come back to Florida," the young couple agreed. "After searching the state up and down, St. Petersburg came out on top."

"We had several reasons for choosing this area," the doctor remembered. Many of his patients had moved to St. Petersburg when they retired. "We wanted to come back anyway, so we followed them down," Pete laughed.

Lois, a busy mother and homemaker, believes "St. Petersburg has a variety of things to hold your interest." She plans to go back to school and study to be a teacher. Future plans also include volunteer political work and helping out at the Little Theatre. She's taking bridge lessons at the YWCA and passes on her new-found information to her husband. Water skiing and sewing are favorite hobbies, too.

Though Lois claims her husband is "married to his profession," Pete plans to find time to be an active member of Kiwanis and the Jaycees. He's also a do-it-yourselfer — likes to "tinker" around the house.

According to Dr. and Mrs. Fernandez, St. Petersburg compares favorably with any other place they've lived. "In Fort Lauderdale they concentrate more on tourism. St. Petersburg is more relaxed. It has everything Fort Lauderdale has, and more."

Reproduced courtesy St. Petersburg Evening-Independent.

Reprint of article, March, 1966.

HOW I RUN A THOUSAND DOLLARS PER WEEK PRACTICE

In *SHARE Magazine,* January, 1967, the article entitled "How A Series of Three Letters in Six Weeks Brought $1700," I reported a successful system of getting my new practice started quickly here in St. Petersburg, Florida — a city of over two hundred thousand people.

Since that time nearly two years ago, my practice has done very well. Now, as a result of my office procedure, I am able not only to operate and maintain an income of a thousand dollars per week, but continue to grow.

I would like to share with my fellow D.C.'s the procedures which I believe are basically responsible for this.

I follow the latest of office management techniques religiously. In a few instances, I have developed innovations which have helped. In other instances, I have altered forms to fit them into the personality of my practice. In still other instances, I have overprinted forms to make them personalized, but this has not in the least changed my distinct adherence to planned procedures.

The following outline describes this procedure in detail.

I. THE PATIENT'S FIRST VISIT

A. The patient enters the office and is greeted by the Chiropractic Assistant.

B. The Chiropractic Assistant instructs the patient to fill out the Pre-Consultation Questionnaire.

C. Using the information on the Pre-Consultation Questionnaire, the C.A. fills in the pertinent data on the following items:

    1. ADJUSTING CARD. This card contains spaces for regular progress reports and will accompany the patient on each future visit to the office.

    2. PHYSICAL EXAMINATION.

    3. PATIENT'S FINANCIAL LEDGER, CARD, OR SHEET.

    4. X-RAY NAMEPLATE.

D. The Chiropractic Assistant then escorts the patient in street clothes to the consultation room.

E. The doctor receives the folder containing all of the abovementioned material from the C.A. and studies it prior to greeting the patient.

F. The doctor then enters the consultation room and introduces himself to the patient.

G. In the beginning of the actual consultation, the doctor questions the patient according to the previous article on consultation.

H. The doctor then follows the procedure of the descriptive close of the consultation, i.e. "Why don't you slip on a gown [remove your shirt] and let's see what's causing your problem?"

I. The doctor then conducts a brief but informative preliminary examination.

1. He palpates pain parts to tie the complaint into the spine, using such statements as, "There doesn't appear to be a problem here. . . . Sometimes a pinched nerve in the spine can cause almost all, if not every bit, of the problem you present here."

2. He makes a range of motion study. When limited motion study is apparent, comments are made, such as, "No wonder your hip hurts. Your back is in a rigid spasm, not allowing your spine to bend. When your back is fixed in an out-of-normal position like it is today, this is an effort on the part of your body to protect a seriously injured joint in your spine by placing a 'splint'-like muscle spasm around the vertebra immobilizing the weakened joint so you won't further injure yourself."

3. The heel-drop test is performed eliciting pain on the injured side to re-emphasize the problem to the patient.

4. A temperature differential instrument reading is made, followed by comments, such as: "We have found that the very best thing to do in cases like yours is to take a picture [x-ray] from front to back and from side to side to see exactly what is causing your problem."

a. 14x36 A to P and lateral films are made routinely, along with indicated spot x-rays of crucial areas.

b. During the process of x-raying the patient, the doctor explains the purpose of the x-ray study, as follows: "Mrs. Jones, when you take an x-ray from the back only, you may miss a problem in the front of your spine. That's why we are x-raying all around. If there is a problem with your spine, whether it be at the back, on the side, or in the front of your spine, we won't miss it."

J. The doctor then instructs the patient to get dressed and be seated and he will return in just a moment.

K. The doctor presents the patient with the Cornell Medical Index Questionnaire, and a white paper bag with a urine specimen container in it. He explains as follows: "Mrs. Jones, we are going to develop and study your x-rays this afternoon. We want to see you tomorrow and we'll let you know exactly what we have found and whether or not we can help you. In the meantime, I would like you to fill out this questionnaire for me. I know it looks rather imposing. There are about two hundred questions, but they are very easy and will take only a few minutes of your time." [The doctor reads a few easy questions from the questionnaire at this point, to show how easy they are.] "I appreciate your help in filling out the questionnaire. I can learn more about your health in ten minutes with this questionnaire than I can in five hours of talking with you. In this bag there is a urine container. I would like your first morning urine sample so I can check out your kidney function."

L. The doctor checks the services rendered on the fee slip and familiarizes the patient with the services that were rendered that day. He then folds it and presents it to the patient, saying: "Give this slip to my assistant, and we'll see you tomorrow." He then leaves the room; the patient gets dressed and goes to the C.A.'s desk.

M. When the patient arrives at the assistant's desk, the C.A. states: "The doctor says he wants to see you tomorrow for further examination and report on your x-rays. Would you like a morning or afternoon appointment . . . an early or late appointment?" The C.A. then opens up the fee slip, totals up the charges of services rendered, and writes the total on the fee slip. She then says: "Today the doctor performed the following services [whatever was done]. The total charges are . . . . . Will that be cash or check?"

II. THE PATIENT'S SECOND VISIT

A. When the patient arrives for her second visit, the Chiropractic Assistant collects the completed Cornell Health Index Questionnaire and the urine specimen container.

B. While the patient is in the dressing room getting ready for examination, the C.A. gives the questionnaire and the urine container to the doctor. He checks over the information on the questionnaire and examines the urine specimen prior to seeing the patient.

C. The patient is moved to the examining room and the C.A. enters the room, followed by the doctor. The C.A. has a comprehensive examination form on a clipboard with her.

D. The doctor makes the following statement: "Mrs. Jones, we have found something on your x-ray that could be causing most, if not all, of your problem. Today we are going to examine you further to see if we can correct that which we have already found." At this point, the doctor will ask pertinent questions from the questionnaire.

E. The doctor then performs a complete orthopedic, neurological and physical examination, and the C.A. records his findings. (*Note:* Some doctors write down their own findings or dictate them.)
The C.A. does not interrupt the doctor under any circumstances during this procedure. If any questions arise in the mind of the C.A., she waits until after they have left the room to clarify them.

F. When the doctor completes his examination, he states: "Mrs. Jones, we are now going to correlate our physical examination findings with the urinalysis, questionnaire answers, and your x-rays. I want to see you tomorrow for a report of my findings. When you come tomorrow, we are going to give you a written report showing what we have found, what results you can expect, and our recommendations. At the same time, we will show you your x-rays so you can fully understand the cause of your health problem and what should be done. Please tell my assistant to give you a time to come in tomorrow. I want to reserve at least one hour for you so we won't be interrupted as we go over your case. [A half hour might be ample for some.] See you tomorrow."

G. The patient then dresses and reports to the C.A.'s desk for an appointment for the third visit.

III. THE PATIENT'S THIRD VISIT

1. The doctor's desk is clean.
2. The patient's x-rays are in the viewbox.
3. All necessary materials are at hand.
4. A copy of the patient's written report is on the desk.
5. Real-Izer; Motion-in-Life; Muscle, Spine, and Nerve Charts, such as the Roll-Up Wall Chart are all in readiness.

A. The patient is escorted by the C.A. to the consultation room.

B. The patient is seated in the consultation room and given a copy of the written final report (complete), and allowed the necessary time to read it.

C. The doctor spends the first few minutes going over the written report with the patient, especially that portion pertaining to the nerve charts contained within the final report. (See pages 231 and 232 for copies of these nerve charts.)

    1. The doctor says: "Mrs. Jones, the nerve charts are one of the most important parts of this written report. As you'll notice, one contains a picture of the spinal column and pelvis and their relationship with the cerebrospinal nervous system. This is called the Voluntary Nervous System because it controls all muscles on command."

    2. The doctor holds up his hand and moves his fingers to demonstrate voluntary muscle control.

    3. This explanation is given in simple layman's language because it is not for the purpose of impressing the patient but of teaching the patient something about chiropractic and how it works.

    4. The doctor then continues: "The other chart also shows an exact duplicate of the spine and pelvis, but the nervous system is different. This is called the Autonomic Nervous System. The reason we show you both nervous systems is sometimes when a vertebra slips out of place, it can produce a dual set of symptoms. For example, when the first thoracic vertebra is misaligned, the nerves going to the arms are often affected, causing a neuralgia or a loss of strength and, at the same time, the nerves will be pinched going to the heart, which can cause heart distress. Therefore, one misalignment can — and often does — cause two entirely different sets of symptoms."

    5. The patient's complaints are tied in directly with this explanation. For example, in a case of sciatica and poor circulation in the legs, with tension in the neck and sinuses, the doctor will say, "Now, Mrs. Jones, these charts are individualized to your case. They show you exactly which vertebrae are misaligned in your spine, what nerves are being pinched, and what conditions are being caused in both nervous sytems."

    6. Through the use of these charts and with a knowledge of neurology, the doctor can often pinpoint problems that

the patient might be having, even though the patient may have neglected to tell the doctor about them. This is a pleasant surprise and the patient is amazed at the thoroughness of the doctor's investigations.

7. The use of the charts allows the doctor to explain several different problems that are within the realm of chiropractic care, such as poor circulation, sciatica, headaches, stomach pain, etc.

D. The balance of the report of findings covers the following points:

1. The explanations of the positive orthopedic and neurological tests.

2. The explanation of the patient's x-rays.

3. The doctor's recommendations for corrective care.

(*Note:* After careful study of these charts and their applications, Dr. James Parker of the Parker School of Professional Success, Fort Worth, Texas, said: "This is one of the most valuable and most useful additions to the Final Report that has come to our attention recently.")

This idea came to my attention from a medical doctor in North Carolina who performed surgery on one of my patients before that patient came under my care. The patient showed me a chart that the M.D. had done, showing the entire alimentary canal. He had drawn on the chart the surgery he had performed and noted the results that the patient could expect. I adapted the idea to chiropractic from this. Each chiropractor should secure supplies of both of these charts and underline the patients' individual problems and circle the vertebrae with felt marking pens showing the effects. This is a most useful explanation.

IV. PATIENT MANAGEMENT

A. "A Suggestion for Faster Recovery" pamphlet is given to the patient on the visit when he receives his first adjustment.

B. "A Family Plan" folder is given to each patient as soon as improvement is noted, assuming of course that the patient has a family.

C. An exercise program is recommended for the patient as soon as symptoms have abated to the extent that the performance of exercises will not unduly aggravate his condition. It is wise when recommending an exercise program to mark specifically the exercise recommended for that particular patient.

D. In cases where overweight is a problem, a folder — which is

EFFECTS OF SPINAL MISALIGNMENTS ON THE CEREBRO-SPINAL NERVOUS SYSTEM

C1
C2
C3 Misaligned vertebrae in the upper neck will impinge the nerves leading to the head and face. The result of this impingement is tension along the base of the skull, nervousness, nerve system involvements, insomnia, headaches, certain eye disorders, facial pain (tri-facial neuralgia), and torticollis (wry neck).

C4
C5 A subluxated vertebrae in the mid-neck will cause pressure on the nerves leading to the throat. Neck pain and spasm, throat pain, swallowing difficulties, and speech problems may be the result.

C6
C7
T1
T2
T3 A malpositioned vertebrae in the lower neck and upper back will irritate the nerves leading to the throat, shoulders, arms and hands. The result of this continued nerve irritation is neuritis, or bursitis of one or both arms and hands, numbness of the hands and fingers, pain in the lower neck and upper back, tension across the shoulders, and swallowing difficulties.

T4
T5
T6
T7 A vertebrae out of its normal position between the shoulder blades will produce slight pressure on the nerves in this area. This "pinching" will cause pain and tension between the shoulder blades, pain radiating outward under the shoulder blades and to the front of the chest. Continued pressure on these nerves may lead to shingles.

T8
T9
T10
T11 A subluxated spinal segment in the mid-back will cause pain and tension just above the belt line, possibly impinging the nerves radiating outward between the ribs producing shingles.

T12
L1 When the vertebrae in the lower mid-back have slipped out of place the result is pain along the belt line and pain in the side just under the ribs.

L2
L3
L4
L5
S1 Whenever the vertebrae in the lower back are misaligned pressure on the nerves radiating outward to the hips, pelvis and legs is the usual result. Sustained pressure on these nerves may cause pain and tension in the lower back, sacroiliac pain, lumbago, painful neuritis of one or both legs, sciatica, pain in the legs, pain into the groin, pain into the hips and buttocks, disc difficulties, and pain at the end of the spine while sitting.

CORRECTION OF THE MISALIGNED VERTEBRAE LISTED ABOVE WILL RELEASE THE IMPINGED NERVES, ALLOWING THE AFFECTED PART TO RETURN TO NORMAL FUNCTION.

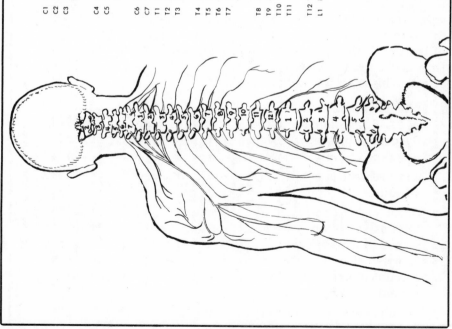

EFFECTS OF SPINAL MISALIGNMENTS ON THE AUTONOMIC NERVOUS SYSTEM

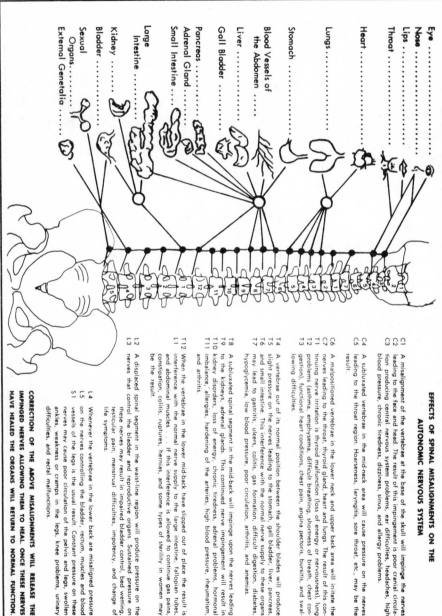

Eye ....
Nose ....
Lips ....
Throat ....

Heart ....

Lungs ....

Stomach ....

Blood Vessels of
the Abdomen ......

Liver ....
Gall Bladder ......

Pancreas ....
Adrenal Gland ......
Small Intestine ......

Large
Intestine ....

Kidney ....
Bladder ....
Sexual
Organs ....
External Genetalia ......

C1
C2
C3
A misalignment of the vertebrae at the base of the skull will impinge the nerves leading to the face and head. The result of this impingement is poor cranial circulation producing central nervous system problems, ear difficulties, headaches, high blood pressure, chronic tiredness, dizziness, sinus, and allergy problems.

C4
C5
A subluxated vertebrae in the mid-neck area will cause pressure on the nerves leading to the throat region. Hoarseness, laryngitis, sore throat, etc., may be the result.

C6
C7
T1
T2
T3
A malpositioned vertebrae in the lower neck and upper back area will irritate the nerves leading to the throat, thyroid gland, heart and lungs. The result of this continuing nerve irritation is thyroid malfunction (loss of energy or nervousness), lung problems (asthma, emphysema, difficult breathing, shortness of breath, chest congestion), functional heart conditions, chest pain, angina pectoris, bursitis, and swallowing difficulties.

T4
T5
T6
T7
A vertebrae out of its normal position between the shoulder blades will produce slight pressure on the nerves leading to the stomach, gall bladder, liver, pancreas, and small intestine. This interference with the normal nerve supply to these organs may lead to gastritis, ulcers, colitis, gas formation, difficult digestion, diabetes, hypoglycemia, low blood pressure, poor circulation, arthritis, and anemias.

T8
T9
T10
T11
A subluxated spinal segment in the mid-back will impinge upon the nerves leading to the kidneys, adrenal glands. This continued nerve impingement will result in kidney disorders, loss of energy, chronic tiredness, adrenal problems, hormonal imbalance, allergies, hardening of the arteries, high blood pressure, rheumatism, and arthritis.

T12
L1
When the vertebrae in the lower mid-back have slipped out of place the result is interference with the normal nerve supply to the large intestine, fallopian tubes, and abdominal muscles. . . . If this interference is allowed to continue gas pains, constipation, colitis, ruptures, hernias, and some types of sterility in women may be the result.

L2
L3
A displaced spinal segment in the waist-line region will produce pressure on the nerves that control the bladder and reproductive organs. Sustained pressure on these nerves may result in impaired bladder control, bed wetting, testicular pain, menstrual difficulties, impotency, and change of life symptoms.

L4
L5
S1
Whenever the vertebrae in the lower back are misaligned pressure on the nerves controlling the bladder, rectum, muscles and blood vessels of the legs is the usual result. Constant pressure on these nerves may cause poor circulation of the pelvis and legs, swollen ankles, weakness or cramps in the legs, knee problems, urinary difficulties, and rectal malfunctions.

CORRECTION OF THE ABOVE MISALIGNMENTS WILL RELEASE THE IMPINGED NERVES ALLOWING THEM TO HEAL. ONCE THESE NERVES HAVE HEALED THE ORGANS WILL RETURN TO NORMAL FUNCTION.

called the "10/10 Diet" — is given to the patient with instructions to follow for loss of weight. This is the well-known grapefruit diet which appeared in *Cosmopolitan* magazine.

E. All patient with lower back pain are given copies of the article, "How Your Patients Can Rise Painlessly."

HOW YOUR PATIENTS CAN RISE PAINLESSLY

Most patients with low back pain invariably rise from a lying or sitting position incorrectly. These patients usually complain that their back pain is intensified upon rising from one of these positions, and yet it is the actual manner in which they get up that causes their pain. Therefore, simple rules for painless rising from a lying or sitting position are in order.

How to Rise from a Lying Position
Without Pain

Fig. 1: Lie on your side, close to the edge of the bed.

Fig. 2: Push up from the bed with your hands and elbow, keeping your spine at right angles to your pelvis. Do not let your spine sag in this maneuver. It is the sagging of your spine that produces the pain. At the same time, bend your knees and slide your legs off the edge of the bed. Keep your legs at right angles to your pelvis. If you drop your feet to the floor during this maneuver, it will produce pain.

Fig. 3: With your hands, walk yourself upward toward a sitting position, keeping your spine and legs at right angles to your pelvis.

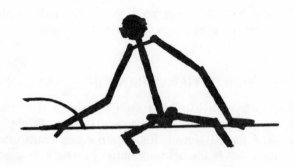

Fig. 4: When almost in a sitting position, place your uppermost hand on the opposite side of your body on the bed. Remember to keep your spine at right angles to your pelvis. Do not drop your pelvis onto the bed, as this will produce pain.

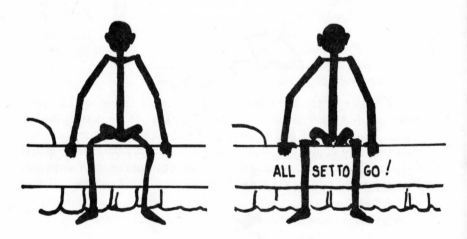

Figs. 5 & 6: Swing your body weight up onto your hands as you come to a sitting position. Ease your body weight onto the bed. Remember, keep your spine at right angles to your pelvis. Don't sag your spine at any time.

How to Rise from a Sitting Position Without Pain

Fig. 7: Place your buttocks very close to the edge of the chair (bed, etc.). Place your feet under the chair, directly under your buttocks and approximately one foot apart. Lean your body slightly forward in order to be in a balanced position.

Fig. 8: Rise to a standing position by pushing upward with your thigh and calf muscles. Do not push up with your hands on the chair or on your thighs. Rising from the sitting position is to be accomplished by your leg muscles only. If you attempt to rise by bending forward and pushing up with your hands, you will place the weight of your upper body forward of your injured spine and, therefore, will further strain your spine in the attempt to stand, thus producing pain.

By following these simple steps in rising from a lying or sitting position, you should be able to do so without pain, no matter how painful your spinal condition may be.

Doctors, keep these suggestions handy. Your patients will appreciate knowing how they can avoid unnecessary pain.

Front

Happy Birthday

It seems hard

to believe

you are ONE

year older . . .

Excellent example of Birthday Card to send to your patients.

Inside

and so,

of course,

is your SPINE!

A very *Happy Birthday* to you both!!

Even though the main theme of this book has been devoted to the acquisition of new patients, what good does it do to have a steady flow of new patients entering our practices when, at the same time, we have an equally steady stream of present patients quitting our care? New patients are not the answer to building a successful practice. Plugging up the leaks in our practices is the *secret*, the new patients are then the icing on the cake. Read these *118 Ways to Chase Patients Away*, and perhaps you will discover leaks in *your* practice. Once your "leaks" are plugged, your practice will automatically fill up.

* * *

1. The appearance of the chiropractic office and doctor. Is your office in a deteriorating neighborhood? Are your patients reluctant to come to your end of town? Has the socioeconomic level of the neighborhood in which your office is located gone downhill? If so, move!

The best location for a new office will be in an area of town that is middle-class. The average age of the people surrounding your new office should be approximately 45 to 55 years old. This is the age bracket that mostly utilizes chiropractic care. The mortgages on their homes have been eliminated, their children are through college, and they are now in a position to afford chiropractic care.

2. How is the parking situation at your office? This is a parking world! Some doctors don't have any parking and wonder why they don't have any patients. People don't like parking two or three blocks away and walking to your office. If you don't have parking, get a new office.

3. Is your sign visible? Have you had the annoying experience of searching for a street address only to find that none of the houses had visible numbers? If so, you can imagine the problem and annoyance some patients will have locating your office if you don't have obvious identification. Also, how can you attract walk-in business if the prospective patients don't know your office is in their neighborhood? If you have poor visibility, eliminate the problem with a large, appropriate professional sign and floodlights to light up your office at night. An electric timer will reduce the great electrical expenditures of the floodlights.

4. Is your office difficult to get into? That is — unsafe walkway, bushes overgrown on the walk leading to your office, a second-floor office without an elevator. Make it convenient for a patient to come to your office. Trim the bushes and repair the walkway, etc.

5. Do you have a second-floor office without an elevator? If so, move to a ground-floor location or an office building with an elevator.

6. Is your office neat and clean? Quite often doctors are very dedicated and they don't even see the dirt that surrounds them. Is this the case in your office? You should get someone to come to your office — such as a fastidious lady friend (not a patient) — to come through and critique your office. You can imagine the lady patient of yours that is a fastidious housekeeper and she walks into your unclean office. You won't keep that lady as a patient and she will not refer. All doctors' offices should be impeccably clean, almost sterile!

7. How is the soundproofing in your office? Can your patients overhear your conversation with other patients? If so, contact an architect to help remedy this problem. No one wants to relate items of a personal nature to their doctor when they are sure someone will overhear them. The lack of soundproofing will stifle the patients' free expression to you, their doctor. When patients can't confide, relate or express themselves to their doctor, they will quit. Wouldn't you? Soundboard, carpeting, acoustical tile, solid core doors, wallpaper, etc., will stifle sounds. Ask your architect; he will be happy to help.

8. Do you have poor lighting in your office? Your patients don't want to come to a dingy office. Get the aid of an interior decorator to help you with adequate, cheerful lighting. Most paint stores will have an interior decorator come to your office free of charge to advise you on painting, lighting, etc. Take advantage of this service to brighten up your office. Your contact with the manager of the paint store and the interior decorator may result in their becoming new patients and possible referrals.

9. Does your office smell bad? Cigar and pipe smoke may smell like the aroma of the Gods to you, but stale smoke smells repulsive to most people. Improved air-conditioning and a room deodorant will aid in eliminating unpleasant odors. Perhaps you should consider a "No Smoking" policy in your office.

10. Do you have badly outdated magazines in your reception room? If so, who wants to spend time in your waiting room reading two-year-old news articles? Spend two dollars per month to give your patients up-to-date reading material. Remember, it is the little things that count in building a successful practice!

11. Don't have a cluttered office. People equate a cluttered office with a cluttered mind. If your patients see a big mess in your office, they will not stick with you because they want and expect their doctor to be organized. How would you like to have your gallbladder taken out by a surgeon who couldn't find his instruments? You wouldn't like it! If you walked into a surgeon's office and it was cluttered and messy and he couldn't find his examination instruments, you certainly wouldn't let him operate on you! These same facts are to be considered when a patient comes into your office. If it is cluttered — Goodbye!

12. Do you have inferior equipment? If your equipment looks like it was made before D. D. Palmer was born, get rid of it. Have nice looking equipment, even though it may not be the latest model. Make sure it looks nice, is well polished, and well cleaned. Is the upholstery on the table worn or tattered? If so, re-upholster it. Appearance is what counts.

13. Don't be too wild a dresser. Historically, the older patients — middle age and older — have a mistrust and a lack of respect for the younger generation. If the doctor's dress is too "mod" or he dresses in "hippy" clothes, he will lose a certain percentage of his patients. Dress nicely, expensively, but slightly conservatively for the best effect on all patients.

14. Do you look too young to be a doctor? Patients equate age with experience, knowledge, wisdom, etc. If you are young and *look* young, grow a moustache, a beard, etc., to give the older image. Also, dress older to give an older impression.

15. Do you have unclean personal habits? That is — dirty hands, bad breath, rotten teeth, dirty fingernails, dirty shoes, body odor, dirty clinic jacket, full ashtrays, unclean tie, need a shave, unkept hair, etc. If so, clean up your act! Your patients notice what you look like. If they don't like your appearance, they will quit your care and most definitely won't refer to a doctor they consider unclean. Adopt a "No Offense" policy in your office. Have an arrangement with your staff that if any member of your staff, including yourself, has an offensive anything, that another member of your staff will tell them for their own good, and they won't be offended. If your hair looks like a birds' nest or is too long, etc., get it styled slightly on the conservative side. Perhaps your new hairstyle will be a little more "straight" than you would really like it to be, but remember, you are styling your hair to please your patients, not yourself.

16. Do you have bad mannerisms? That is — drumming your fingers on your desk, picking your nose, biting your fingernails, twitches, etc.? If so, make every effort to correct these mannerisms, as it detracts from your image as a doctor.

17. Do you use slang or bad English in your conversation? There isn't anything that more sharply identifies an individual as under-educated than bad grammar, slang, etc. If you project an under-educated image, this will have a serious detrimental effect on your practice. Take classes at your local junior college to eliminate problems you may have with the English language.

18. Are you a "poor-boy" doctor? A doctor should be as well-dressed as his best-dressed patient. If a banker or a lawyer is your patient and he is pleased with your care but you are a poor-boy doctor and you look and dress like one, he will not refer any of his friends, of his same socioeconomic level, to you because he doesn't want to send his friends to someone who is in a lower socioeconomic level than they are. Therefore, you will lose out on the majority of this man's referrals. Again, be as well-dressed as your best-dressed patient.

If you are in the first year of practice, get Master Charge or Visa, and buy yourself some new clothes. Patients like their doctor to be very successful. They want him to drive a Cadillac. They want him to have an attractive, well-dressed wife. They want him to be well-dressed because people go by status symbols that indicate a doctor as a success. They reason that if a doctor is any good, he is successful, and if he is successful, he is well-dressed. This isn't necessarily true, but this is the way people look at things. You have to be successful in their minds. So, don't be a "poor-boy" doctor — dress to the teeth. Have a nice car, and keep it washed. Impress your patients and they will be proud to send their friends — who might be lawyers, doctors, bankers, etc. — to you. Don't eliminate a large portion of your practice population because of shabby dress.

Doctor's Attitude

19. Negativity: Are you a negative doctor? If so, a negative attitude will drive patients away from your practice. Remember, sick

240

people are negative already. They need a positive person to take care of them. If your patient is negative and you, too, are negative, this will be like trying to touch two poles of a magnet . . . two *negative* poles of a magnet! The negative poles repel each other, just as two negative people repel each other. Think about it, and change your attitude.

20. Timidity: A timid, mild-mannered doctor will not inspire confidence in his patients and they will not stay with him, nor will they refer. If you are this kind of a doctor, take a course at Dale Carnegie and learn how to be more positive, more interesting, and more definite. A timid doctor will not go anywhere.

21. Indifference: An indifferent attitude on the part of a doctor will drive his patients away. If you have an indifferent attitude, your patients will pick it up. They will feel that you don't need them and will go elsewhere. Indifference is the greatest loser of patients! Who wants to go to a doctor who is not interested in them, a doctor who has the attitude that he doesn't need the patients and who takes them for granted? An excellent test to determine if you have the indifference disease, too, is to pick up a patient file folder that you have treated for three or four months, and determine how much you have learned about that patient's condition, his family, etc., since he has been under your care. If the only thing you know about the patient and his condition is what you learned on the first few visits, then you are indifferent and are driving your patients out of your practice.

22. Dedication: Are you dedicated? People like to go to dedicated doctors. Patients like to tell their friends that their doctor is dedicated, of the seminars he attends, and so on. They love a doctor who is totally interested in his work and his profession. It is a better image to be dedicated.

23. Insecurity and Dissatisfaction: Are you infusing your patients with your own insecurity? I find this prevalent in our profession. If you are not sure, or are dissatisfied with the results you are getting, the patient will pick up your attitude, and you have then lost a patient. If you have confidence in yourself, the patient will pick up your confidence and he will stick with you and get results. If you are insecure, he will not continue as your patient!

24. Do you have lack of appreciation? Do you thank your patients for keeping their appointments, following your recommendations, referring their friends, for the flowers they brought to your office? Do you send Thank-U-Grams and thank-you letters to your patients? If you don't show appreciation, your attitude will stymie your practice. Who wants to go where they are not appreciated?

241

25. Are you strictly a technician? Do you solely treat the patient's physical problem? Is it beneath you to listen to their emotional or family problems? I have had a number of associates who felt that their job was strictly to reduce nerve pressure, and to heck with treating the patient for a psychological overlay. Needless to say, they didn't develop much of a practice and are no longer associated with me. A holistic doctor treats the *whole* man. He takes care of the patient's physical problem and then gives him something else: concern, compassion, empathy, etc. Be the total doctor and treat the whole man.

26. Are you accepting responsibility for the patient's recovery? If so, you are falling into the worst and most destructive trap a doctor can fall into. A doctor is responsible for rendering the best service he is capable of to his patients. He is not responsible for the recovery. A patient's recovery is dependent upon many factors, i.e., age of the patient, length of sickness, diet, rest, bad habits, etc. The patient might not psychologically want to get well. If he gets well, what would he complain about to get attention? It is important to remember that it is our responsibility to give our best service. We are not responsible for the patient's results!

27. Do you have an "acute only" practice? Do you dismiss patients as soon as they are symptom-free? If so, you are playing the part of an aspirin doctor. We all know aspirin relieves the pain, but it does not fix the cause of the pain. This is exactly what *you* are doing in your practice! The professional doctor of chiropractic accepts patients on the basis of objective findings and dismisses them when the objective findings have been eliminated. The professional doctor realizes that the symptoms are due to the objective problems an examination has ascertained and that the elimination of the symptoms is solely the first stage in the correction of the objective problem. Many times a patient will go to a D.C. three or four times for pain relief, and be relieved. But he will become a chiropractic "knocker" because he went to a D.C., was relieved of the pain, but the problem returned and, therefore, chiropractic wasn't any good. Try giving a package of care beyond relief of pain in order to correct the patient's problem. It will pay great dividends.

28. Are there certain conditions you can't treat? All doctors eventually — intentionally or unintentionally — narrow their scope of practices down to the conditions they are most successful in treating. These same doctors repel patients with conditions they are unsuccessful in treating. If you are not successful in treating a certain condition, for example, shoulder problems, you are in effect eliminating a potentially large portion of your practice. Are you weak in treating extremity problems, ulcers, migraine headaches, etc.? If so, attack your weakest areas by attending seminars on how to treat that weakest area. Once your weakest area becomes a strong part of your practice, then attack your next weakest link in your practice until you are able to successfully treat all the major conditions that fall within the realm of chiropractic. Once your weak spots are eliminated, you will more than double your practice. (Refer to Practice Expansion Wheel on Page 39.)

29. Are you afraid to go to court? If so, you are diminishing your practice by elimination of all litigated cases. The courtroom scene can be exciting, rewarding, and challenging if you know what you are doing. Your exposure to the jury in the courtroom, to the plaintiff and defense attorneys, to the judges, bailiffs, courtroom spectators, etc., will enhance and spread your reputation, increase your referrals, etc. If you are not confident in this area, there are many courses available to help you in this field. Don't put a stranglehold on your practice by not caring for litigated cases.

30. Do you have goals for your practice? Do you have definite ideas on where you want your practice to go? If not, your practice is like a ship without a rudder: totally uncontrollable and most definitely not rewarding. If you don't know where you are going (your goals), how will you know when you get there? Set goals and set staff meetings to explain your office goals, and start moving your practice upward.

31. Are you a "blabber-mouth" doctor? Do you make people wait while you talk excessively with another patient, or while you are on the phone? Trying to overwhelm the patient with excessive chiropractic verbiage while, at the same time, making other patients wait, is very discourteous. The patients who are made to wait will quit your care because they can't waste their valuable time in your "waiting" room.

32. Do you talk with patients about your outside interests? Do you talk with friends on the phone during office hours? If so, set a firm policy of no phone calls until morning or afternoon patients are through. Don't talk with patients about your outside interests! And, don't waste excessive time trying to sell chiropractic to the patient while, at the same time, making other patients wait until you are through with your chiropractic snow-job. Stick to business!

33. Do you have outside interests that are more important than your chiropractic interests? Are you more interested in the stock market, golf, or a weekend away? Are you emotionally involved in outside-the-office activities? If you are, it is going to show. Patients can sense when their doctor's mind is wandering. If they think you don't care about them, they will quit. Compartmental-ize your mind. Once you are in your office, think chiropractic only. If you don't, you will suffer the consequences: patient attrition.

Detrimental Actions on the Part of the Doctor

34. Foul language and dirty jokes. Do you like to be "one of the boys" and crack jokes with your patients? Stay away from foul, dirty jokes! Can you imagine telling a dirty joke to a patient or having them tell you one, and both of you having a good laugh? Is this patient then going to refer his wife, his daughter, or his mother to you? Of course not! By using foul language or telling off-color stories in your office, you will successfully eliminate all the female patients that this man would have normally referred to you. Keep the barroom talk out of the office!

35. Don't make too light of the patient's problem. Don't tell the patient, "Don't worry about it. You'll be okay," or "You don't have anything to worry about." The patient doesn't feel he is in a "don't worry about anything" situation. When the patient hurts, his pain is the most important event in his life at that moment. Don't ever say it's nothing. It is better to amplify the patient's condition a little than it is to downgrade it. Remember, it's their life, their pain, and they are concerned about it. You should show an equal concern.

36. Don't be overly friendly with your patients. They look at your friendliness as if you were giving them a "snow-job." They are thinking, "Why is he so nice? There has to be something phoney about this doctor because he is trying so hard to be friendly." Just be professional! Be friendly, but don't be overly friendly.

37. Don't be too open about your personal life and problems. The patients are not in the office to psychoanalyze you. They are there to get well. Spend your time on the patients' problems, not yours!

38. Don't bad-mouth other doctors. One of the worst mistakes a professional man can make is to try to upgrade his image by stepping on and downgrading another professional. Frequently, a patient will quit a doctor, not because he is a bad doctor, but because he doesn't understand or can't heal a certain condition. They still have respect for their original doctor, but are coming to you for a certain condition that their original doctor couldn't handle. If you say anything derogatory about their original doctor

244

— whom they respect — they will have an immediate disrespect for you, and you have lost a patient. If a patient comes to you from another physician of another discipline, simply say, "Dr. Blank has an excellent reputation and the reason I found your problem was because I performed a chiropractic examination on you, which is my specialty." Build up the other doctor and, at the same time, you will be building yourself up in that patient's mind.

If the patient quits another chiropractor to come to you, simply say, "I know Dr. Jones and I have known him for years. He is a very good doctor. What was his opinion of your problem? Let's see if I can find something that perhaps he overlooked."

39. Don't be argumentative. It is silly and stupid to win an argument with a patient and lose that patient and his referrals. If you must disagree with him, simply say, "I understand your point of view, but have you ever thought of it in this way. . . ?" In other words, you can disagree without being disagreeable.

40. Do you keep your word? If you tell a patient you are going to do something — for instance, re-x-ray, re-examination, post lab work, post urine work-ups — you had better keep your word. If you don't provide what you promised, the patients will feel you are slighting them and you will have lost a patient.

41. Are you active in local and state chiropractic associations? If not, you are losing a great source of practice building information. The technical speakers at your society meetings will improve your ability to treat your patients. The contact with other successful D.C.'s will give you new ideas to apply in your practice. I can personally attest to the fact that I have been honored by holding every elective office in my local and state association, and have never found it a detriment to my practice. The converse has held true. Each time I have held an elective post in my association, my practice has increased due to the contacts with other successful chiropractors. Try it — you'll like it!

42. Do you refer most of your patients to other health practitioners? If so, you should avail yourself of the many seminars that increase a chiropractor's competency. There isn't anything wrong with chiropractic. It works! Sometimes a D.C. doesn't know how to make chiropractic work. Attending technique seminars will increase your competence in this area. Don't be a referral service for other doctors! Learn how to make chiropractic work.

43. Are you unavailable? Do you have an unlisted phone so your patients can't reach you after office hours? You can't build a practice by hiding from your patients! I have been fortunate to practice twenty years and have never had an unlisted telephone and have never had any patients abuse the privilege of calling me at home. Are you practicing to serve your patients or to hide from them? It is your choice.

44. Fractionalizing of office time. Whenever a doctor rushes into a room to see a patient, fills out half an insurance form, takes personal phone calls, visits at length with a good friend-patient, and on and on, this is called "fractionalizing" of office time. Frankly, the very nature of a chiropractic office lends itself to this drip-and-drab approach to a number of jobs. Obviously, a truly cluster-booked practice is by far and away the most efficient. If a doctor can condition himself to do certain specific jobs at certain times, then holds himself to such a self-agreement, he is way ahead. For instance, if you pay the bills only twice a month and you do insurance only on Thursdays between the hours of two and five, those types of time commitments really open up holes to do other jobs whenever necessary.

45. Overmanagement of a practice. The second most prevalent time-waster is a doctor's desire for staying on top of everything, with repetitious inquiry as to the status of this and that and the next thing and, in effect, poking his nose into everything that is going on all day long. Oftentimes this grows out of an insecurity that things are not getting done, and an unwillingness to stipulate that the employees are doing their jobs as they are required. Doctors, in many cases, are masters of the bottleneck system. That is, they require everyone to channel things through them for their attention and, consequently, hold up progress for other employees. Don't over-kill as far as management is concerned. Simply delegate a job to a member of your staff and give him/her a time reference to report back to you that the job is done.

Are You Developing a Bad Reputation?

46. Don't be a womanizer in your office. Keep your hands off the lady patients. If you have a sudden sex drive, go home! If you have an incessant sex drive, take care of it before you go to the office! Keep your hands off the women patients! This type of activity will give you a bad reputation, and if you develop this kind of reputation, you will not have a practice.

47. Do you have bad personal habits? Do you hang around the pool hall or the local bar? Are you one of those doctors who drinks too much, likes to smoke "funny" cigarettes? If so, do it privately. Don't let your town know about your bad habits. If you get a bad reputation from your habits, it will destroy your practice. Use common sense.

48. Are your friends a bad influence on you? Are your friends negative, down-trodden, bearers of gloom and bad tidings? Do they have bad reputations that can rub off on you? If so, get a new set of friends. It is a proven fact that all bums are friends of bums. People on welfare have friends who are on welfare. Drunks hang around with drunks, and so on. If your friends are not the uplifting type, discard them as they will hold you back. Do you associate with D.C.'s who are not successful? If so, you will remain unsuccessful. Only associate with successful D.C.'s. They will help you up the ladder. If your practice is down, call another D.C. who you know is doing well. Talk with him and he will lift you up. Remember, you are judged by your associates.

49. Do you have NO reputation? It is equally bad to have no reputation at all, as it is to have a bad reputation. How are people going to come to your office if they don't know you are in their town? Is your lifestyle like that of a hermit: not circulating in the community? There is an old axiom that says, if you want to double your practice, you have to double the amount of people who know you. Don't hide yourself. Circulate in your community. Join civic clubs, athletic leagues, etc., to get yourself known.

50. Do you have a strict "cash only" policy in your office? If so, you are making a mistake and keeping patients out of your office. Eighty percent of our patients have insurance and want to utilize it when coming to our offices. Many doctors have policies that the patient pays the doctor and the doctor fills out the patient's insurance forms. The insurance company then pays the patient. This type office policy works well if the patients are all wealthy. However, since most patients are not wealthy, this type office policy will not greatly help the patient and will have a deterrent effect on the doctor's volume, income, etc.

For example, if you can imagine a typical, middle-class, insured patient who has a take-home income of two hundred dollars per week, has a wife and two children, mortgage payment, etc., his insurance coverage is probably a hundred-dollar deductible and pays eighty percent of all bills above the deductible. Before his insurance company will be of any benefit, he will have to spend a hundred dollars or more for services which he probably can't afford. Then the insurance company will pay only eighty percent of any future services. Even then, he will have to pay for your services before he will be reimbursed two or three months down the line. Just exactly how much more can this middle-income patient pay you before he runs out of spare cash? A hundred dollars? Two hundred? Therefore, you are placing a ceiling on how much this patient can pay your office before he has to quit for financial reasons, after two or three hundred dollars.

If the doctor would just reverse his procedure — that is, accept insurance assignments, accept eighty percent from the insurance company and then let the patient pay off the difference in installments to stay under chiropractic care longer, to get better results, and bring his family in to see you under insurance assignment, etc., etc. — the doctor's practice would go up in volume, income, etc., and everyone would be happier. Think about it!

51. Do you have too liberal a cash policy in your office? This type policy is exactly the opposite policy described in the previous point. By letting your patients charge their services, building up large balances, you will again be holding down your patient volume and income.

It is a psychological fact that patients who owe doctors money (lots of it), will end up quitting the doctor, and they will become "knockers" in order to justify why they shouldn't pay their bills and will possibly sue the doctor for imagined malpractice cases whenever he pushes for collection. A good middle-of-the-road policy is: Patients be allowed to charge in your office if you have an assignment on their insurance coverage, and they should be allowed to charge in your office without insurance if they have previously demonstrated their ability and willingness to pay. For all other patients, have a cash only policy. With the above described policy, your office procedures won't be too strict or too liberal.

52. Do you have fluctuating fee schedule? Don't fluctuate! Don't fluctuate your care. I find this with a lot of chiropractors. They charge one patient $20 for a service and charge the next patient $10 for the same service. You have to understand that people talk to each other, and when they start comparing fees, they'll find that the one patient is paying a certain amount for your services and the other patient is paying less for the same service, and you have lost both patients because both of them become disgruntled with you. You have to have continuity of office procedure.

53. Try to keep your regular office visits below $25 a visit. Statistics show that a patient will pay three or four office visits over $25 and still remain an active patient. However, if the over-$25-an-office visit continues above four or five visits, the patient will quit for financial reasons. Office visits in the $20 to $25 range will not cause hardship on the patient and he will remain under your care.

Naturally, the above described guidelines will vary with the area in which you practice.

In small communities, the described dollar figures would be lower and in the more affluent communities, in the larger cities, the dollar values would probably be higher. Again, common sense is your best guide.

54. Adjust all financial disagreements to the patient's benefit. If a disagreement comes up with a patient concerning small amounts of money, credit the patient's account this small amount, in order not to lose that patient. If the patient is positive he has paid off his account yet you still have a $20 balance on your record, don't force the patient to pay the $10 or $20 and lose the patient, his family, and possibly their referrals. Use common sense!

55. Do you have proper office supplies — all the supplies that you need? This pertains to vitamins, orthopedic supplies, and so on. If you don't have the proper supplies, how are you going to take proper care of your patient? If you put yourself in the position of the patient and you tell the patient certain vitamins that you want him to take and he goes out to the receptionist's desk to pick up the vitamins and none of them, not even part of them, are there, this reeks of inefficiency and the patient doesn't like it. Besides, if you do not have the proper supplies, how are you going to dispense them? If you cannot dispense them, obviously you will lose income. More important than the loss of income is the negative effect that it has on the patient who goes out to get the proper supplies that are not available in your office. Be well stocked and have a tickler or card system on all vitamins and orthopedic supplies to make sure that you are up to date at all times with these necessary items.

56. Don't keep your patients waiting too long in your reception room. It is obviously important to keep your reception room full at all times. But keep the patients moving in and out of the reception room. You should adopt a policy like I have in my office: one half-hour from the time the patient enters my office he/she has waited, undressed, been treated, and is gone from the office! Naturally, this refers strictly to the normal office visit. There are exceptions to the rule, which would be the initial office visit with consultation, x-ray, examination, and so on, which obviously take longer periods of time. But the normal office visit should be no more than thirty minutes. Remember, a patient can afford to schedule three half-hours a week in your office, but can's afford to schedule three *afternoons* a week! So, get the patient in and out!

57. Try not to let the patient see an empty reception room. Naturally, if you are starting out in practice, this is difficult to do. If you are just starting in practice, it would be a good idea to hang someone's coat or hat in the reception room to give the patient coming into the room the impression that someone else is being treated in the office. If you have an already-established practice, group the patients together. Do not schedule one patient where he won't see another patient. People don't like to be experimented on. When a patient goes into a doctor's office and sees that he is the only person in the office, it gives him an eerie feeling and he might feel he is being experimented on. Therefore, group your patients together. If you have four patients to see in one hour, schedule all four at exactly the same time so that they will see other people in the reception room. They will have someone to talk to whilst waiting and they will feel more secure.

An excellent example of this is when I practiced as an associate for a doctor in Georgia. Our office saw from a hundred and fifty to two hundred patients a day. One Saturday, we were supposed to fly to another city to attend a seminar, but the weather became bad and we couldn't fly out, so we went back to the office. So there we were — two doctors and the receptionist in an empty office! The office was a very large, expensive facility that could care for, as I said, two hundred patients a day. Well, a new patient was scheduled. The lady sat in the empty reception room and looked up at us: two doctors and a receptionist with no one else in the office. She said, "Well, you doctors couldn't be any good or you would have an office full of people. I'm not going to allow you to experiment on me." And she left! It's ironic that in a busy practice, like the one described here, that just because there wasn't anyone in the reception room, the patient left.

When you have new patients, schedule them with your regular flow of patients. For example, if you have a hole in your schedule for new patients at ten thirty in the morning, don't schedule the new patient at ten thirty so that he comes in and sees an empty office. Schedule him at ten o'clock so that he can come and see a full office. By the time the receptionist gathers the pre-history information: address, telephone number, etc., you will have finished with your first group of patients and will be ready to see the new patient without the pressure of any patients in the office. Then, when the new patient is through and walks out, the next group of patients have arrived and the new patient again sees a full waiting room and doesn't feel like he is being experimented on.

58. Are you too rushed? If you are too busy and appear rushed, the patient will feel short-changed, feeling that you didn't spend enough time with him, and he will quit. There is a technique that you should use when you are busy. *The busier you are, the slower you must go.* If you speed up, you are going to make errors. You will then have to undo those errors, and the next thing you'll know is that you are further behind schedule. The technique is very simple: When you walk into the room, ask the patient how he feels, then shut up and listen to him. Then you say, "Let's find it." Then you can say you have found it. Next, you can say, "Let's fix it." Then say that you have fixed it. Tell him the results he can expect from the adjustment and tell him when next to come in. This is about a two-and-a-half-minute office visit, but the patient feels it has taken half an hour. You are not talking about anything other than what you did to that patient that day. You have given total concentration to that person. When you are really busy and you try to hurry, stick to the script!

59. Are you always behind schedule? Many times a doctor feels that he runs behind schedule because he is a busy doctor. I have a friend who is a pediatrician and, even with the little kids who are sick with the flu or vomiting all over the place, and even with the emergencies he has, if an appointment is at ten o'clock, he see that patient promptly at ten o'clock, and he never has over three or five minutes' waiting period. If he can run this tight a schedule with the chaos that is prevalent in that kind of practice, so can you! So move the freight! Get the people in and get them out! Don't make them wait. If you make them wait, they can't come to you. The patient cannot schedule three afternoons a week in your office, but he can schedule three half-hours per week.

I remember many years ago I hired a practice management consultant to come through my office because I was always running an hour to an hour and a half behind schedule, and I thought that my receptionist and staff had something to do with the screwing up of my schedule. I knew that I was efficient, but somewhere my office wasn't efficient. So, therefore, I hired a high-priced consultant to come in and review my procedure. This man spent two days in my office reviewing what the staff was doing, watching the operation of the office, watching me, etc. Then he sat down and talked to me. I was waiting to hear what my staff was doing wrong. He told me: "Dr. Fernandez, your staff is perfect. Your receptionist is doing a good job. It is your big mouth that is holding your schedule up. You are talking too much, and you are keeping everyone else waiting." It was a hard lesson to learn. It was my *mouth* that was causing me to run behind schedule! When I quit talking and started taking care of patients, making sure I only talked about their condition, all of a sudden I was right on schedule and I was able to get a patient in and out of the office in a period of thirty minutes. Needless to say, my practice doubled, and I was still on schedule. Patients were happier, my staff was happier, and obviously, so was I.

60. Are you in a hurry to leave your office? Do you like to be home at a certain time and rush through the last few patients to get out of your office? This is a great way to lose patients! The doctor should continue practicing until the last patient is competently cared for. Never set appointments for out-of-the-office activities or have dinner within one hour of your closing time. If you are rushed to get out of the office, the patient will sense that you are in a hurry. When you are rushed, the patient may be hurt, and he will not be able to comfortably relate some of his problems to you. He will feel slighted that you are not interested, and so you will lose that patient. Start your office hours fifteen minutes earlier and end as the last patient is seen. Remember, the patient will sense that you are in a hurry and will quit your care.

61. Do you have a tight-ship practice? Do you have a practice that runs on an appointment-only schedule? Do you have a practice where you see new patients at certain times and give reports of findings at certain times? Is everything done in clusters? Is everything on time? I have heard from many doctors that it is impossible to have this kind of practice in chiropractic because people come in sometimes in pain, and they take longer than a patient who is not in pain. As I have previously stated, if a busy pediatrician can be on schedule and see seventy patients a day, so can a D.C.! In other words, don't kid a kidder! If you are not on time, if the patients have to wait, there is something wrong with you as a practitioner. There is something you are doing that is wrong!

62. Do you have an appointment-only practice? It is obvious for the efficient running of an office that a strict appointment schedule is needed. I am not suggesting that you kick patients out of your office who don't have appointments! But I am suggesting that you schedule patients with appointments and that you keep those appointments. If a patient walks in and would like to see a doctor, you tell him you will be happy to see him once your regularly scheduled patients are seen. In other words, if you have a tight appointment schedule from nine to ten thirty in the morning and then from eleven to noon, and a patient walks in the door at ten o'clock, you will be happy to see him. Have him sit out in the reception room until you are through with your ten-thirty patient, and then see the walk-in. Under no circumstances should you take a walk-in patient ahead of a patient who has an appointment. If a patient doesn't have an appointment, have him wait until the patients with appointments are seen. Frankly, most patients are happy to keep their appointments in your office if they know they will be seen relatively close to their appointment times.

63. Don't let telephone calls interrupt the doctor unless it is an absolute emergency. All personal calls and requests from patients should be noted on a memo pad; then, when the doctor has a break in his schedule, he can call back the people who just called him. Do not interrupt consultations, reports of findings, x-raying of patients, or regular office visits with telephone calls. You can imagine yourself in a position of the patient, how you would feel if, when you were ready to ask the doctor a question and the doctor was called out of the room for a telephone call and then, when he returned to the room, he had forgotten the question! Of course, you would be very upset. The doctor should devote his entire time when he is with a patient to that patient! He should never be interrupted for any phone calls other than the most dire of emergencies.

64. Develop a "running late" code. If the doctor starts to run behind schedule and the patients are waiting a little too long, his office should have a code between office staff and doctor, to inform the doctor that he is running late. This will let him know that he has to speed up the process. In my office, the code is very simple. The receptionist calls me over the intercom and says, "Doctor, the films are in the developer. Do you think they have been in there too long?" Or, "Doctor, the films are in the developer and you wanted to take a look at them." This gives me an obvious excuse to leave the room or cut short an office visit when I am talking too long with a patient. The patient won't feel miffed because he knows that I have to go and look at an x-ray film. Obviously, the doctor and the receptionist will have to work out a code that will suit them best, and the doctor should never get offended at the receptionist notifying him that he is running behind schedule or talking too much. Naturally, you should use a code that the patient won't understand. Remember, the receptionist is the captain of the ship. She is the one that is responsible for moving the practice and the doctor, too. This is a responsibility you have assigned to her. Don't be upset when she gives you the secret code word so you can move faster.

65. Are you constantly behind in your office? Do you always have a stack of thirty or forty x-rays that have to be filed or ten or fifteen narratives that have to be written? Do you have twenty to thirty insurance forms that have to be filled out? If this applies to you, then you are cutting off a tremendous flow of new patients strictly because you are bogged down due to inefficiency in your office procedure. It is a known fact that psychologically you will push away any new patients who have insurance, who are litigated patients, who need narrative reports, or who need x-rays, simply because you are behind. It is a very negative feeling to walk into your business office and see twenty insurance forms sitting on your desk. You think, "My God, do I have to do this?" Well, you are surely not going to go out and push for more insurance business when you hate to do the insurance you already have.

The same thing is true of the narrative reports, the litigated cases, and so on. If you want to increase your practice in insurance areas and litigation, x-raying patients, and so on, get up to date, and stay up to date! Schedule a certain period in your practice, say a Tuesday afternoon or a Thursday morning, that it is strictly designed as "catch up" time to do insurance forms, to do narrative reports, and so on. Get the job done and keep it done weekly. When your office is up to date, then you can concept and attract new patients who have insurance or are litigated cases, etc. In this way you will increase your practice. If you are behind, you will not increase your practice.

66. Do you have a lack of continuity in your practice? Many doctors are guilty of: When one patient comes into a doctor's office and he follows a certain procedure, then the next patient comes in, he blows it by having a completely *different* procedure for that second patient. I find this true with doctors who use written reports. When they are not busy, they give written reports to their patients, but when they *are* busy, they drop the written reports altogether. In other words, they are not consistent. Well, what happens is that when you give a written report to a patient, he becomes a "booster" and tells his friends. They, in turn, tell their friends, and so the word gets around that you give neat, written reports to all your patients. But when a friend of the patient whom you had given a written report to comes in and you *don't* give him a written report, well, it is obvious that he is going to feel short-changed. So now you have lost the referring patient, the patient he referred to you, and any other patients he might have referred to you. Get a standard procedure, and stick with it if you want your practice to grow.

67. Are all activities in your office organized? Or, do you do one activity when it comes up, and then jump to another one, come back to the first one, see a couple of patients, dictate a narrative report, see two more patients, develop x-ray film, and have a constant chaos in your office all day long? It is better to practice in clusters. Cluster all the patients that you are going to see into groups. See the patients, get in the rhythm of treating the patients. Then, when you are through, sit down and do all your insurances at one time. An excellent way to do this is to reserve, say, a Thursday morning or Tuesday afternoon strictly for billing patients, writing narrative reports, filling out insurance forms, etc. Organize your activities in clusters. Treat in clusters . . . dictate in clusters . . . examine in clusters . . . and so on! This will make your office procedure much more efficient. You will then be able to see more patients yet be more relaxed at the end of the day because the day hasn't been chaotic.

68. Don't handle the same piece of paper twice. If you have a request to do an insurance form, there should be a place on your desk for these forms so that when the time of the week comes that you do insurance forms, you can pick up the form, fill it out, and get it out of the way. Then you can pick up the next form, fill it out and get it out of the way. Don't grab the paper, look at it, put it in another stack and constantly shuffle the papers back and forth. Don't massage the papers. Only handle them once. When you have a form in your hand, fill it out and get it over with. "Do It Now!" should be your motto.

69. Are you a lazy doctor? Do you procrastinate any chance that you get? Do you follow the motto "Don't put off till tomorrow what you can put off till three days after tomorrow"? In your office, you should have a "Do It Now" attitude. If something needs to be done, do it without thinking. Many times during the course of a busy day, a doctor will have a tendency to let slide procedures that should be followed. For instance, he knows he should x-ray a certain patient on a particular busy day, but puts it off until a later visit because he is so busy. Unfortunately, at the next visit, things are just as pressured, and he lets it slide once again. When you have a break in your schedule, sit down for a couple of minutes, pick up some insurance forms and write the diagnosis on them to help the receptionist or the insurance girl. Or, start the process of dictating a narrative report. Make every second count in your office. The motto here is "Work hard, and when you're through with office hours, then play hard." Don't be a lazy, procrastinating type of doctor. You are there to do a job, so do it! Try and keep everything up to date. I cannot stress this too many times.

You can imagine how many procedures that you don't do on

patients that could bring additional income, but because you were too lazy they weren't done. For example, blood work, urinalysis, additional x-rays, nutritional evaluation, and so on. You can imagine what would happen in an average middle-of-the-road chiropractic practice of a hundred patients per week if the doctor was lazy. He probably would lose $20,000 to $30,000 in income! A good procedure is: At the beginning of a patient's case, map out your plan of attack on his problem — not only how many treatments you feel he should need, but also what tests you would like to do on him. Then schedule these tests and have a tickler file to tell you automatically when the tests are to be performed. Then schedule the time to perform the tests. In other words, map your plan and then work your plan on each and every patient.

70. Do your office hours vary? Do you have certain hours for the winter and certain hours for the summer? Do you start at ten o'clock in the morning one week and nine o'clock in the morning another week? Or do you decide that you are going to take off all day on a Thursday and then change your mind to half days off on Thursdays and half days on Saturdays? Are you constantly varying your office hours? If so, you are driving your patients crazy! Set definite office hours so that patients will know exactly what times you will be in your office. Year in and year out, you should be available to see patients during regular office hours. Patients must feel that when they call in, you will be there. Don't let them quit your care because they never know when you will be in your office. Let them know you are available to them in your office Monday through Friday, nine to five (or whatever your office hours are). They will then know that you are sure to be in the office at those hours and that they can see you or talk to you during those working hours.

71. Do you have an appointment-book practice? Is everything that takes place in your office noted in your appointment book? Memos to call people when they get back from vacation . . . deposits that you make daily . . . accounts receivable totals . . . telephone calls made by your receptionist or by you . . . and so on? If you are going to run an efficient practice, you must have a master control log that controls the practice, and that is the appointment book. Everything revolves around the appointment book and everything is noted in it. Then, if four or five months down the road, you want to check and see when that certain man called, or when you called so-and-so, you can flip back through the book and — there it is! The more efficient a doctor is, the more patients he can see. Therefore, the more patients he sees, the more care he renders and, obviously, the more income he makes. Be efficient! Have an appointment-book practice!

72. Do you pay attention to details in your office? Do you make sure that whatever you assign to your staff is carried out? Do you make sure that recall on present patients is done? Nationally, across the country, nine percent of patients call daily to cancel their appointments or to reschedule them. You should have accurate figures on hand of how many people call and reschedule, and how many people call to cancel appointments. The combination of these two should not exceed nine percent. If it does, something is wrong with your office procedure. You should check what you are doing wrong and correct it. Pay attention to details. How many recalls are done daily? How many birthday cards are sent out daily? It is the man who pays attention to details who moves his practice ahead!

73. Do you schedule multiple appointments? If you don't, you are overworking your C.A. It is an excellent procedure in a chiropractic office to set the patient up on three months' care, and give him a calendar that has the entire year on it, and then set up all three months' appointments at one time. Put all these appointments in your appointment book to make sure you reserve that time for that particular patient. The patient will appreciate knowing that he has a time reserved with you, because he knows that you are on a strict appointment system. It also shows that the doctor is very serious about the patient following the care exactly as he has programmed it. When he says "three months," he means "three months," because he gave that patient a calendar of his office visits with all the dates entered.

74. Do you schedule ten-visit appointments? Another excellent procedure is to go ahead and schedule the patient ten visits at a time, giving him a ten-visit appointment card. The C.A. posts all the appointments on the appointment card and, at the same time, notes in the appointment book the ten visits. This also lets the patient know that you expect him to come for the next ten visits. It lets him know you are serious about his care. When a patient knows his doctor is serious about his care, that patient will also be serious about keeping his appointments. These type procedures greatly cut down the receptionist's work time and, eventually, she will find herself with eighty percent of the practice already having their appointments made. The patient will walk out the front door and say, "See you later, Joan. I already have my appointment for Friday." It cuts down the C.A.'s work time and also shows the patients that the doctor is serious and efficient. This will increase referrals.

75. Do you send out birthday cards, Christmas cards and Thanksgiving cards? These are the little things that make the patient feel warm and welcome in your office. You will be surprised how many patients whose only birthday card is the one they receive from your office. They feel warm towards you and refer to you because of this procedure. There are many people who never get a Christmas or Thanksgiving card. Think of these people, and give them a little bit of extra care by sending greeting cards to them.

76. Do you have a good "medically necessary" recall system on your past patients? Do you send out reminder notices and cards to remind your past patients of their annual chiropractic checkups or their annual physical-orthopedic checkups? Do you have your C.A. call the patients in order to bring your files up to date, to find out how they are doing with their conditions, whether they have had any recurrences, etc.? If you don't do this, you will lose a great source of patients and income for your practice. Frankly, this is the mainstay of my practice: a constant recall of former patients. If I have a constant flow of former patients through my office, I really don't need a constant flow of new patients to keep me booked up. Actually, you are not chasing the patient; you are accepting the responsibility of being a doctor and caring for your patients . . . caring that they get the correct care to stay well. Don't shirk it.

77. Do you have a tickler or reminder file in your office? Do you contact a patient and tell him that you are going to re-examine him in six weeks and also re-x-ray? Do you remind him that, as he is on a certain nutritional and vitamin program, that he should re-order now? These things were promised to the patient and are expected by him. If you are busy, obviously you cannot remember the recommendations that you gave each and every patient as to when they should take vitamins, when they should re-order, when x-rays should be taken, and so on. You can't remember all those facts. Therefore, you should have a filing system of index cards that you can refer to about each patient's needs. The vitamins a patients needs would be noted on the card and also the date when to re-order. When that day comes, you check your cards and your C.A. can call the patient, or you can see him in the office and ask him if he re-ordered. The same is true of re-x-rays. If you know you want to re-x-ray a patient in sixty days, note it on an index card and put it in the file sixty days hence. Then, when that time comes, the receptionist simply schedules the patient for re-x-rays and you walk in the room and take the picture. Obviously, this tickler file has many uses: it coordinates your office; it gives you a strict office policy; it shows the patient that you are efficient, that you know what you are doing and what you expect him to do: you are going to do your part, and he has to do his. This is the hallmark of an efficient office and the patients love it. Naturally, the reverse is true. If you promised a patient you were going to do something and you don't, he will feel short-changed, feel that you are disinterested and that you don't care. No one goes to an office where the people in that office don't care.

78. Do you have a good recall system for present patients? Do you have a system in your office that requires that when a patient doesn't keep his appointment, he is called immediately within twenty minutes of his missed appointment? Or do you wait two or three weeks hence until your practice has a good-sized dip, to go out and scream at the receptionist to do a recall? An important fact to consider is that if you can recall the patient within thirty minutes of his missed appointment, you have a ninety-eight percent chance of recapturing him. If you recall him at the end of the day, you'll have an eighty percent chance of recapturing him. If you call him the next day or the next week, you'll only have a three percent chance! That's how important a daily recall system is. You should recall immediately upon learning of a missed appointment. Usually the patient is busy and forgot, and so will appreciate the recall. If you don't bother to call until two weeks has elapsed, the patient will think that the office visit wasn't that important. Remember, when a patient drops out of your care, it is "out of sight, out of mind." You should definitely have a good recall procedure on your patients.

79. Are you keeping in touch with your patients? Do you have a recall system to call old patients? Do you mail to the patients monthly, giving them an update on chiropractic information? Or, are you letting the patients forget that you're around, so that when they hurt, they will go to a different doctor? In my first years of practice, I used to send a mail-out to my patients every month. Naturally, I kept up a good flow of former patients. However, there was a year's period of time when I got lazy and didn't mail out anything to my patients. One day, my associate had a new patient come into the office who he examined, x-rayed, and started to treat. While walking through the office, I noticed the patient's file folder and recognized the name on it as that of one of my former patients. I walked into the dressing room and said to my former patient: "Did you ever go to a chiropractor before?" He replied, "Yes, sir." I said, "Well, who did you go to?" He said, "Oh, I went to some doctor on 9th Street in St. Petersburg, but I don't remember who he was." I said, "It was me, sir. You forgot." Then he said, "Oh, yeah, I forgot." Isn't it amazing that when you mail to a patient monthly for years and then forget for a period of time, that that patient will forget you and go to another doctor? Is this happening to your patients? Are they forgetting who took care of them and are now going to another doctor? Keep in touch with your patients!

80. Do you have poorly written literature in your office? Have you taken even ten minutes a day to read the literature that you have in your office? Or do you just order a bunch of literature from your favorite supply house and just stick it in your reception room and adjusting room? It is amazing that quite a large amount of our chiropractic informational flyers have misspellings, poor punctuation, poor sentence structure, and even relate chiropractic information which you may feel is not accurate. And yet, this type of literature is given to your patients! They walk out your door with it, read it, and then have a disbelief in you because you had that kind of trash in your office. Any literature in your office which is worthwhile buying, obviously should be worthwhile reading! Read it yourself to make sure it says what you want it to say. Another good idea is to give it to someone who you know is an expert in the written English language and let him read it to see if it is written in the correct grammar, spelling, etc. If it is worthwhile to have something informational to read in your office, it is worthwhile to make sure it is something good!

81. Do you have your telephone covered at all times? When you are not in your office — throughout the night, over your lunch period, in the evenings — do you have an answering service to catch those calls made by your patients at those times? Or do you have an answering device in your office which will pick up the patients' messages? If not, you are losing a tremendous source of new patients, former patients, etc. A study was made about ten years ago by a national practice management organization where they tried to reach ten thousand doctors by telephone. Unfortunately, they could only reach about two thousand! The rest of the doctors could not be reached by phone. If this is the case with your office, you can imagine how many phone calls a day are not getting through. You are losing practice volume, practice dollars, and so on. Keep your phone covered at all times! An answering service or answering device will only cost about twenty or twenty-five dollars a month. It is very obvious that one new patient will more than pay for this service. If you are interested in your business, take care of it by covering your phone at all times!

82. Do you have poor telephone procedures in your office for you and your staff? Have you taken courses on how to answer the telephone for you and your staff? Have you ever had the experience of calling someone's office and the receptionist or the assistant was gruff, or they gave a bad impression over the phone? We have all had such an experience. What is the experience of your patients when they call your office and listen to your voice or your receptionist's or a member of your staff's voice? Some day, when you are at home and your staff is at work, call and see what they sound like. The same is true for you. Have a friend call and see what you sound like when you answer the phone. Have him do it when you don't know the call is coming through. Take the many office procedure courses offered to our profession and learn how to properly handle the telephone. After all, this is the first contact that any patient has with your office. It should be very pleasant, efficient, warm, and welcoming. If you are not relating this impression, you are going to decrease your income and your patient volume, and you are going to start off a new patient on a negative foot rather than on a positive one.

83. Do you examine your patients? Do you perform a thorough orthopedic or neurological examination to find a reason for your patient to be under chiropractic care, other than just for pain? Patients have tendencies to minimize their problems and hope they only have small problems which would need only little care. But if you examine a patient thoroughly, you will probably find objective findings that are brought on by a long duration of a disease. The patient will then realize that he doesn't have a minor problem but a major one, and is therefore more ready to stay under chiropractic care until the objective findings are corrected. If you don't examine your patients thoroughly — orthopedically and neurologically — the patient, having only come to you because he was in pain, will "self-destruct" or dismiss himself as soon as he is out of pain. After all, why should he hang around and get more treatments when the only thing wrong with him in the first place was pain — or so he thought?

84. Do you re-examine your patients? If you perform an excellent orthopedic and neurological examination at the beginning of care and then set up a treatment program for the patient — one which seems to last for ever and ever — and then never re-examine that

261

patient thoroughly to show him the reduction in his objective signs, the patient is going to quit your care because of his assumption that there is no end to the treatment. It is therefore a good procedure to examine the patient every month and compare objective signs, to show you and your patient how he is progressing, and also to show him a reason for continuing under your care. If the patient, after two months of treatments, is examined orthopedically, and fifty percent of his objective findings are eliminated, he is going to be very pleased. At the same time, the remaining fifty percent will give him good psychological reasons to continue under your care, even though he may be asymptomatic at that point. Your motto should be: "Examine, examine, examine, and re-examine!" — for good patient control.

85. How good is your consultation, examination, and report? Consultation is where it's at! In consultation, the doctor will figure out ninety-five percent of the diagnosis. The examination basically rules out some things. The consultation is where you do your job. The consultation tells the patient that you are interested in him. In consultation, you dig until you find an answer. The examination should be extensive. It should blow the patient's mind! It should be more thorough than that of any other doctor who has examined that patient before, and the report should not be a "snow" job. Sit down with the patient and explain what is wrong with him — in simple English — and tell him how long it will take to treat. These three steps: the consultation, the examination, the report, are the most important!

86. Do you examine and x-ray the patient's pain part? We all know that, with the majority of patients who come into our offices with shoulder or arm problems, the problem is actually in the patient's cervical spine or upper thoracic spine. When a patient says his arm hurts, his hand is numb, his shoulder hurts, etc., etc., the doctor immediately goes to the spinal column in order to find the cause. Well, the patient said his shoulder hurts (or his arm) and he wanted that part examined and x-rayed to make sure something wasn't pathologically wrong in that area. And, who knows? If the patient has a shoulder problem (perhaps he has a carcinoma in the shoulder or an arthritic spur or tendonitis or calcific bursitis), you don't know until you examine; you don't know until you x-ray. And the patient knows that you don't know! So, a hard and fast rule in your office should be: Examine and x-ray the pain part. If a patient has four pain parts, examine and x-ray them all. Then, when you give the report of findings, you can tell the patient, "This is a picture of your shoulder. There isn't anything wrong with it. Actually, your problem is coming from the cervical spine. Let me show you your neck and show you where your problem is coming from." Your patient will know then what is wrong with him and what is *not* wrong with him. You don't know what is not wrong with the patient until you have examined and x-rayed the pain part.

87. Are you disorganized in your presentations to a patient during consultation, in your report of findings, or in the mini-report of findings that you give after performing orthopedic or neurological examinations? Patients appreciate efficiency and organized thought. If you go into a report of findings with a patient and shuffle through papers to find the correct one — the one with that patient's problem noted on it — if you ramble during your presentation, the patient is going to think you are disorganized. This won't build up his confidence in you and he won't stay under your care. The report of findings, and even the mini-report of findings, should be canned and planned. Know exactly what you are going to say when you confront the patient. Get to the point, with no extraneous thoughts thrown in. The patient will see that you are efficient, that you know what you are doing, and he will realize that you are a professional and not an amateur. Be professional, be thorough, and be organized!

88. Are you guilty of not telling your patients how long they have to stay under active care or how much their care is going to cost? Or, do you go ahead and start treatment of a patient, saying, "Well, you will be relieved shortly. Just stay with me and I will do my job"? The patient feels he is taking treatments under your care forever and ever, and the costs for that care gets higher and higher. He doesn't know when his treatment is going to end and he will have uncertainty in his mind about your care. He will quit as soon as his symptoms are relieved sufficiently to please him, and then you have lost a patient. An efficient doctor covers all aspects of care with a patient. An inefficient doctor doesn't! An efficient doctor has a large practice. An inefficient doctor has a helter-skelter mess in his office and, consequently, a smaller practice!

89. Don't let patients see you or your staff standing around doing nothing. Remember, patients like to go to busy doctors. They feel that good doctors are busy doctors, and they like to see the staff busy. If a patient sees the doctor standing around, he will think he is not a good doctor because he isn't busy. In my office, we have a ten-second zone around the receptionist area. No doctor is allowed to stand in this area for more than ten seconds. A doctor may state his business to the receptionist and then move on. This

263

is an essential procedure in your office if you want to keep your patients.

90. Take notes and show interest. A recent study showed that patients in hospitals felt slighted by their doctors' care. A doctor, in most hospitals, simply goes into the patient's room, examines the patient, says a couple of words, and then leaves. That patient then feels that he didn't receive enough of his doctor's time. He didn't realize that the doctor, prior to entering the patient's room, had read the patient's chart, made notations on the chart, then entered the room, examined the patient, left the room, and then spent five to seven minutes writing his findings on that patient's chart. The doctor spent half an hour or more with that patient! Yet the patient only saw the doctor for maybe ten minutes or less. So, reverse the procedure in your office. Read the patient's chart in front of him. As you talk to him, show interest in him. When you are through, write your notes on that patient's file — in front of him. After that, say, "goodbye," and leave the room. This lets the patient know that you are interested in him and that you are noting various aspects of his treatment as you progress with his care.

91. Are you guilty of the Peter Principle? There was a book published recently about the Peter Principle. This is about people in the service, or any large organization, who, when they are very efficient, are promoted to higher positions which they can handle efficiently and competently. They keep getting promoted higher and higher up the ladder until they are promoted into a position which they are no longer qualified to handle competently. They have been promoted into a position of incompetency. Is this the way you are in your practice? Are you only competent to handle a certain number of patients per day? Are you only competent to see so many new patients per week before you become inefficient? An excellent example of this is the case of a doctor who recently came to town. He had practiced in another locale and saw thirty patients a day for ten years. When he came to St. Petersburg, he bought a practice that was seeing seventy patients a day. Within three months, that practice went down to thirty patients a day. He couldn't assimilate, handle, and keep the fifty-eight new patients he had because his level of competency was thirty patients a day! Take a realistic appraisal of yourself. What is your competency level? What would be your incompetency level? If you want to build your practice, look realistically at your competency level and then attend seminars to learn how to handle more patients, how to more efficiently treat patients, in order to increase your level of competency. When this level is increased, your practice will increase to that level. You have to constantly upgrade your level of competency in order to build a larger practice. You cannot see more people than you can competently handle.

92. Do you listen to your patients? Do you really listen to your patients? Many times a patient will come into your office and tell you about a friend of his who has been in an automobile accident, but, because you were so busy or your mind was somewhere else, you didn't hear what he was saying and, therefore, you didn't tell him to schedule his friend to come into your office for an examination. Or perhaps a patient tells you about a relative who has a certain problem, but your mind is somewhere else and you don't listen to him. You don't pick up what he is telling you and, consequently, you cut off a source of referrals. Your patients will sometimes tell you where your new patients are coming from — so listen to them!

93. Do you leave a patient guessing? Do you neglect to tell a patient what he can expect to gain from chiropractic care, or the normal progression of the healing process? Do you reinforce your results on each office visit? It is not enough to tell the patient that once the vertebra is set in its proper alignment that his condition will heal. We all know that conditions heal in stages. First one thing heals, a certain pain is relieved, and then another pain will be relieved. It is a steady, slow healing process. The patient doesn't really know what to expect unless you tell him. Remember, to a patient his physical condition is a scary thing. Whenever his symptoms change, the patient gets scared, thinking his condition is getting worse, and he imagines all kinds of fearsome thoughts. Therefore, the doctor should tell the patient, once he is started under your care, the sequence of events he can expect. Lay it out for the patient and then, when the patient comes in and you ask him what symptoms have changed, you can say, "That's good! That's part of the healing process. What you can expect now is . . . ." You should keep on explaining to the patient, reinforcing your care all the way down the line, until the patient is well.

94. Are you guilty of keeping poor records? Have you ever had a patient come in with a pain in his neck, arm pain, and his whole hand was numb? You treat that patient for three months, and he comes in one day and says, "Boy, am I mad at you!" You ask why and he replies that his finger is numb. You ask him about his neck, and he says that is fine; his arm is fine also, etc. If you didn't have good written notes on that patient's condition, you would never have been able to refer back to his original complaints, enabling you to point out the symptoms that have improved when he was complaining to you about his finger. Without detailed notes of consultation and examination, you would never have been able to change that patient's negative complaints to a proof of positive results, and you would have lost a patient because he would still be mad at you. Think about it.

95. Don't treat more than one condition at a time. The patient comes in and his problem is that he has back pain, pain going down the leg, as in sciatica, and you delve into his past history and find out he also has sinusitis, asthma, a heart murmur, high blood pressure, and ulcers! Don't tell the patient you are going to treat all of these conditions, because if you treat all the conditions and you expect all to be cured, and you tell him so, you may fail on one or two of these conditions and the patient will quit your care because you failed to cure only one or two of those conditions. So, treat one condition at a time! If the patient says his main problem is low back pain and leg pain, treat that problem first and relieve that problem. Then you are a hero! If you treat all his problems and they do not resolve, then you are a failure in that patient's mind. You will lose that patient and you will have a "knocker." It is well known in our profession that ten percent of any particular condition does not respond to chiropractic. Just like the disc condition: we all know that ninety percent of all patients who have disc problems will get well, or be much improved. But ten percent will not be helped, and they will possibly need surgery. The same is true of whiplash or brachial neuralgia: ninety percent improve and ten percent do not. Therefore, if you are going to treat five separate conditions, your ten percent failure ratio is staring you in the face on each one of these conditions. In other words, if you are going to treat five conditions on a patient, you have a fifty percent chance of failure. Who wants those odds? Treat one condition at a time.

96. Question your patients to see if they are following your recommendations at home. Quite often a doctor will tell a patient that he wants him to do certain things at home: exercise, use hot packs, ice packs, take tub baths, sleep on a firm mattress, walk two or three blocks a day, etc. Once you tell a patient these things, you should always follow up on it. I feel the doctor should nag, cajole and push the patient into following the recommendations that help the patient get well. Patients do not mind the doctor's concern for them when he badgers them to do things for their own benefit. It shows the patients that the doctor has concern for them

266

and wants them to get well. Whenever you show a patient that you want him well and that you do have concern for him, then he will become enthusiastic over you and your services and will refer his friends, and your practice will increase. The reverse is true: If you don't follow through on your recommendations by questioning your patients, they will feel that you don't really care and, if the doctor doesn't really care, then they won't either. They won't stay under your care, and they won't refer.

97. Do you keep patients coming to you too long without sufficient results? If you tell a patient that you feel his symptoms will be relieved within thirty days, and yet, at the end of thirty days, his symptoms are not relieved and you are still treating him, that patient is going to feel short-changed and will wonder if he is being treated by the right doctor. I feel the proper procedure to utilize in this type of circumstance is, if the patient doesn't respond as you expect him to, re-x-ray and re-examine the patient, re-evaluate your position, and then report to him your findings. If there is no change in his condition, tell him that you had expected better results by this time, and that his body has not responded as anticipated. Apparently the patient's body is going to take longer than normal in recovering. Simply tell him that you will be happy to continue treating, but that it is going to take longer to get well than you had anticipated. Also tell him that, if he wishes, you would be happy to refer him to another doctor, and you would send the x-rays, etc. on to that doctor. You should give the patient the opportunity to continue under your care or to go to another doctor. It has been my experience that ninety percent of these patients decided to stay with me, even though it was explained to them that their conditions would take a longer time to heal. If the patient does take the elective of going to another doctor, he will still have good feelings toward you and will continue to refer to you. However, if you keep dragging the patient's treatment on and on with no satisfactory results, and don't give that patient the option of choice of doctors, he will discontinue coming anyway because of the unsatisfactory results, and if he leaves your care under such circumstances, he will obviously not refer patients to you.

98. Don't reinforce the negative. If the patient has a health problem, don't ask him during each office visit how his health problem is, and have him repeat the horror story of all the symptoms, pain, etc. Change his mind from negative to positive by asking him what is better. Ask him to explain each and every symptom that has improved. What has he noticed that shows improvement, and what can he do now that he couldn't do before? Take the patient's mind off his problems by saying, "Where are you going on vacation? What about that hobby you have, how are you doing with it?" By changing the patient's mind from negative to positive, you will speed up his results. The better results you get, naturally the more patients will refer, and your practice will increase.

99. Are you guilty of improper timing? Do you try to teach your patients about chiropractic when they are in pain? Do you try and give them a chiropractic lecture whenever they are in a hurry to leave your office to keep another appointment? Proper timing is important to motivate patients. When patients first come to you and they are in pain, they don't want to hear about other conditions that chiropractic can take care of, or that you want them to refer other people to you. At this point, they simply want to talk about their condition and what they can expect as they get well. Tell them about other patients, of the same age and sex, with similar problems, and how they responded to your treatment. Give them hope. Once a patient is out of pain and feeling good, and once he appreciates the benefits of chiropractic, *then* you can start educating him! Don't try to educate him when he is in pain. He won't listen. Would you? Watch your timing . . . it is important.

100. Are you slovenly in your approach to your patients? The patients want a thorough doctor. They don't like to go to a doctor who overlooks problems or who leaves many stones unturned. Years ago I sent out questionnaires to all my patients, asking them to anonymously answer the ten questions on the questionnaire, all pertaining to my practice. One of the questions asked was whether or not they thought my examinations of them were thorough, mediocre, or poor. Naturally, I expected a "thorough" answer! I hate to relate my percentage of results on this question, but it ranged from "poor" to "inadequate"! That's how my patients felt about my examinations, and I thought I was an excellent examiner. Your patients want thorough examinations. Perhaps they are not getting them. Be extremely thorough and leave no stones unturned when examining and questioning your patients in consultation and examination. I have a friend in St. Petersburg who is a physician, and every patient who comes into his office, regardless of his problem, is thoroughly examined — orthopedic, neurologic, physical examination, and a huge barrage of blood work, are all carried out. All of his patients say the same thing: "Boy, is he expensive! But he certainly is thorough! He found out what was really wrong with me!" This particular doctor sees over a hundred and fifty patients a day, five days a week, and is always extremely thorough when examining them. The patients love it and tell their friends how good their doctor is. He doesn't need their referrals because, obviously, he is too full taking competent care of his regular patients. Think about it!

101. Do you make your lady patients put on gowns, completely disrobe, when they come to you for a cervical problem only? Many times you can have the lady patient simply wear a dress that zips down the back and not wear a slip. The doctor can then simply unzip the dress, unsnap the bra, and the spine is exposed for his examination. Many lady patients don't like to disrobe in front of anyone, including their doctor. There are many reasons why they don't like to disrobe in front of people. One is when she is on her menstrual period — for obvious reasons. Another reason is if a lady has her hair done just the way she likes it. When she takes off her dress or blouse, she messes up her hair and this puts her in an unresponsive mood, because she is now already irritated. Naturally, there are certain times when she has to disrobe and get into a gown: to utilize therapy on a lumbar problem or thoracic problem. That is understandable. But, if you know you are not going to use therapy, simply unzipping the back of the patient's dress will suffice. If the patient has only a cervical problem, there isn't any real need for her to disrobe, and she would be more comfortable if she didn't have to. The more comfortable your patients are, the more cooperative they will be and the more they will refer.

102. Do you explain chiropractic to a patient? I don't mean: Are you giving a chiropractic "snow" job? What I am referring to is, are you explaining to each and every one of your patients what chiropractic can do for a multitude of conditions? It is a well-known fact that headache patients refer headache patients; backache patients refer backache patients, and so on. It is rare that a backache patient will refer a headache patient, unless they know that you can cure headaches. Unfortunately, in a busy practice, the majority of patients don't know that you can take care of multiple conditions. An excellent procedure that was started in our profession fifty or sixty years ago was the "touch and tell system." Whenever the doctor of chiropractic has the patient on the table and he is going to adjust the second thoracic vertebra, he explains to the patient which vertebra it is, where the nerves go, and for patients who come to him who have arrythmia of the heart, heart pains, chest pains, etc., this is the area in which he works. He corrects their problem. When he adjusts the upper cervical area, this is the area which causes headaches, and with all the headache patients you have, this is where you find their problem. If he adjusts the thoracics, he tells the patient this is the area that controls the stomach, this is the area that ulcer patients have problems with, and when we treat them, the ulcers clear up. Each and every time the doctor adjusts a vertebral segment, he explains to the patient where the nerves go, the conditions caused, and how he helps people with these conditions. It is a good, slow, subliminal way to educate your patients to the many conditions that chiropractic can take care of. Then, the headache patients can leave your office and refer ulcer patients, patients with shoulder problems, kidney problems, low back problems, discs, sciatica, etc. If you don't have a good system like this in your office, obviously you are cutting down on the number of referrals you can obtain from each and every one of your patients!

103. Do you inconvenience your patients? It is silly to expect patients to keep appointments when the doctor doesn't keep them himself, by being fifteen minutes late in the morning or in the afternoon. If you are really serious about your practice, arrive at the office fifteen minutes before your morning and afternoon appointments. Start fifteen minutes early and end as the last patient is taken care of. Do not end the day by the clock! I wouldn't like to be the patient of a doctor who has a habit of oversleeping in the morning and who takes too much time for his lunch period, making me wait while he is out doing something that doesn't pertain to his patients. Patients appreciate efficiency, and a doctor who is on time and sees them on time is the doctor they will continue to see.

104. Are your office hours inconvenient? Do you have screwball office hours like 10:00 to 11:30 in the morning and 2:30 to 5:00 in the afternoon? If so, how is your patient going to get in before work or after work. or during his lunch hour? Try to schedule your office hours to meet the needs of the majority of people in your community. If you are working in an industrial area where there are many different factories, evening hours are an excellent idea. If you know that most of the people in your area work from eight in the morning until four in the afternoon, then your heavy workload should be from four in the afternoon until eight or nine at night. I know many doctors feel that the patients can take off work if they need care. Just visualize yourself in their employers' shoes; how would you like to have your staff taking off work three times a week to go to a doctor during your office hours? You wouldn't like it, nor would you permit it. Why, then, would you expect your patients' employers to permit it? Again, if you are interested in seeing patients and interested in seeing volume in your practice, have office hours that suit your patients' needs.

105. Are you thorough enough with your patients? Do you examine, examine, and then re-examine? Do you dig for chronicity? Do you dig for past history? Do you impress your patients with your thoroughness? Or, are you so anxious to treat the patient that you skip a detailed past history? Or, do you skip taking questionnaires or urinalysis? Do you skip indepth examinations in order to get the patient into an adjusting room to try and relieve his pain? Patients like a thorough doctor, and if you are not doing these aforementioned things, then you are cutting down on your practice volume.

106. Is your staff negative? Do you have employees who are down in the mouth, negative, and always looking at the bad side of everything? If so, get rid of them and hire a new staff! As I previously stated, patients are negative when they are sick. When a negative person comes into your office and comes in contact with a negative member of your staff, they will repel each other like two negative poles of a magnet. Therefore, everyone in a chiropractic office should be positive and enthusiastic in order to lift the patient up out of his negativity and help get him on the road to positive, good health. Under no circumstance should you have a negative person on your staff.

107. Is your staff interested in the patient? Is your staff courteous toward the patient? Do they smile at the patient? Is the atmosphere in your office warm? Have you ever had the experience of walking into a business office (it could be another doctor's office or an attorney's office, etc.) and the receptionist was a "cold fish"? Maybe she was efficient, but her attitude was a Zero! Are you interested in doing business with that office? Not on your life! Probably exactly the opposite! Have you ever gone into an office where the receptionist was cheerful, who welcomed you and poured you a cup of coffee? She made you feel welcome. Do you like doing business with that office? You bet you do! There is no doubt that you *still* do business with that office! The doctor should instruct his staff to be courteous, to smile at the patients, to give them a warm welcome and make them feel at home. If they don't feel at home in your office, then they are not going to go there. If your staff is not interested in the patient, the patient's family and also the patient's problem, then it is time you fired that staff and hired another. Taking care of sick people is an avocation, not a job! You take care of sick people because you like to help people. People who feel similarly are the kind of people you need on your staff: people who are interested in helping people. If they are not interested, you should not be interested in having them work for you!

108. Don't have your patients come into a "dead" office. This section pertains to the music that you play in your office. I have previously mentioned about your staff not being interested in the patient . . . not courteous, not smiling, etc. It is equally true that you don't need a staff who has a dull attitude and who walk around like they are the living dead! The music in your office should be peppy, such as mambos and sambas, and so on. It is a mistake to play music such as classical or country and western in your office, because these types of music will turn away certain patients. You can imagine a patient who is used to listening to country and western music; he is not going to sit in an office where he has to listen to Beethoven or Bach. The same thing is true of someone who likes classical music; he sure isn't going to like to listen to country and western. Therefore, make sure the music played in your office is good — a good FM station, Muzak; music that has a peppy beat, but a middle-of-the-road type of music. Pep up your office. Remember that sick people are always down in their attitude to begin with, and you don't need the music in your office to bring them further down. Play music in your office so that it peps up people and makes your office a good, warm-feeling place to come into.

109. Are you a playboy doctor? Do you party all night and then come into the office half hung-over and half asleep? If so, I am sure you are wondering why your practice isn't doing well. When you are half asleep or half hung-over, it is obvious you can't be listening to your patients' problems. The patient will pick up when your mind is wandering or when you are not paying attention to him. When he feels the doctor is not paying attention, obviously he will quit coming. So, if you are a playboy doctor, do your playing on weekends and holidays. Get plenty of sleep on Sunday and come to work refreshed on Monday!

110. Always call a patient by his/her last name, especially older women. Many older women are offended when someone calls them by their Christian names. They do have last names, and prefer they are used. A seventy-year-old woman will become offended when a twenty-year-old receptionist calls her by her first name. So use courtesy in your office and don't upset your patients by using such terms as "Honey," "Dearie," or "Sweetheart," to a woman who is old enough to be your grandmother. Show her respect and she will show you respect. People are proud of their surnames and would like them to be used!

111. Don't be an exaggerator and claim to be able to cure everything. This causes a lack of belief in the doctor. Many doctors of chiropractic feel that their science is an evangelical cause and therefore preach it to each and every one of their patients. They claim they can cure anything from acne to cancer, etc. Remember, you are dealing with the public and you have to tell them what is believable to them. Once they understand what chiropractic is and how it can help their condition, you can slowly amplify what other conditions chiropractic can successfully treat. But, if the patient has a preconceived concept of chiropractic solely treating neuromusculoskeletal problems and you tell him that chiropractic can treat cancer, etc., he is not going to believe you, and if he does not believe you, he will quit and won't let you treat his neuromusculoskeletal problem. Use common sense! Don't turn your office into a lecture hall. It is a professional facility, rendering a professional service. You can spread the word of chiropractic, but use common sense and go along with the patient's believability quotient at the time. Once he is sold on the benefits of chiropractic, then you can expand his concept, and successfully so.

112. Do you re-examine your patients regularly? Do you examine your patients every tenth visit? Many patients go to chiropractors and receive the same treatment month after month, with no progress examination or report. The patient feels he is getting the same old treatment over and over again, and so becomes dissatisfied. If you *re*-examine your patients on a regular basis, they will see their progress and will continue to stay under your care. If you don't re-examine and make new reports regularly, your patients will discontinue your services.

113. Don't promise the patient too much. If you examine a patient, and while interpreting his x-rays you see pathology on the film that cannot be reversed, or if you find irreversible pathology during a physical/orthopedic examination, tell the patient you feel you can relieve the symptoms he has but you cannot cure his problem. There are some cases that cannot be cured by chiropractic, or by any other measures. The patient should be so informed in these type cases. It is absolutely preposterous to promise a patient a cure when you know you cannot provide it. Simply state to the patient that you feel you can relieve his problem within a certain length of time and that you can honestly figure on a fifty to seventy percent positive result in his case. Tell him that he will always have a residual problem because the damage is there, and he will always have to be treated for that residual problem. He will understand this. Patients know that some conditions never get totally cured. Pertaining to this point, the old axiom, "Once a back problem, always a back problem" is definitely true! This applies also to a patient who has high blood pressure. There isn't a cure for high blood pressure, but it is a condition that can be controlled, and the patient should be told that it can be controlled. The same is true of hypoglycemia and many other conditions. Therefore, don't promise your patient a cure if you cannot produce results. Simply give him a realistic outlook as to what he can expect. If you promise too much and then can't deliver — even though the patient receives good results under your care — that patient will criticize you and not continue his treatment. Perhaps we should take a lesson from our allied profession, the medical profession: they never promise cures to patients. They simply treat the patients to control their problems. Think about it!

What About Your Treatments/Adjustments?

114. Do you rush your patients? Do you rush your patients in and out of your office too quickly? If so, they will feel short-changed and quit your care. You'll soon find your patients going down the street to one of your colleagues' offices, to where the patients' problems are given time and careful consideration.

115. Do you spend two hours with each patient? People don't like a two-hour treatment or even a one-hour adjustment. They don't have time for it. Do your job; tell the patient what you've found; tell him what you did; tell him what he can expect from your treatment. Don't delay him in your office unnecessarily. He wants to leave. Your patients' time is valuable.

116. Are you a sadist? There are a lot of doctors who try to get their patients well in two days. They are excessively rough and hurt their patients. If you hurt the patient, you may lose his business. If you can make a positive change painlessly by extending the patient's treatment over three visits, do so. Don't do it in one visit, painfully. Don't hurt the patient! Patients who are hurt while being treated will not return.

There is an interesting phenomenon that has occurred with the recent influx of female practitioners into the chiropractic profession. The female doctors are kept quite busy adjusting their male colleagues. Why? Because they don't give painful adjustments. The lady doctors "kiss the bone in" instead of forcing it in! The male doctors don't want to be hurt any more than patients do. Therefore, the male doctor seeks out a female doctor for his treatment.

If you don't like to be hurt when given an adjustment, extend the same consideration to your patients.

117. Are you a masseuse? Use chiropractic. You don't have to mash blackheads, give rubdowns, etc. to keep your patients. If a patient wants a massage, send him to the local spa or YMCA! Basically, our profession is extremely simple. If there is a pressure on a nerve, we get the pressure off the nerve, and the patient gets the results. That is what our patients come to us for. We don't have to give a glorified massage!

118. Are you guilty of giving monotonous treatments? Once you have secured the patient during your report of findings, do you then proceed to give him the same treatment each and every visit? If you do, then that patient, before too long, will begin to feel that he has become part of a treadmill and may quit your care.

A WORD FROM OUR GRADUATES

"I want to tell you how enthused our entire office is about the Clinic Management Associates' practice consultancy. The "up-to-date" concepts in insurance procedures, P.I. work, and patient control, have greatly broadened our perspectives. The course is all the other practice management courses rolled into one, and then some."

— G. Stanford Pierce, D.C.P.A.

"With three hours of instruction, Dr. Fernandez increased my practice by $50,000.00 a year. Need I say more?"

— Dr. Jerry Goforth

"I was well versed in practice and confident of my skills, but this program has added so many new dimensions to my practice that I want to publicly thank CMA. The first class is worth thousands of dollars to anyone's future. In just the first month, my practice doubled without raising my fees."

—Donald F. Housh, D.C.

"The hours of consultancy I have received on the management of my practice have been stimulating, constructive, and very rewarding. I doubled my practice every year for the first five years. And now, continuing consulting, I am still experiencing steady growth."

— Dr. William A. LaTorre

"Dr. Fernandez doubled my practice in the first month . . . and then doubled it again without advertising or gimmicks. I can't praise this program enough."

— Dr. Steve Newton

"By using Dr. Fernandez' methods, my income increased immediately and in only six months, it tripled! All this without the prepayments and case fees required by some other consultancies."

Dr. Robert Malone